Get more out of G Suite - A Teacher's Guide

Independently Published

ISBN: 9781980822974
First Printing: 2018
Updated and republished 2020

Contents

Introduction

Welcome to 'Getting more out of G Suite - A Teacher's Guide'. This book has been specially written for teachers and educators who use G Suite within their organisation. My goal and aim for writing this book is for the reader to save time in their busy lives by using the tools offered by Google to improve the way they work and maximise their use of the programs available. Through reading this book and trying out some of the tools and techniques available you will learn how to use all of them to your advantage in your day to day role as a teacher.

Initially each section will summarise the basics of how to use each of the Google App tools and then move on to how you can use this as a teacher in the classroom and outside of the classroom for admin and additional tasks. There are definitely two different uses of G Suite which are those for the students and those for the staff which both have equal value in the life of the teacher and can help many different people to manage their workload and collaborate with each other effectively.

Once we have gone over some of the fundamentals of G Suite and how these can be used in all manner of ways in an educational environment this book will look at Google Chrome extensions and also Google Drive add-ons to show you just how much time these tools can save you and also show you some of the more advanced functions you could be using to greatly improve what you are using with G Suite. Every reader of this book should find something new they have not used before or not tried before and be able to easily implement these new ideas by using this book as a guide and a how to manual.

Due to the unprecedented situation occurring in 2020 with the outbreak of COVID-19 I have spent time updating this book. The main updates are about using Google Meet for remote learning as well as updating a variety of other sections in the book such as the Google Classroom section. A full break down of the updates is included at the end of the book in the Acknowledgements section.

Look out for these icons which indicate that there is an example file on the website that you can take a copy of: https://sites.google.com/view/gsuite-teachers-guide

Google Drive

By choosing to read this book hopefully you already have a full understanding of how Google Drive works and its function however if this is completely new to you then these initial pages should explain some of the basic functionality of Google Drive.

You need to think of Google Drive as an online storage area where you can upload any type of files to the cloud for access from any computer or device with Internet access. However, Google Drive is much more than just an online storage area as it also provides real time collaboration with other people through the additional G Suite tools such as Docs, Sheets and Slides, but more on those later.

Once you are logged into your Google Drive you will see a view similar to what is shown below. In this image my Google Drive is currently set to the 'List View' option which I find easier to view all of my files however you can select 'Grid view' which is more of a thumbnail view of Google Drive. In order to change this, you simply use this button to toggle between the two different views.

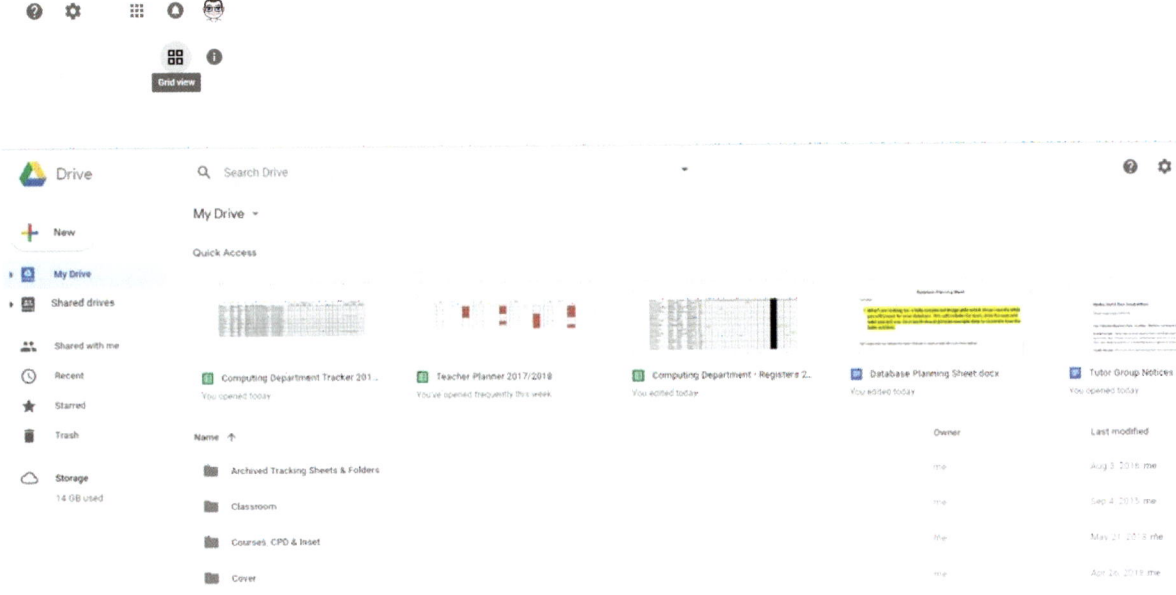

Drive Main Menu

+ New	1	1. Click here to create a new Google File (Folder, Docs, Sheets, Presentation etc)
☑ Priority	2	2. Click here to load your Priority Drive Workspaces
▸ 🔺 My Drive	3	3. Click here to display all of the files and folders that you own or have created/added to your Drive
▸ 👥 Shared drives	4	4. Click here to access your Shared Drives
👥 Shared with me	5	5. Click here to view all of the files and folders that have been shared with you but you have not added to your Drive
🕐 Recent	6	6. Click here to see recent Google Files you have opened
☆ Starred	7	7. Click here to see your Google Files you have 'Starred'
🗑 Trash	8	8. Click here to see the files and folders you have deleted, to permanently delete, you need to delete from the Trash can too.
☰ Storage	9	9. Click here to manage your storage use

You can also use Drag and Drop to upload files to Google Drive

'New' Button Menu

New

Folder (1)

File upload (2)

Folder upload (3)

Google Docs (4) >

Google Sheets (5) >

Google Slides (6) >

More (7) >

1.Click here to create a new folder to organise your files

2.Click here to upload an existing file to your Google Drive

3.Click here to upload an existing folder of files to your Google Drive

4.Click here to create a new Google Document (Google equivalent of Word)

5.Click here to create a new Google Sheet (Google equivalent of Excel)

6. Click here to create a new Google Slides (Google equivalent of PowerPoint)

7. Click here for more options

More Options

1. Click here to create a new Google Form (Survey or Assessment)

2.Click here to create a new Google Drawing (Google equivalent of Paint)

3. Click here to create a new customized Google Map

4. Click here to create a new Google Site

5. Click here to search for other apps that you can connect to your Google Drive

Google Forms (1)

Google Drawings (2)

Google My Maps (3)

Google Sites (4)

Connect more apps (5)

In the top right hand corner, you have the Settings button

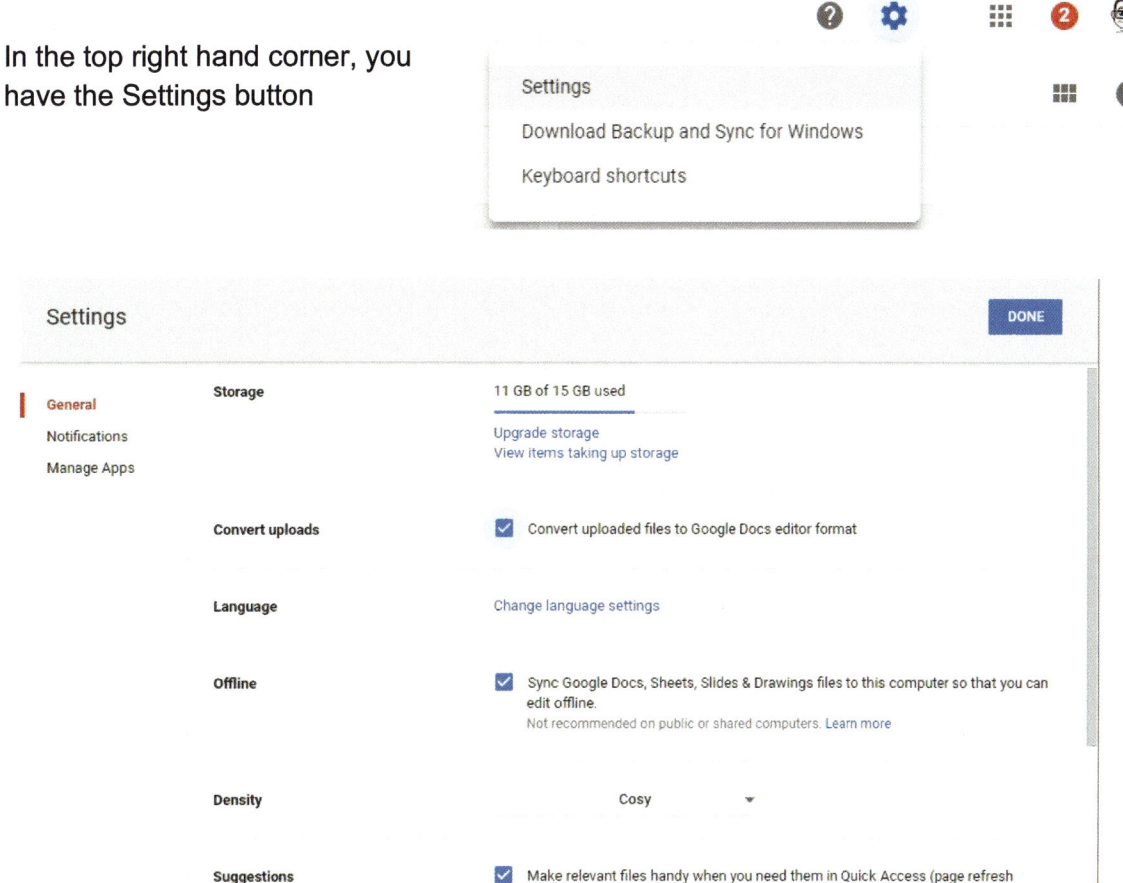

In the settings window shown below you can adjust a few options for Google Drive however generally you will not need to use this very often. One thing I would always advise you to do is to make sure that the checkbox is ticked so that when you upload files to Drive they are automatically converted into editable versions. This means you can edit and work on the file online using Google Drive.

As a teacher you will use Google Drive all of the time and there are many specific teacher uses that I will go over however these will be covered in the explanations of the other G Suite applications such as Docs, Sheets, Slides and Forms.

Priority Drive

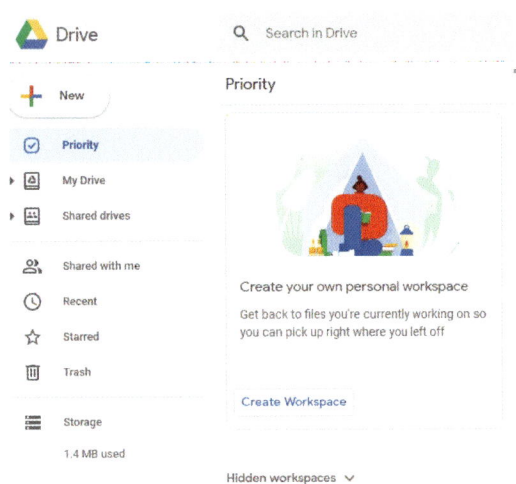

This is a new feature of Google Drive that allows you to create 'Workspaces' within your Drive meaning you can access files that you use regularly from this area.

To get started you need to click on the 'Create Workspace' button shown here.

Next you can give your new workspace a name and add the files you would like.

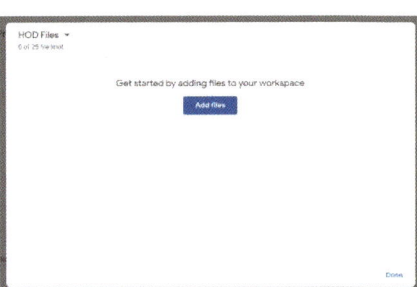

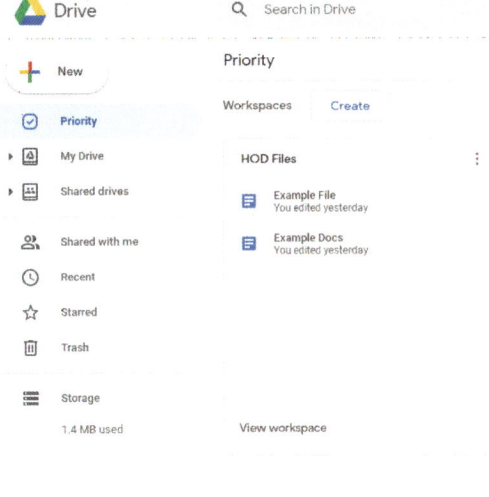

You can add lots of workspaces to your Drive and you can have up to 25 files in one workspace. You can also hide workspaces once you are finished with them and do not want to delete them.

You can control whether Priority Drive loads when opening Drive by changing a checkbox in the settings of Google Drive as shown on the previous page.

Shared Drives

Shared Drives are a relatively new addition to G Suite but a very welcome and useful addition. Shared Drives are essentially Google Drives that are owned by the domain rather than the individual. They work in exactly the same way as a personal Google Drive however you can add and remove members to the Drive and manage their access restrictions as required. You can also create as many Shared Drives as you require for the different aspects of your role within the organisation. Shown here is one Shared Drive for a Computing Department however I am sure you can all think of many Shared Drives it would be useful to have such as Yr7 Team or Heads of House as two examples.

There are different access restrictions that the owner or 'Manager' member of a Shared Drive can assign to the different members of the team.

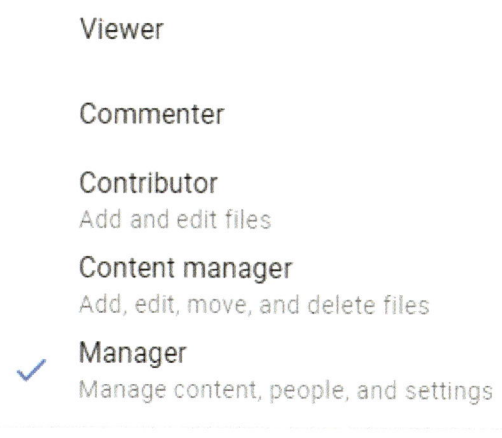

Anybody who is a member of a Shared Drive at the very least will be a 'Viewer' allowing them to see all of the files within the Shared Drive.

Like a Google Doc you can have 'Commenters' and 'Contributors' which are like editors. A new addition to these options was the 'Content Manager' as this gives a user the ability to organise and delete files but not add users to the Drive.

This has some large advantages for the organisation and also the users of Shared Drives. I suspect that most of you have used or are still using shared network areas for storing either your own personal files or shared department files for everyone to use. There is of course nothing wrong with this however there are some good advantages with using Shared Drives for network storage instead. Firstly, Google Admin's for your domain can manage the users of any Shared Drive and add and remove people as required very easily but also meaning that any user who leaves and therefore has their account suspended also loses access to the Shared Drives.

One of the major advantages of using Shared Drives over normal network areas is the fact that you can keep a department scheme of work on a Shared Drive including all of the resources. As soon as you need a resource added to Google Classroom for example you can insert it directly from the Shared Drive and then everyone in the department can access and do the same. This saves plenty of time in uploading to your own Google Drive and then inserting to Classroom from there.

Other advantages of Shared Drives are the use of having a Shared Drive for a certain group of staff who have meetings as all of the files for the meetings can be stored on Shared Drive for all to access and staff can simply be directed to access the files from Shared Drive. This can be easily used with students as well and for example you may have a Duke Of Edinburgh Shared Drive for all student members to access files they need and have staff members with full or editing rights so they can add and change files as required.

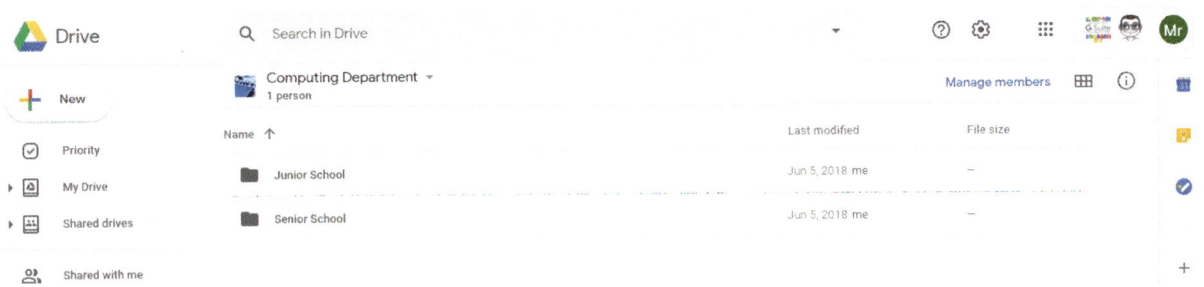

As you can see from this screenshot a Shared Drive looks and works exactly like a personal Google Drive.

Controlling the Shared Drive is very simple and at the top you have a drop-down menu next to the name and on the right-hand side a blue 'Manage Members' button that loads the following screen.

As you can see here the window is similar to the file sharing box for most Google products and gives the user the ability to enter email addresses of new members and select the type of access they will require to the Shared Drive.

You can also personalise the email message here as well.

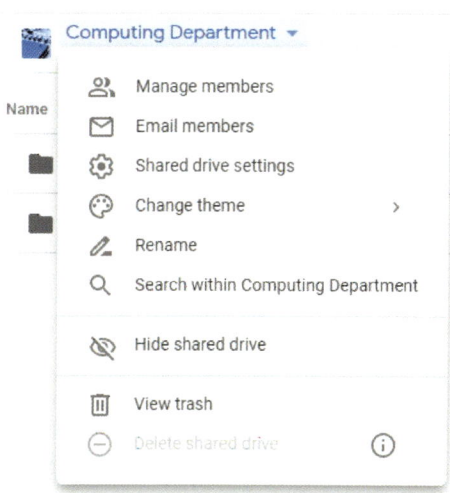

You can control all of these options and more by clicking on the drop-down menu next to the name of the Shared Drive.

These are fairly self-explanatory allowing you to 'Email members' of the Shared Drive or change the theme and colour of the way it looks. You can rename the Drive and also just search within the Shared Drive and not include your own Drive.

Shared drive settings will open this window and allow you to further customise your Shared Drive.

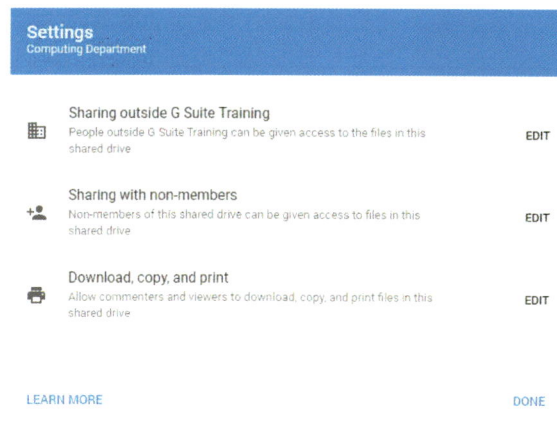

As you can see in this image you are able to apply additional restrictions to all the files saved within your Shared Drive. Sharing outside of your domain may be set higher at admin level however you may like to stop members from sharing files with anyone outside of the Shared Drive members and also disable the ability to download, copy or print any of the files. This is particularly useful for more sensitive Shared Drives such as an SLT drive for example.

Hide shared drive allows you to hide the drive away from your view so you can focus on other drives but still have access if you need to. You can view all hidden Shared Drives from the main shared drive screen as shown in this screenshot. You will see the blue button on the top right-hand side of the screen 'Hidden Shared Drives'.

View trash allows you to see anything deleted just in case of accidents. You can also delete the Shared Drive but only once all the files within the Shared Drive have been deleted.

File Sharing & File Management

I have already touched upon file sharing when talking about Google Drive and Shared Drives and this has got to be the best thing about Google Drive. The ability to share a file with another person via their email address and decide upon their access restrictions to enable real time collaboration on documents has amazing impacts and consequences for the efficiency people can work together and collaborate on projects.

The sharing process is fundamentally the same whether you are in Google Drive, Shared Drive or any of the G Suite applications such as Docs, Sheets or Slides etc however there are some slight differences in how you initially share the file or folder.

To share within a Google file such as a Google Doc you simply click the blue Share button at the top right of the Google Document and the box shown below will open.

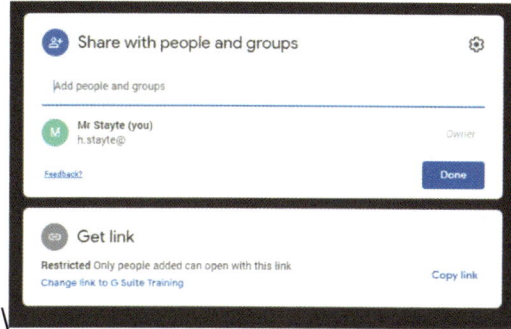 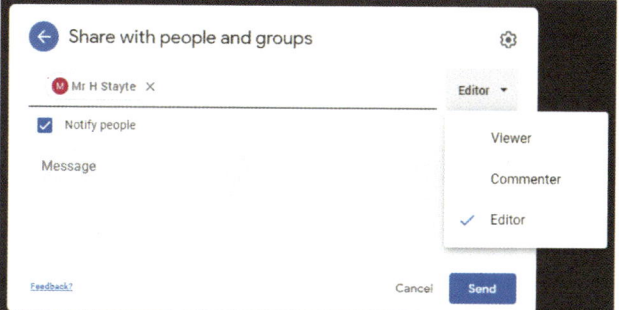

Here you can enter any email address to share the file and then also choose the access rights for the individual. If you need to have different access restrictions for different people or need to adjust the settings already set, then you can click on 'Change link to *domain name*' which will turn on sharing for anyone in your domain.

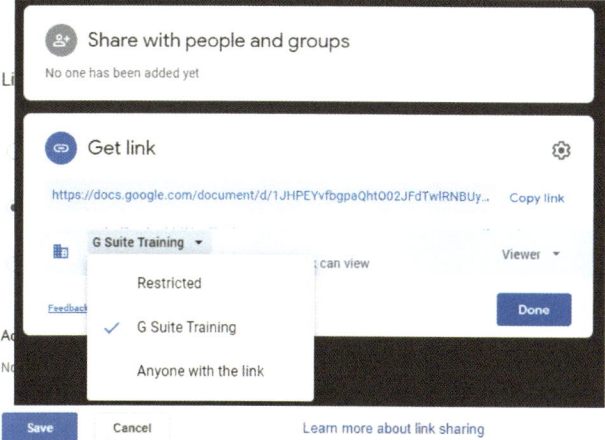

Here you can see that you can then adjust the settings you require so that the document can be on the web to anyone or Anyone with the Link. You can also adjust whether you want these settings to mean they are a Viewer, Commenter or Editor at the side.

You can use the 'Copy link' button here to easily get the link that you can share with others.

Sharing in Google Drive & Shared Drives

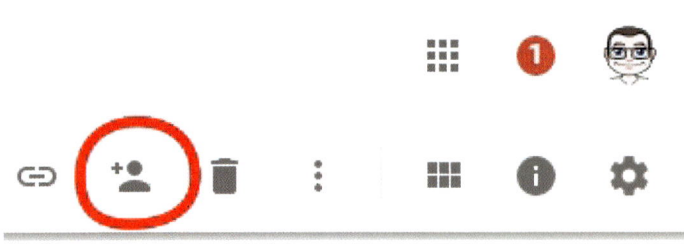

Within Google Drive and Shared Drives you can simply click on a folder or file/s and then at the top right hand side you have this 'sharing' icon that will allow you to manage the sharing of the file/s selected.

File Management in Google Drive & Shared Drives

The best way to conduct file management within Google Drives is to use your right click menu by right clicking on the file you want to manage, and these are very similar in both My Drive and Share Drives. The only difference between the two is that you 'Remove' a file from your My Drive whereas you 'Delete for everyone' from a Shared Drive.

My Drive Right Click on a file

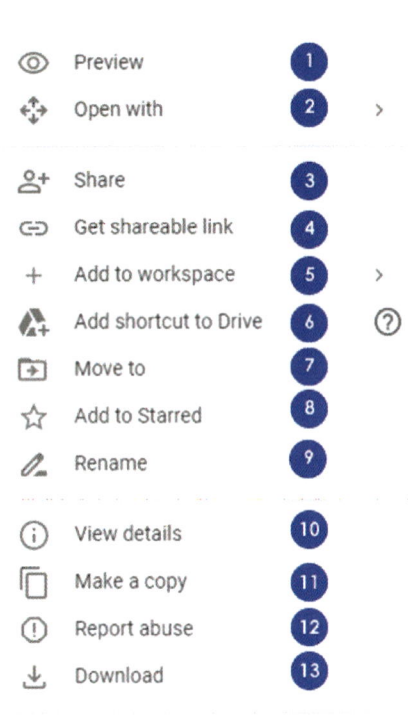

1. Previews the selected file
2. Allows you to select the app to open the file with
3. Opens the sharing dialogue box
4. Automatically opens the sharing link if previously shared via a link
5. Allows you to add the file to a workspace in your Priority Drive area
6. Allows you to add a shortcut to the selected file in another location
7. Allows you to move the file to another area (including a Shared Drive if you have permission)
8. Adds the file to the starred files for quick retrieval
9. Allows you to rename the file
10. Displays some general information about the file including the 'Activity Log'
11. Creates a copy of the selected file
12. Allows you to report the file to Google
13. Will automatically download the file in the default format
14. Removes the file from your Drive (Will not remove from other users if the file is shared)

Google Docs

Welcome to Google Docs. For those of you that have been around long enough you will remember that what is now Google Drive used to be called Google Docs before it was rebranded and Drive introduced. So from that Google Docs is the first and one of the most used G Suite apps due to the word processing and collaboration element of it. This section of the book will quickly go over some of the basic features and functions of Google Docs and then explore some of the advantages of using Google Docs and some of the more advanced features that you might not be aware of. I have identified lots of the detail from the menus in Docs as many of these options are common across G Suite and you will use them in lots of the other applications as well.

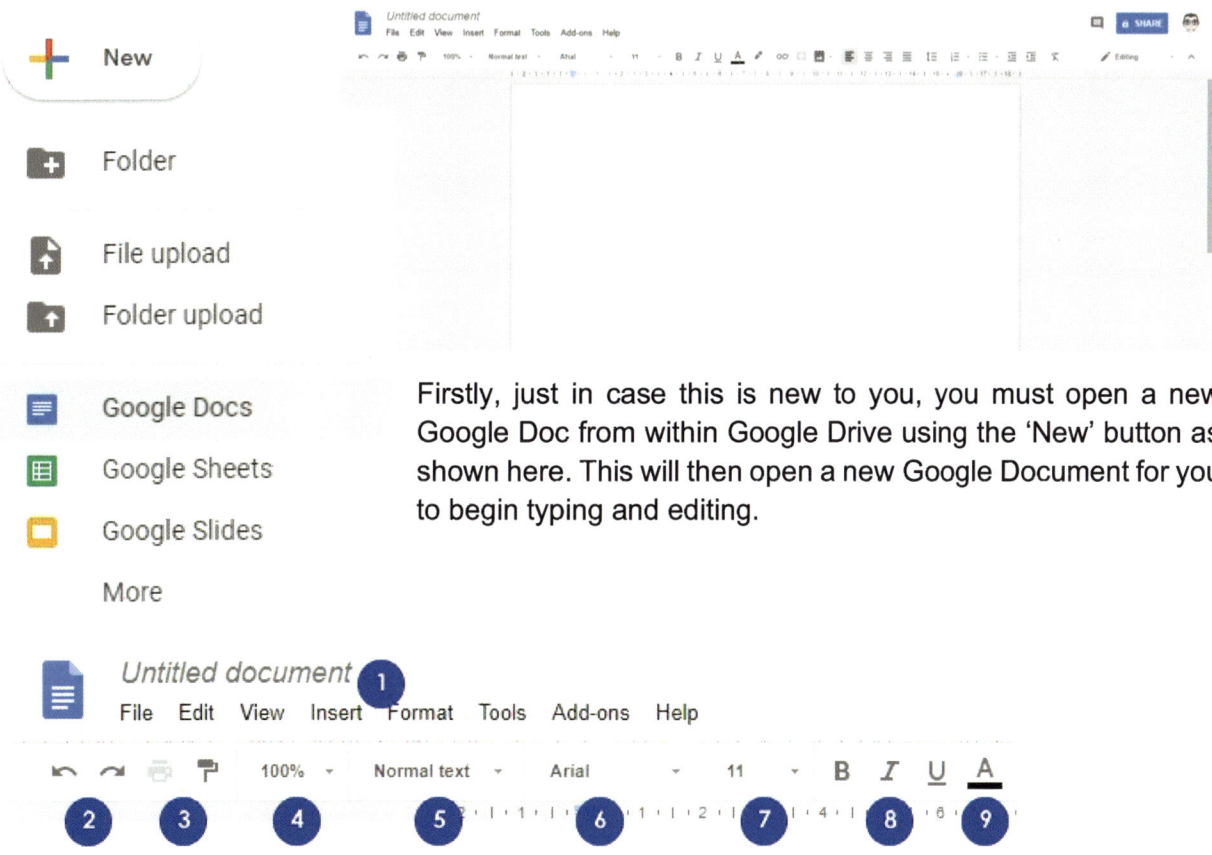

Firstly, just in case this is new to you, you must open a new Google Doc from within Google Drive using the 'New' button as shown here. This will then open a new Google Document for you to begin typing and editing.

1. Click here to change the name of the document
2. Click here to undo and redo
3. Click here to Print or use Format Painter
4. Click here to change the zoom of the document
5. Click here to change the type of text options
6. Click here to format the text font
7. Click here to change the text size
8. Click here to adjust the Bold, Italics or Underline of the text
9. Click here to change the text colour

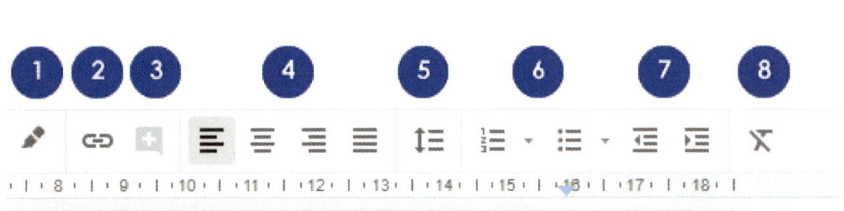

1. Click here to change the Highlight colour
2. Click here to add a link to your document
3. Click here to insert a comment into your document
4. Click here to adjust the alignment options
5. Click here to change the line spacing
6. Click here to adjust the bullets and numbering
7. Click here to increase or decrease the indentations
8. Click here to clear all formatting (Very useful when you have uploaded or copied text)

File Options

Below are all of the options you are given when you click 'File' on your Google Document. Some of these are common through all types of Google files and can be used for Presentations, Spreadsheets, Drawings and Forms as well.

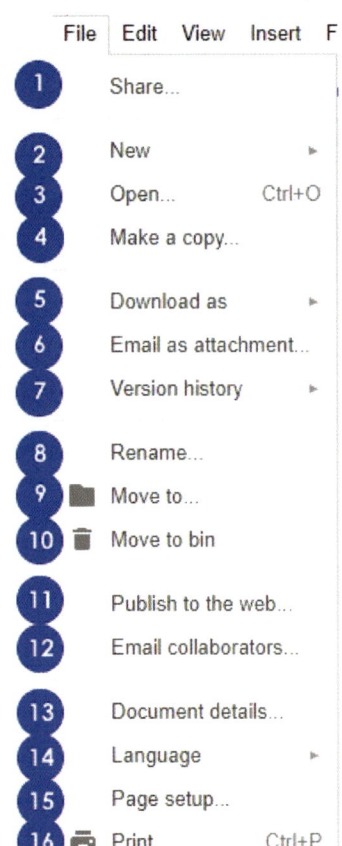

1. Click here to 'Share' your document with others – you can also use the button on the top right of the screen
2. Click here to create a new Google file
3. Click here to open an existing Google file
4. Click here to make a copy of the current file (Very useful if you do not want to edit the original document shared with you but want your own copy)
5. Click here to download a copy of the file in a format you would like (Very useful if you need a local version)
6. Click here to email the document as an attachment
7. Version history allows you to track the changes and revert to an older version of the file
8. Click here to rename your current document
9. Move to allows you to put the document into a folder
10. Move to Bin deletes the document
11. Publish to the web allows you to make public a link for use of the internet or even embed it into a website
12. Click here to email all of the people you have granted access to the document to
13. Click here to see the basic document details
14. Click here to change the language
15. Click here to change the settings for the page
16. Click here to print the document

Insert Options

I am intentionally missing out Edit and View options as I feel these are self-explanatory however I wanted to go through the Insert Menu as there are so very useful tools built in here that you can use as a teacher.

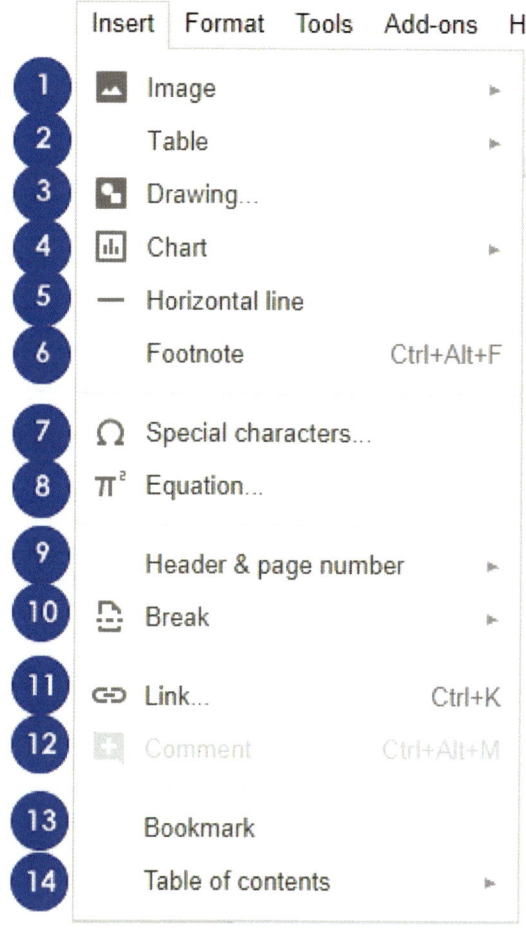

1. Image allows you to insert an image by Uploading, Searching the web, Google Drive, Google Photos, URL or your webcam. The search the web feature is particularly handy and saves you a lot of time

2. Table is similar to most word processors you can insert tables into docs to help with layout options

3. Drawing is excellent for quickly creating graphics using Google Drawings directly into your Google Doc

4. Chart allows you to insert an existing Chart or create a new one using Google Sheets all from within Docs. These charts can be live linked so that they update on the Google Doc if the chart is updated

5. Simple horizontal line to help with layout and separation

6. Use this tool to add footnotes to text that appear at the bottom of the page

7. Use this tool to find special characters. There is also a drawing window to allow you to quickly draw what you are looking for and Google Docs finds the closest matches

8. Equation - a very useful tool for maths and science teachers (create equations)

9. Header and Footer options essentially

10. Insert a page break or column break into your document
11. Insert a hyperlink
12. Insert a comment onto the document
13. Insert Bookmark onto the page
14. Insert and create a table of contents automatically from the headings used throughout your document

Tools options

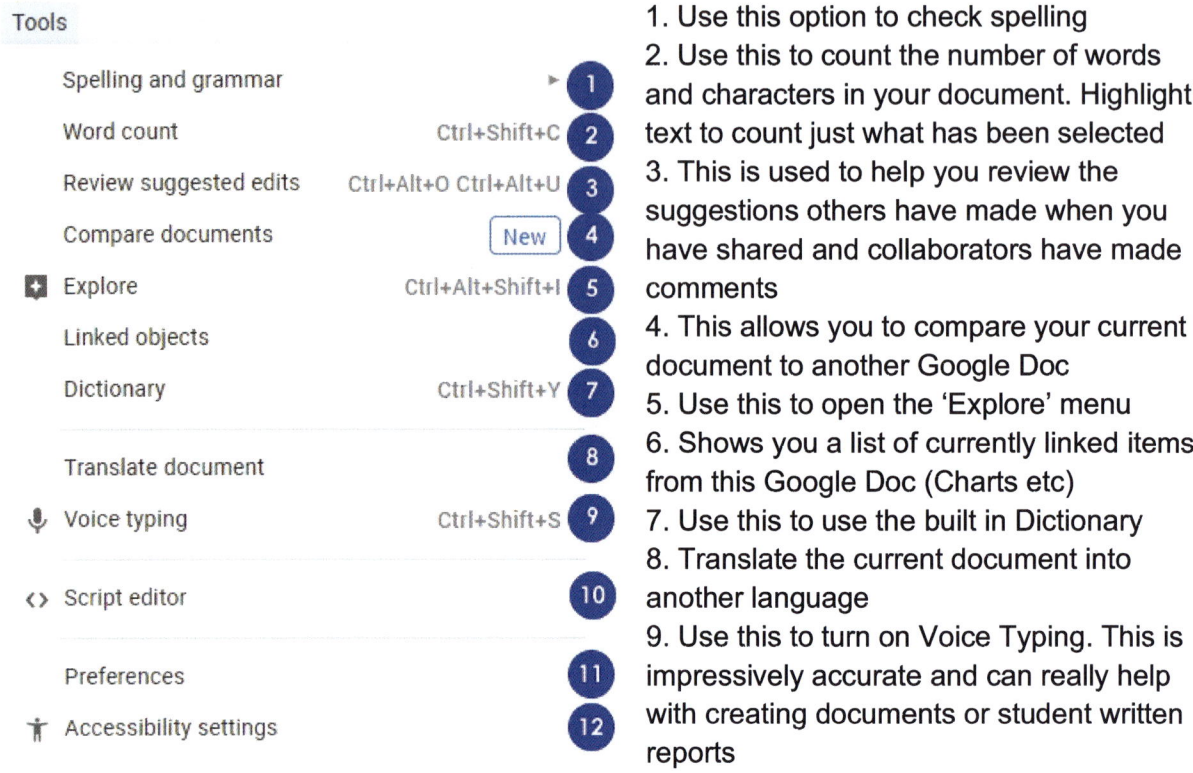

1. Use this option to check spelling
2. Use this to count the number of words and characters in your document. Highlight text to count just what has been selected
3. This is used to help you review the suggestions others have made when you have shared and collaborators have made comments
4. This allows you to compare your current document to another Google Doc
5. Use this to open the 'Explore' menu
6. Shows you a list of currently linked items from this Google Doc (Charts etc)
7. Use this to use the built in Dictionary
8. Translate the current document into another language
9. Use this to turn on Voice Typing. This is impressively accurate and can really help with creating documents or student written reports

10. This is where you can create your own Google Apps Script to enhance the functionality of your document
11. Change Preferences and shortcut keys
12. Allows you to change the Accessibility settings

Get more out of Google Docs

Teacher - Student Use

The most obvious thing you can use Google Docs for is to create worksheets for the students to use. These will of course come in many different types of worksheet and you can also upload all of your existing worksheets to be automatically converted into Google Docs. Once you have created a worksheet one of the best ways to share with your class is using Google Classroom which can automatically create a copy for each student however more on that later. Below are some examples of the different types of worksheet you can create as a teacher within Google Docs.

<u>Questions Sheets</u>

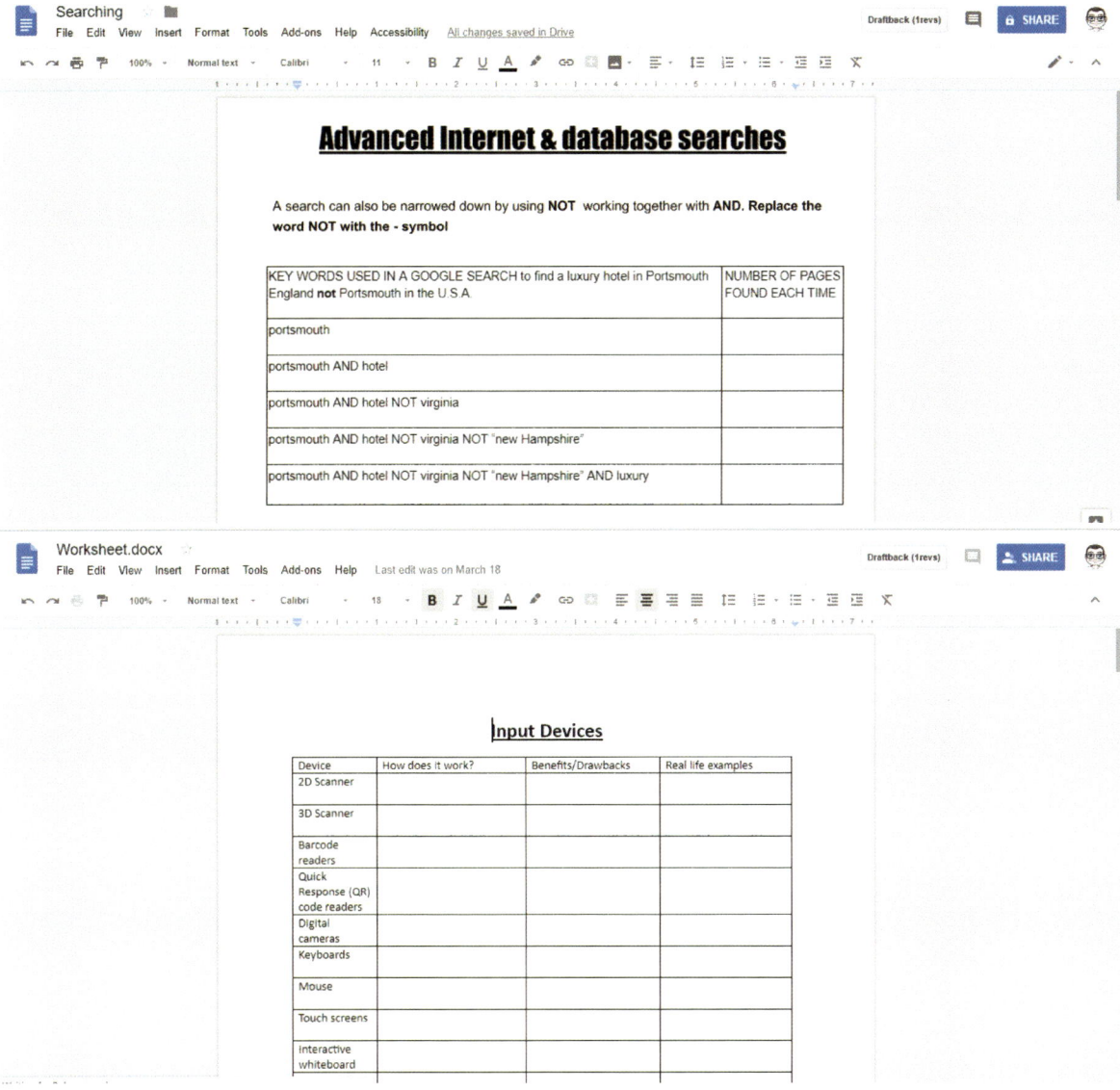

Fill in the gaps

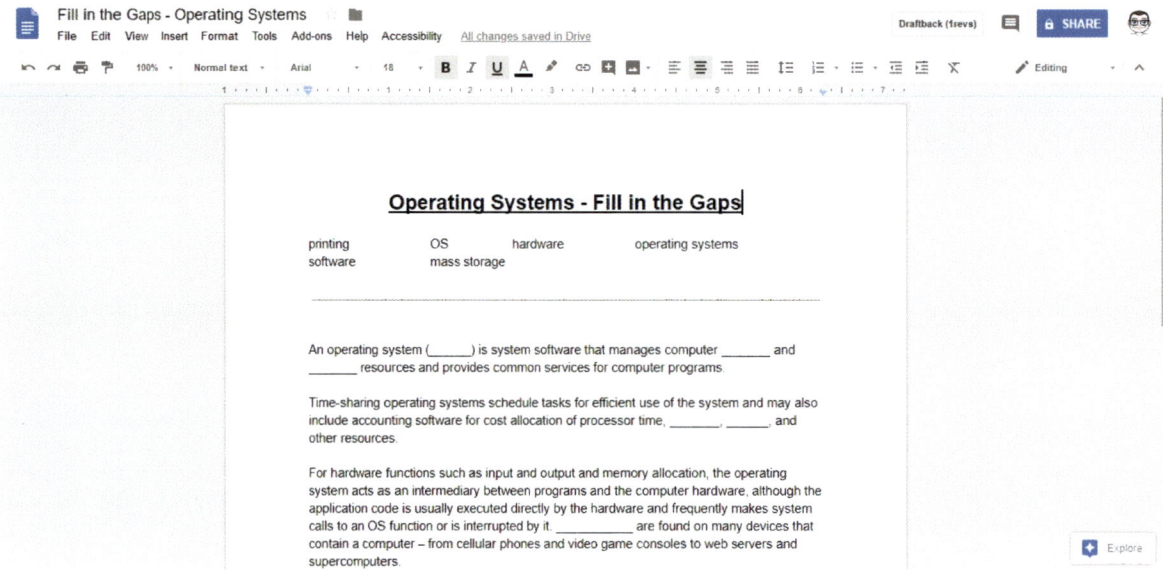

Instructional Sheets

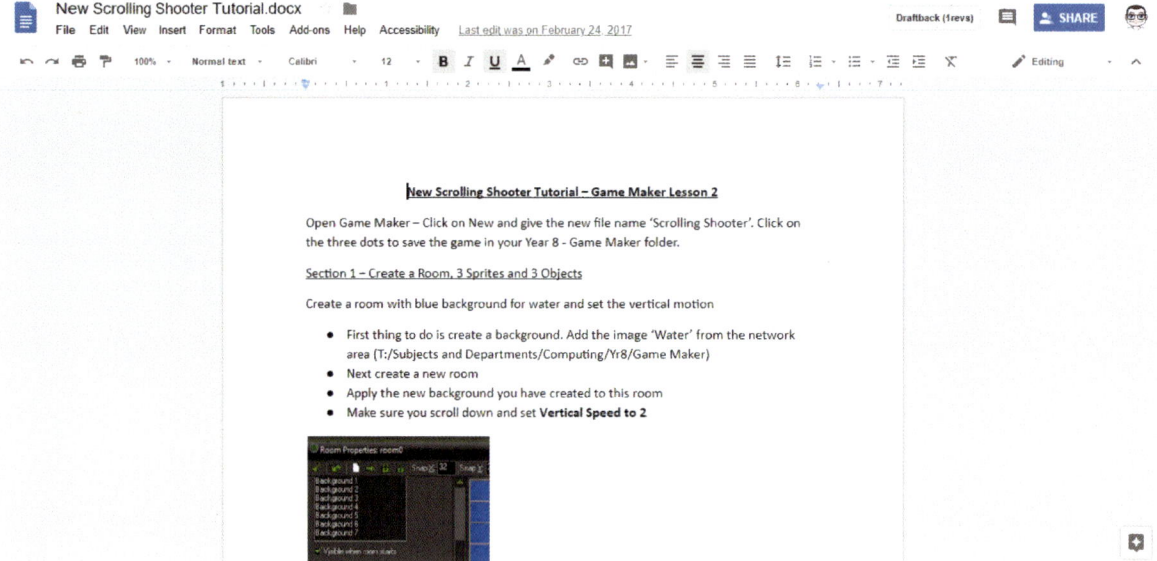

Writing Frames

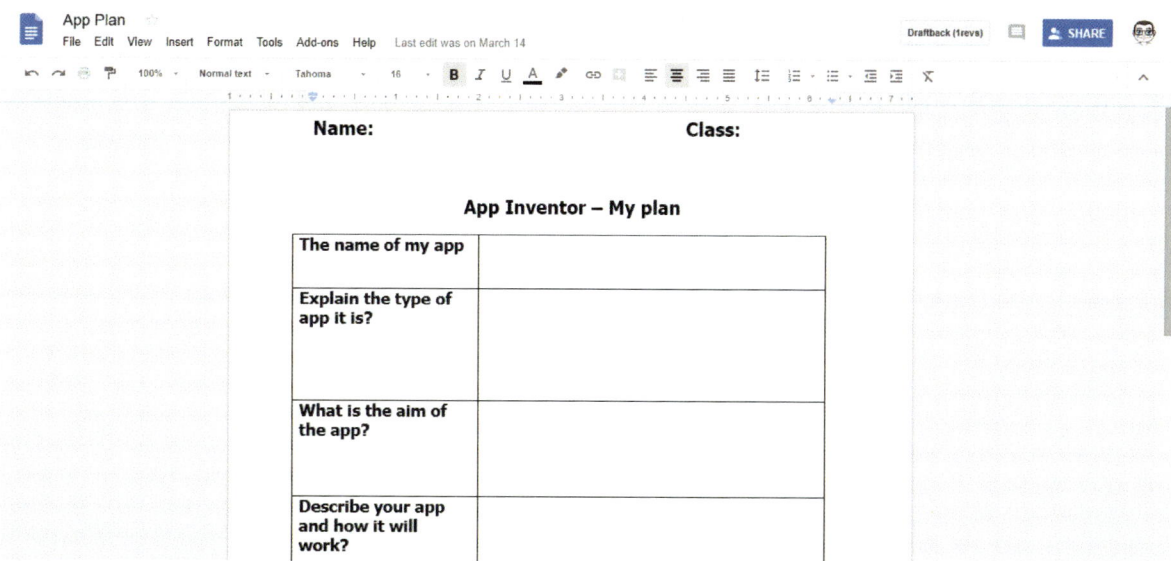

All of these worksheets are just some examples that I have used as Google Docs which are then shared with all students. Before Google Classroom came along you could use add-ons like Doctopus to make copies for all of your students and share with them however Google Classroom has streamlined this process and made the handing out and collecting of electronic worksheets like this much easier and more efficient.

Teacher - Admin Use

Another side of using Google Docs is for the administration side of being a teacher and there are many examples of where using a Google Doc has huge advantages over paper based or network files.

- Meeting Agendas and Minutes

I am sure you have been to many meetings where you are all given a paper copy of the agenda and then there is someone hand writing the minutes as they are discussed. Once typed up the minutes are then shared with all who attended, tragically on yet more paper, which if you were at the meeting you will not pay much attention to. Thankfully many organisations will at least email out the minutes rather than printing them however the power of Google Docs provides a much better solution to this problem.

Create your agenda on Google Docs in advance of your meeting and share it with all of the invitees of the meeting. During the meeting have a laptop, Chromebook, tablet or even your phone where you can type the minutes directly into the Google Doc agenda under the relevant sections.

Even if you still prefer to hand write your minutes and then type up by typing up onto the Google Doc the minutes are already shared with the relevant people and they can easily be directed to them or expect the agendas to be updated and changed. You can also use Shared Drives to help with this as well and simply direct staff to the relevant section on the Shared Drive for them to access the agendas and minutes.

The same process for a standard meeting can also be used for line management meetings as well. You can also use Google Sheets for this process which I will talk about later but this definitely lends itself better to the line management meeting where the same agenda items are repeated each meeting and therefore duplicates of the worksheets can be made easily.

- Typing notes

This may seem like a really obvious thing to say but I know so many people who carry around tablets and yet still choose to hand write everything despite the fact that they may very well type some of it up. The beauty of using Google Docs for note taking is that it saves automatically and you do not have to worry or mess around with saving issues. Another major benefit that I have seen some people use is to take advantage of the voice typing for their note taking and using Google Docs built in voice translator that I mentioned earlier. This does work remarkably well and is accurate enough to make it worthwhile using and a long way from when the technology was first introduced.

- Lesson Observation Forms

This is another use of Google Docs that may be a little dependent on your organisation's requirements but if there are no objections to word processed lesson observation sheets then using a Google Doc for this purpose is also very useful. Some of the reasons identified earlier such as auto saving are also very apt for this purpose but also the sharing ability of a Google Doc lends itself well to the observation collaborative process as you can easily share the Google Doc with the observee and also any line managers or SLT as required. Assuming there is a section for the observee to comment and respond, having it on a Google Doc means there is only one copy that has been updated and all of the revisions can be seen and tracked by the editors. Obviously the document can be exported and hard copies made as required but if they are not needed then the file can be left as a Google Doc ready to be accessed by anyone who needs it.

- Appraisals

Similar to the lesson observation, using Google Docs for appraisal documents can be very beneficial as managers can complete the form in advance of their conversation or in collaboration before, during and after any appraisal meeting. Using Google Docs in this way simply saves everybody a lot of time and can lead to better conversations during the appraisal meeting as some form of collaboration and discussion could have already taken place within the Google Doc in advance.

- Writing School Reports using Google Docs

This can mean two different types of reports but again all of the same advantages of using Google Docs can be applied to this. The first type of report is the one of parent reports home at the end of a term/year where the teacher will be giving comments on the performance of the child. Again just as with the other uses of Google Docs the voice typing is a huge advantage here is it allows the teacher to speak their written report and Google automatically translates this into digital text. This can save teachers hours of time in thinking about what they want to say and how to write it when they can actually just speak it and then edit it a little bit afterwards. Along with the advantages already discussed another advantage you have is spell checker which obviously can be set to whatever language you require and this will again speed up the process of error checking and fixing all problems. Of course one of the problems with using voice typing is occasionally there are going to be mistakes so anything that is created must also be double checked however this seems to be much quicker than actually writing it all out yourself.

The second type of report the Google Docs is really useful for is any kind of school report that you need to write to the senior management about a certain topic. The advantages here are simply the collaboration aspect of Google Docs. Often you are working in collaboration with other colleagues when producing reports for senior management and therefore the use of Google Docs allowing the sharing of the same report to multiple people and collaboration just speeds up the process. Of course no email attachments will be sent back and forth between colleagues as well.

- Proposals

Proposals are very similar to reports and it follows much the same line as the reports to senior management as often the proposals are going to be to senior management and by having them as collaborative documents the people you are working with on the proposal can all contribute and can edit the same document. I have written many proposals and every single one of them has started as a Google Doc and some of the other advantages you forget about are that you can be editing it from anywhere and from any device. So you can catch up a little bit on your phone on the train home and then you can then do a quick bit more on your laptop at home and then of course do some more on your school computer the next day. Just having one document in one place accessing from whichever device you are using at the time makes life so much easier.

- Letter writing to parents

Letters home to parents is another obvious way that Google Docs can help you as a teacher. With most schools and organisations letters home to parents are vitally important and also vitally important that they are error free. Therefore, being able to share the document with another colleague or a member of senior management for checking and to make sure that everything that has been sent out is error free is much easier using Google Docs. You can also use templates so a school can have a template set up across its domain that many members of staff can use. This can save lots of people lots of time and also mean that corporate image is maintained in all of the documentation sent out.

- Curriculum Plans

This is another area that may be better suited to Google Sheets however it does really depend on the template you are using as both can work well. These are fantastic as Google Docs because they can be shared and edited by everyone in the department so can be created in collaboration. Having in Google Drive in this way also means they are easily accessible for all who need them and can be shared with senior management as required. The plans can even contain links to files stored in Shared Drives for all to have access to making the plans an interactive and live useful document.

- Comparing Documents

Using the new option available in the Tool menu to 'Compare documents' allows you to use this in two main ways. If you are working on a report or document of some description and someone uses a new Google Doc (or even something else which you can upload) then you can use this tool to compare the document and track the changes between them ready to approve or reject the changes. You could also use this tool for comparing different students work to see if there are any identical passages. A brand new document is created and it highlights the differences between the two documents as you can see below.

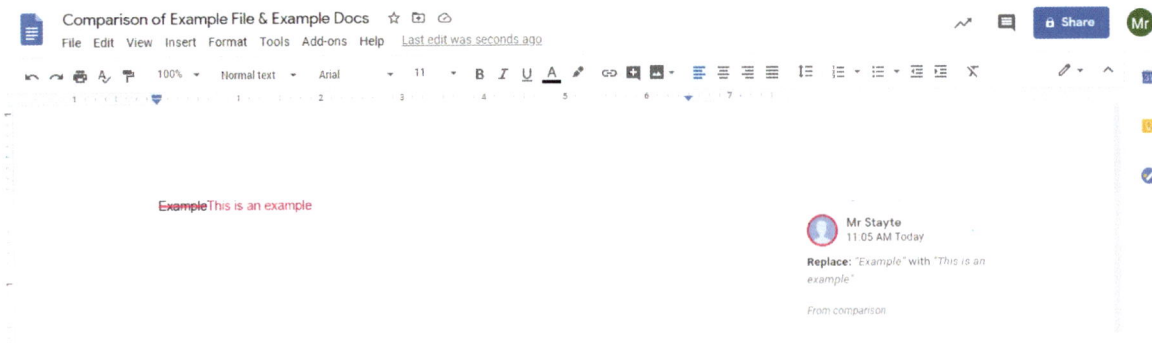

Google Sheets

As a teacher I would probably say that I use Google Sheets more than any other G Suite application simply due to the ease of using a spreadsheet program to create some of the resources and tracking sheets that I use on a day to day basis. I am going to go through some of the basics of using Google Sheets and demonstrate some of the most useful tools that are built in. The vast majority of these are tools that you can do on any spreadsheet program but I want you to be able to do them in Google Sheets and I suspect that also some of these tools will be things that you may not have used before or known you could do.

The one thing I will not be doing here is talking about spreadsheet formula as that is an entire book in itself. If that is something you would like to learn more about then I would encourage you to do so as being able to use spreadsheets and formula correctly and efficiently will save you enormous amounts of time.

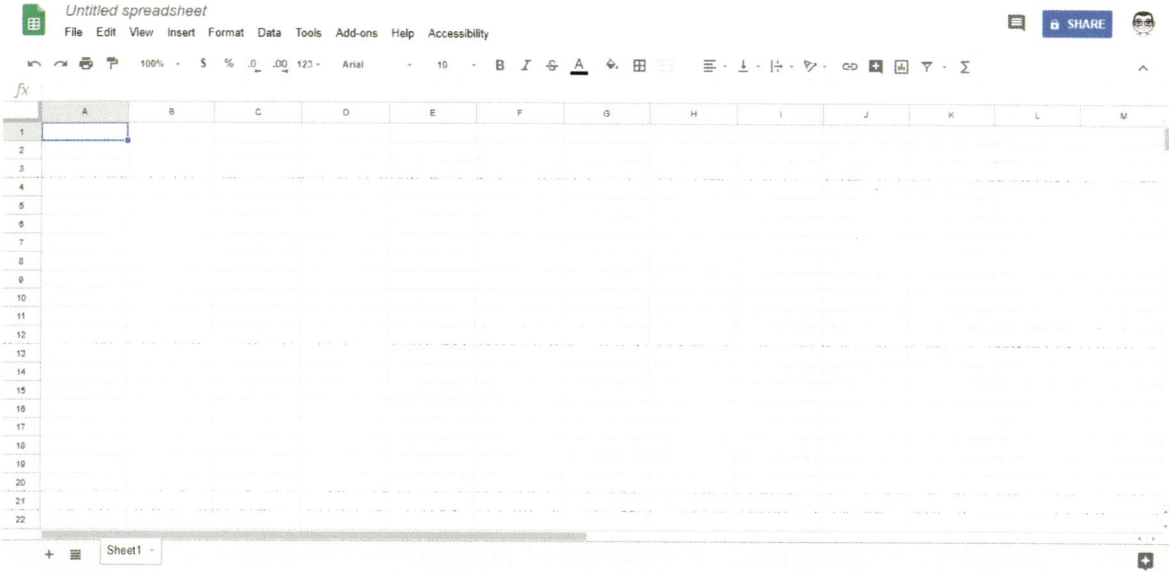

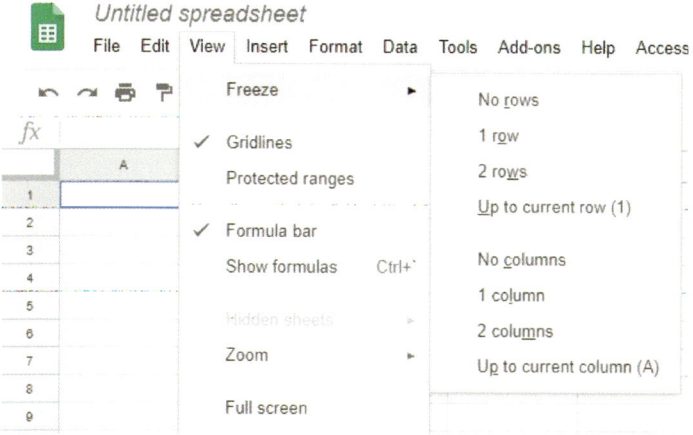

The first thing you should definitely be able to do is freeze your column headings so that you can always see them when you are scrolling through your Google Sheet.

Simply click on 'View' and select how many rows and/or columns you would like to freeze.

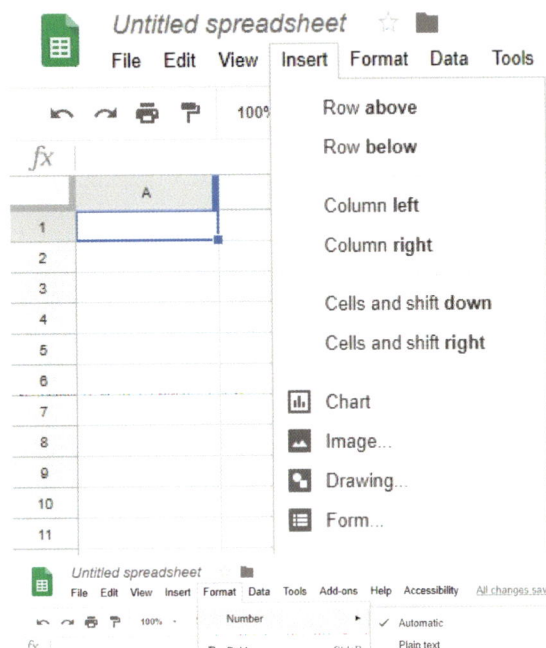

Insert options are very similar to the Google Doc options so I will not go through all of these again however if you are needed to insert columns or rows into your spreadsheet then you can use this menu to do so or right click on the column letter or row number.

Better than other Spreadsheet packages you can specify which direction you would like to insert your columns or rows and you can also do multiple inserts by first highlighting a number of columns or rows first.

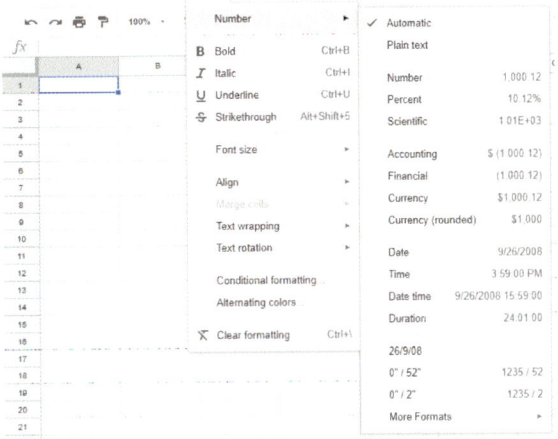

You can also apply different formats to the cell or cells you have highlighted using the 'Format' and then the 'Number' menu as shown here.

You need to be careful if like me you are in the UK and want to use Dates as these are often set to US standard and you will need to use the 'More Formats' option at the bottom in order to get the date to display correctly.

Conditional Formatting

Hopefully many of you teachers out there will already be familiar with the use of Conditional Formatting within spreadsheets and Google Sheets offers this functionality easily as well. If this is something that you were not aware of then conditional formatting is a way that you can make the colours and other formatting on a spreadsheet change depending on the number or values being displayed. For example, if you were using your spreadsheet to keep student's marks on a test then you could have the colours change to red if the student only scores 5 or less as an example. Shown on the next page is an example of using conditional formatting in a Google Sheet.

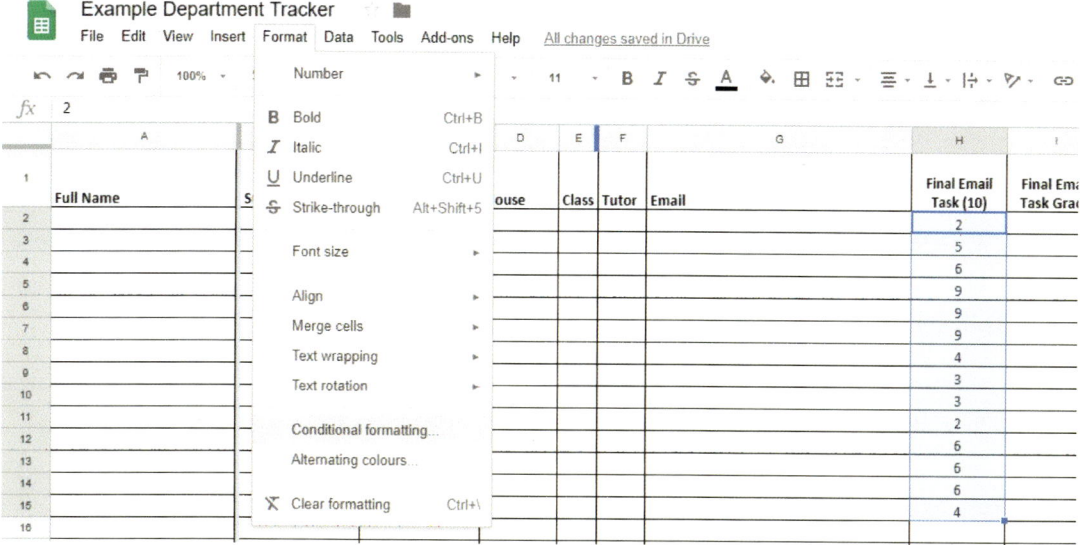

Highlight the data you would like to create conditional formatting on and then go to the Format menu and select Conditional Formatting.

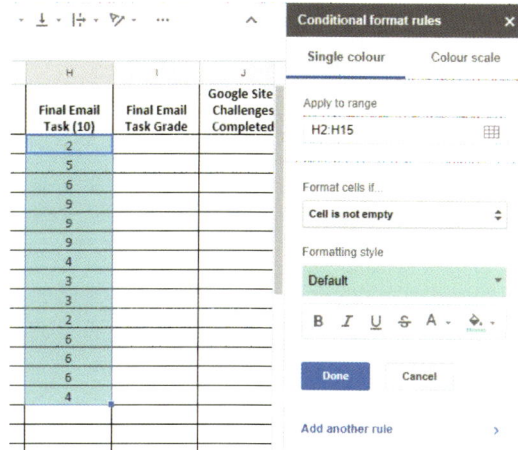

This will load up this side bar menu where you can control the conditional formatting rules that you would like to add to your Google Sheet.

The range is already selected due to your highlighting before clicking the menu. You can adjust the reason for formatting the cell and then adjust all of the formatting colours and options. You can also click 'Add another rule' once you have completed one.

As shown here you can add multiple rules to the same selected data and therefore can do a simple Red, Amber, Green type of conditional formatting.

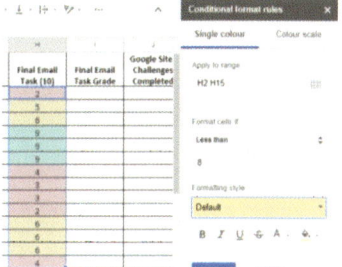
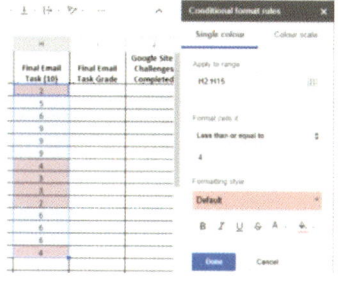

Here are all of the possible conditions that you can use.

Cell is empty
Cell is not empty
Text contains
Text does not contain
Text starts with
Text ends with
Text is exactly

Date is
Date is before
Date is after

greater than
Greater than or equal to
Less than
Less than or equal to
Is equal to
Is not equal to
Is between
Is not between

Custom formula is

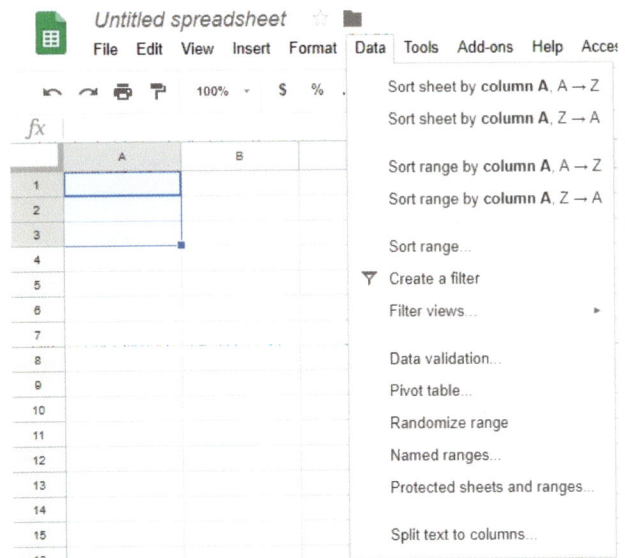

Sort Range

In the Data options you are able to quickly sort the spreadsheet by the column you are currently selected as shown here however for a more efficient sort of data you need to first select and highlight what you want to sort and then select 'Sort Range'.

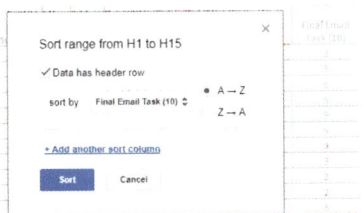

You can also tick the checkbox 'Data has header row' so that Google Sheets knows that the top row of the data selected contains the headings and you can choose to sort by the specific headings rather than column A for example.

Create a Filter

Creating a Filter in Google Sheet is a very fast and efficient way to allow you to only display the data you want to see at that time. Once you press 'Create Filter' Google Sheets will automatically take the top row as the column headings as shown here.

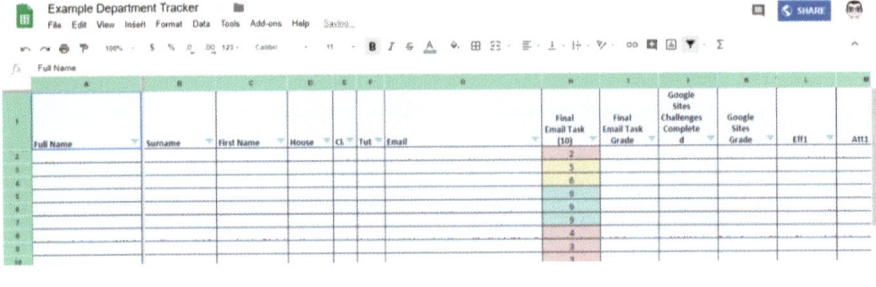

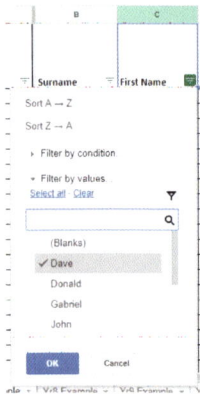

You can click on this icon at the top of your headings in order to adjust the filters being used. This menu will load and allow you to select the data you want to view. In this example I have selected the name Dave and all of the information in the spreadsheet will hide except for the row with 'Dave' in the First Name column.

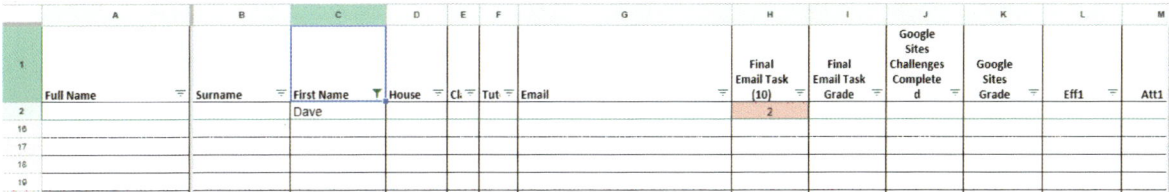

	A	B	C	D	E	F	G	H	I	J	K	L	M
1	Full Name	Surname	First Name	House	Cl	Tut	Email		Final Email Task (10)	Final Email Task Grade	Google Sites Challenges Completed	Google Sites Grade	Eff1	Att1
2			Dave						2					
16													
17													
18													
19													

 You can use this icon to load the menu again and remove the filter or add more. You can also use this icon in the main toolbar menu to remove all filters currently activated on the Google Sheet.

Protect Sheets and Ranges

This is a setting that is incredible useful if you want to share your Google Sheet with others however there a certain worksheets or indeed ranges of a worksheet that you do not want your editors to be able to change.

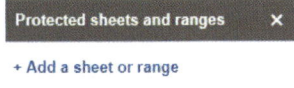 Once you load the menu you will be given this option to add a sheet or range rule.

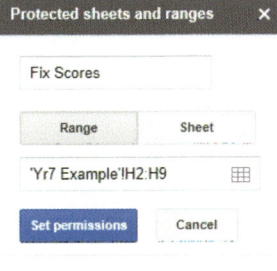 Once clicked you can then give your protection a name and also select the range of cells to be protected. You can click on the 'Sheet' button if you want to protect an entire worksheet.

Click 'Set Permission' to manage who has permission to edit.

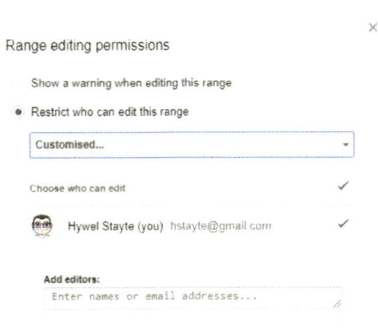 The permission box is very similar to any Google file sharing box and you can choose who is able to edit the range or worksheet you have selected.

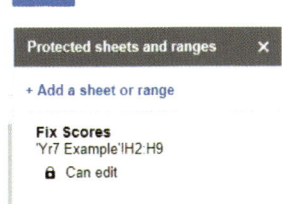 Your protection will be saved into the side menu bar and you can add as many different permissions and rules as you wish.

Split text to columns

I hope that if you have never seen this before you will be glad you read this section of the book as being able to manipulate data in this way is incredibly useful for teachers especially when you are exporting from your organisations MIS or another ICT System and the data comes out all as one chunk. Here is an example of some names that have been exported all in one cell.

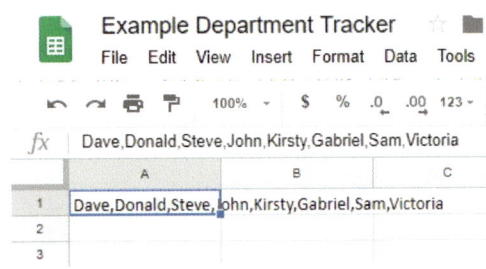

What would be far more useful would be if this data was split across the columns with one name per column. Spreadsheet software allows you to do this and Google Sheets is no exception. First click on the cell that contains the data and then go to the 'Data' menu and select 'Split text into columns'.

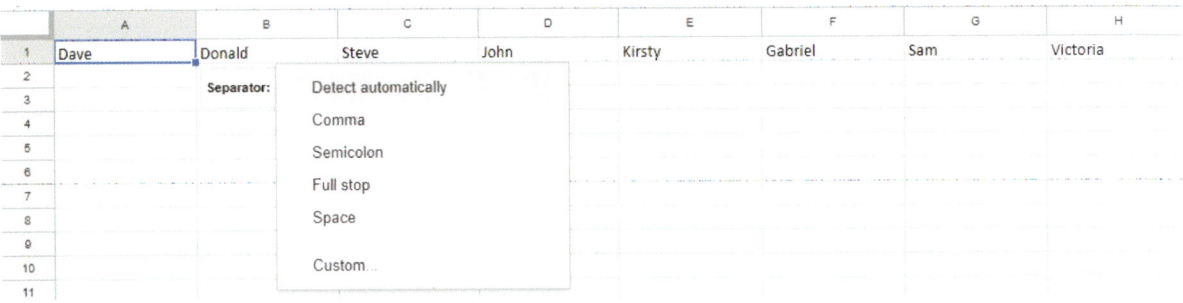

In this example because the names were separated by a comma Google Sheets has automatically guessed the separation and done it however you can specify how to split the data using some of the built in options as shown above and you can also choose Custom to separate data by any character of your choice. Some of you might now be thinking that this is good but wouldn't it be better if the names were going down the spreadsheet rather than across it.

Remove duplicates

Another fantastic feature in the 'Data' menu is the 'Remove Duplicates' option which allows you to select a range and automatically remove any duplicate entries. This was a feature that you would need an add-on or Google Apps Script to achieve so having this built in is very useful.

Trim whitespace

This is also an additional feature (in the 'Data' menu) that has now been built into Sheets meaning that when you import data and it comes in with additional spaces before or after the text you can use Trim whitespace to very quickly standardise your data and make it instantly workable for your needs.

Paste special Transpose

Following on nicely from our splitting of data into columns there is also a method of using copy and paste in order to change the data from going across the columns to going down the rows. Simply highlight the data you wish to change and copy it to the clipboard. (Ctrl + C) Then right click where you want the data to start and click 'Paste special' – 'Paste transposed' as shown below:

Notification rules

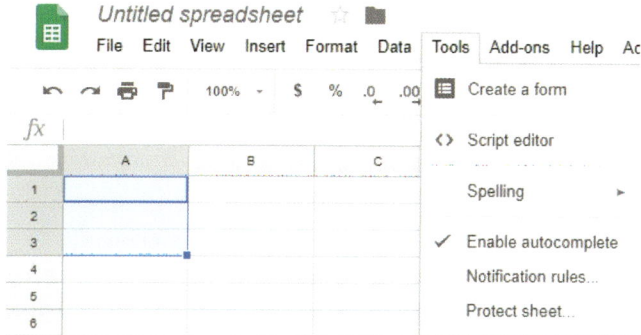

The final useful built in tool I want you all to be aware of are the notification rules that you can build into any Google Sheet. Find the 'Notification rules' option from the Tools menu.

The choices are limited without using Google Apps Script however for the majority of users' needs this menu does enough. You can set notifications every time someone completes a Google Form if there is one attached to the Google Sheet or any time a user makes a change to the spreadsheet.

With both of these options you can choose to be emailed straight away or receive a daily digest of the activities.

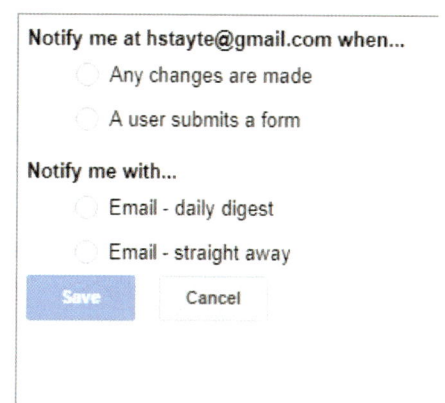

33

Get more out of Google Sheets

In this section about getting the most out Google Sheets I've tried to think of every possible way that I use Google Sheets in and outside of the classroom and within my general teacher admin role and how it can be a real benefit. All you need to do is figure out anything you use a spreadsheet package for and think is there a way I could use Google Sheets for this function and will it improve things. If the answer is yes and it would improve it then there is no reason not to use Google Sheets for this purpose. The following list is by no means exhaustive and I'm sure you can come up with even more ways to use Google Sheets within your teaching role and indeed in a school environment but this should hopefully give you some ideas of things you could do that you might not already be doing.

Teacher - Student Use

- Teaching spreadsheet alternative to an installed program

As a teacher of Computing I feel it is important that students are given a wide range of experiences using as many different types of software and programs as possible and therefore whenever I teach a unit of work on spreadsheets I make sure I use a mixture of local installed spreadsheet programs and cloud based using Google Sheets. One of the great things about using Google Classroom is that I can 'Make a Copy' for each student of the Google Sheet file and all of my students will be able to complete the spreadsheet activity on their own version of the file. This is much easier than emailing the students the file or getting them to get it off a public area on the school network.

- Creation of Graphs and Charts

Some of you may use spreadsheet software to create Graphs and Charts to represent data for reports and proposals etc but there are some advantages of using Google Sheets to create your graphs instead of a local spreadsheet package. If you create a graph in Google Sheets you can insert it into any other Google file such as Slides or Docs and create a link between the files meaning that if the graph is changed or updated, then the Google files where the graph has also been inserted will also be updated. This live link can also be turned off and you can insert static graphs and charts but it is also much easier inserting a graph from a Google Sheet into a Google Doc or Slides presentation than it is uploading from a local spreadsheet file.

- Creating Graph Maps - Geo Charts

This is a combination of Google Sheets and a use of maps. If you open a blank Google Sheet and type in country names down one column and statistics about a topic of your choice down the second column you can use the data to automatically create a world heat map.

Teacher - Admin Use

- Meeting Agendas and Minutes

Very similar to the use in Google Docs is the use of Google Sheets for meeting agendas which then turn into minutes. As mentioned in the Google Doc section a line management meeting may be better suited to Google Sheets as it is easier to duplicate worksheets with standard agenda items on. Of course you can just use copy and paste on a Google Doc but this just comes down to personal preference.

One little tip or trick that you need to be aware of when using Google Sheets for meeting agendas and minutes is that if you need a new line in a cell you will need to hold Ctrl on the keyboard and then press enter to get onto a new line. You can check out an example agenda in Google Sheets in the resources section.

- Lesson Observation Forms

If you want to use Google Sheets for lesson observations this may be easier as a proforma to create and use but again as with the meeting agendas this comes down to personal preference of which Google App you would like to use for this task.

- Curriculum Plans

Curriculum plans can work just as well in Google Sheets as they can in Google Docs but some people may prefer to use Google Sheets as their original curriculum plan was a spreadsheet and therefore it is just easier to upload the existing spreadsheet and convert it to a Google Sheet. Google Sheets are easier to use as Curriculum plans if your plan is in the form of a table as manipulating tables layouts in Google Sheets is much easier than in Google Docs or a word processor.

- Class Trackers / Department Trackers

Department trackers for me are one of the first major advantages which I saw coming from the introduction of Google Sheets because it solves the major problem of 'locked for editing' when someone else in the department was using the Department Tracker when you wanted to. Usually they would have left it open and gone home meaning there was just no way you were going to get on that file today! Google Sheets as a Department Tracker has removed all of this frustration from the equation and allowed the users to all be editing their respective classes worksheets all at the same time and also allowed the head of department to get a real time overview of all of the classes instead of having to ask teachers for mark books or their own personal spreadsheet trackers.

Having the Department Tracker as a Google Sheet also means that colleagues can share headings of their trackers with each other and also see how other classes are progressing in a much more open and collaborative manner. It also makes life easier if teachers are sharing a teaching group as there will only be one tracker for that group that both teachers can add and edit. It makes the head of departments job a lot easier when they receive a phone call from a parent who is in another class and they are able to look up the students' progress within another teacher's class within a matter of seconds.

Having the tracker in the cloud in this way has other advantages for teachers as well because if the tracker was a spreadsheet file stored on a school network then it is conceivable that a teacher may not have access to the drive from home. Therefore, they would be unable to update the tracker with marking and assignment grades until they were back in school however with Google Sheets they can access easily from wherever they are.

- Teacher Planner

This was something that took me a little while to get used to and make the change over to from my beloved paper 'Teacher Planner'. I am sure many of you still have them and use them religiously and by all means please carry on doing so. However, if like me you got fed up with carrying it around or getting frustrated when you left it at school then moving to an electronic teacher planner is the next logical step and Google Sheets is perfect for this task.

There is an example Teacher Planner Google Sheet included in the resources for you to look at but essentially you set up a Master Week (or two Master sheets if Week A and Week B) which you can then duplicate each week. The example has formula setup for the date so that you enter the Monday date and the rest of the worksheet populates with the correct date for that week. You can then record your planning for each lesson and mark off once the lesson is planned and you can add in more columns if you need to about collecting and setting homework for example.

- Timetable

Depending on your organisation depends very much the format of the timetable you are given but I am sure some of you out there like me copy across the timetable into a format they are used to whether that is electronic or paper based. I used to copy mine to a spreadsheet file but now I use Google Sheets for this process for several main reasons. The first one is that once it is only in Drive I have easy access to it wherever I am be it home, school or on the train. Secondly if you ever need to edit or change the timetable you can change the master file on Drive and all previous changes will be saved in the version history. Thirdly you can grant access to more than one person so all of the department can have access as well as trainee teachers as this is often very useful to them. In the example timetable you can see how it is also very easy to add a trainee teachers timetable of lessons below the existing staff making it very easy for all involved to create and manage the timetable. Although there are better ways in G Suite of doing this if you ever need to arrange a time for a meeting you can also share your Google Sheet timetable really easily with other people who can find a time for a meeting.

- Budgets and Tracking

I have met all sorts of heads of department, in fact anyone who managed a school budget, and everyone has their own method and ways of organising and keeping track of spending. Some people are very meticulous and have a ring binder folder for invoices and payments and keep a detailed track of budgets remaining. Other people like me however may very well have a folder but forget to keep track of what they have spent and how much is left!

This is where a Google Sheet has worked really well for me and every time any spending takes place in my department I automatically open my Google Sheet tracker and add the expenditure to it against my department budget. You can see this in the example file but the idea can be applied to an organisation's budget no matter how your budgets are arranged and sectioned up. The reason it works so well for me is being a Google Sheet I have a Chrome Bookmark directly to it so I can open it quickly and I also have it stored on my department Shared Drive.

- Textbook Tracker

Some of you reading this book will be responsible for keeping a track of which students have borrowed textbooks from the department and using a Google Sheet to do this can help make your lives easier especially when you can share it with others in the department to enter the details rather than one person having to do them all.

This also means that at book return time all of the teachers can also enter the return details and complete the Google Sheet from wherever they are and on whatever device they are using. I can already see some of you reeling in horror about giving everyone access to this master spreadsheet file and of course you do not have to give editing rights out to all. Having this type of spreadsheet as a Google Sheet means you could give viewing rights to all teachers so that they can see who in their groups have not returned books and this would help them manage and support getting all of the textbooks returned.

Google Slides

Google Slides is very useful as a teacher and I am sure many other people find the collaboration of Google Slides a life saver when working on a presentation with a group of people. The ability to all edit the same presentation and not have to pass parts of the presentation to one person to put together saves hours of time and hassle.

I do not want to go through all of the elements of a presentation package as that is not the point of this book but I will highlight some of the tricks to Google Slides and some of the elements you may not be aware of or have discovered yourself whilst using.

Import Slides

Under the file menu you can use a tool called Import slides which will allow you to import specific slides from other Google Slide presentations you have saved on Google Drive or indeed from local saved files which you can then upload. This is a great little tool if you want to piece a presentation together from lots of existing files you have or you just need a couple of slides from another.

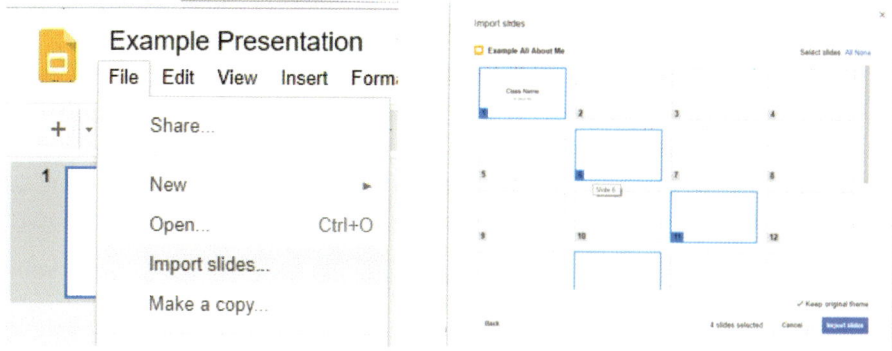

Inserting YouTube Video

Hopefully you have discovered this one yourself already however there are a couple of additional features about inserting from a YouTube video into Google Slides that are fantastic for in the classroom. Firstly, click the Insert menu and then click on Video.

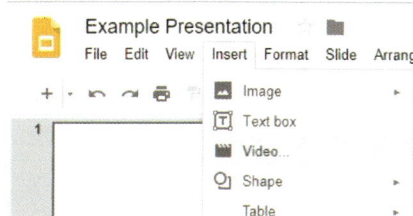

From this new menu you can search YouTube from within Google Slides meaning that whilst working on a presentation you can quickly search and insert a YouTube video effortlessly.

If you have already found a YouTube video that you would like to insert, then you can click on the 'By URL' option and paste the web address of the YouTube clip in. You can also insert any video that is stored in your Google Drive using this menu as well.

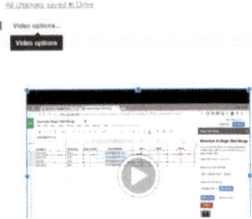

Once you have inserted a video into Google Slides there are some extra options you should be aware of. Whilst you have your inserted video highlighted you can click on the 'Video Options' button to load the side bar menu.

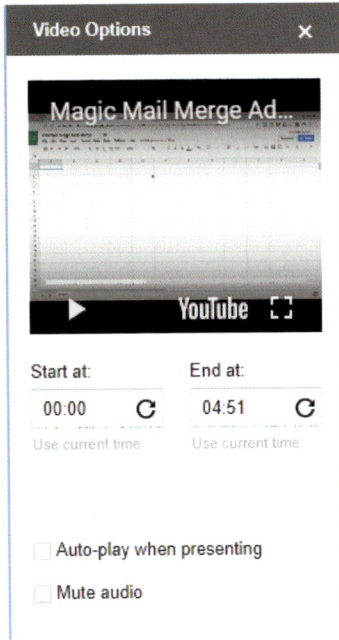

The most useful of the options available to you here is the ability to set a start and end time for the inserted video. Therefore, if you find a 45 minute YouTube video but only want to show 5 minutes of it during your lesson you can have the video inserted and pre-queued to play just the section of video that you require.

This tool saves time and also avoids that awkward moment of trying to find the exact part you need to show the students.

You can also have the video play automatically when the slide is loaded or mute the audio of the clip by using these checkboxes.

Inserting Audio

A recent update to Google Slides has been the ability to now insert Audio onto your Google Slides presentation.

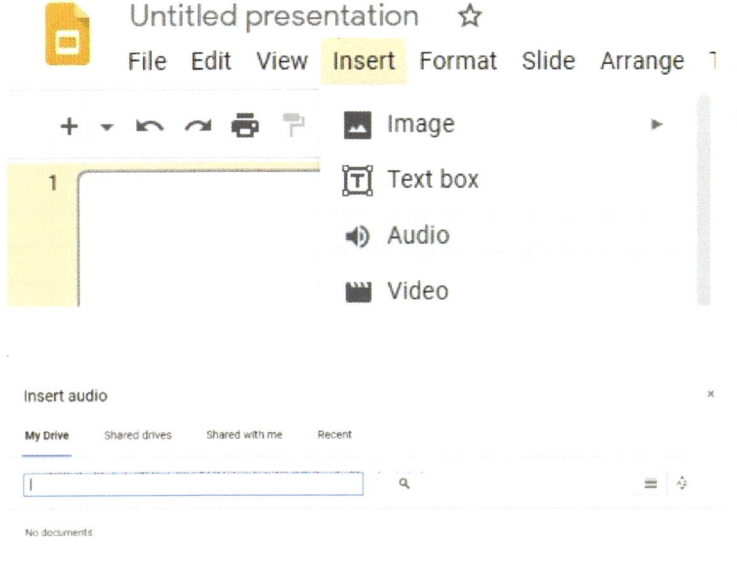

You will find this option next to video in the 'Insert' menu.

The usual insertion dialogue box will appear allowing you to insert audio from your My Drive, Shared Drive, Shared with me or Recent.

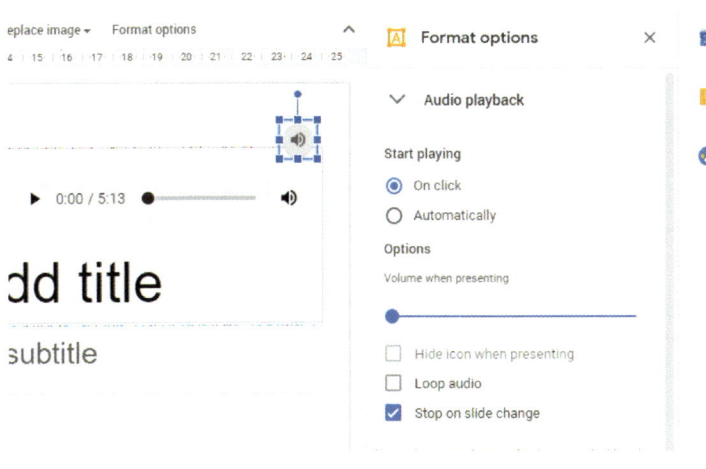

Once inserted onto your Slides you will see the Audio icon on the slides and when you click on it you will have the ability to play to test it. You can also click on 'Format options' in order to load the sidebar menu as shown in this image, giving you more options on how you would like the Audio on your presentation to behave.

Keep Notepad

I will be exploring the use of Google Keep later on but I wanted to highlight that the same functionality is available in Google Slides. Personally, I see myself being more likely to have used Google Keep for making some notes that I would then put into a Google Slides presentation and therefore having the ability to load up Google Keep as a sidebar menu within Google Slides is a huge advantage.

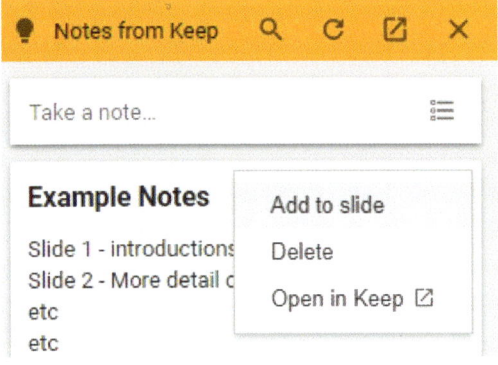

Once opened you can then drag and drop onto the slide you want the information to be on or simply click the 3 dots and click 'Add to slide' and the text will be added beautifully to the slide with your title from Keep as the title of the slide.

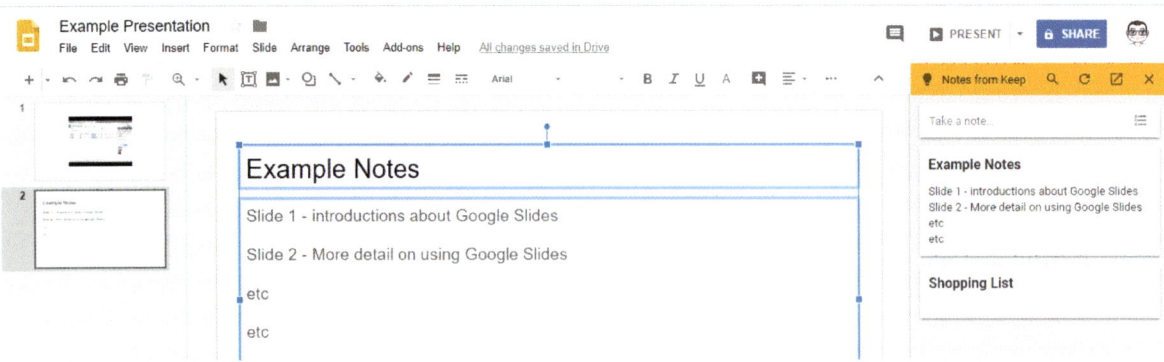

Voice Type Speaker Notes

Just like using within Google Docs you can use Voice Typing within Google Slides to help you with the creation of speaker notes. As previously mentioned the accuracy of this is good and you can create speaker notes very fast and efficiently using your computer's microphone. Voice Typing is also incredibly useful if you want to work using a small tablet or mobile phone as often the keyboard is too small to create something lengthy whereas if you use voice typing then you can create relatively large amounts of text.

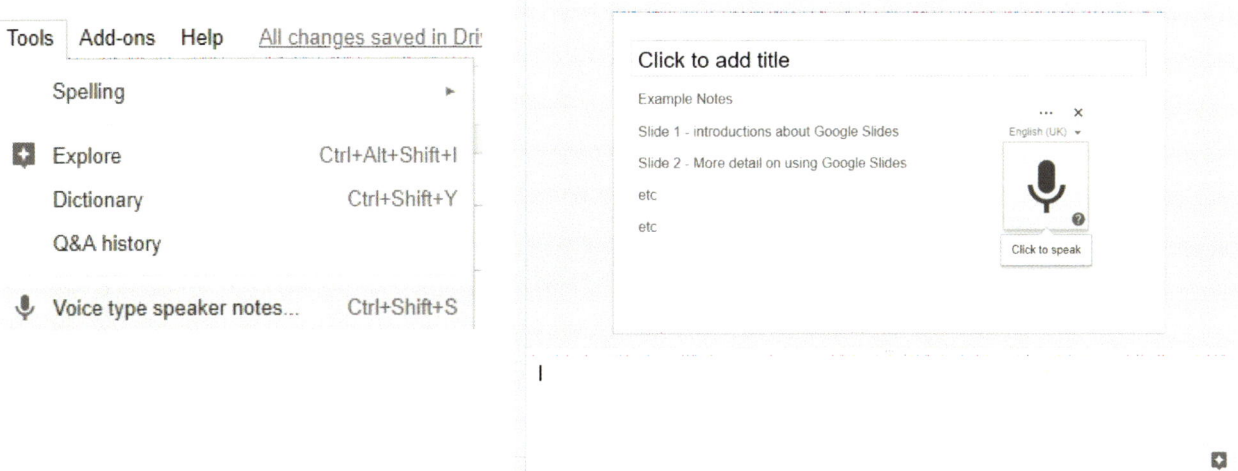

Q&A Feature

In the age of BYOD and the vast majority of people having a mobile device which can access the internet, having the ability to run audience participation from within Google Slides is a fantastic addition. The drop down arrow on the 'Present' button gives you extra options than just presenting such as 'Presenter view' and 'Present on another screen'. Present on another screen makes use of Chromecast and you can send your presentation to another screen that way.

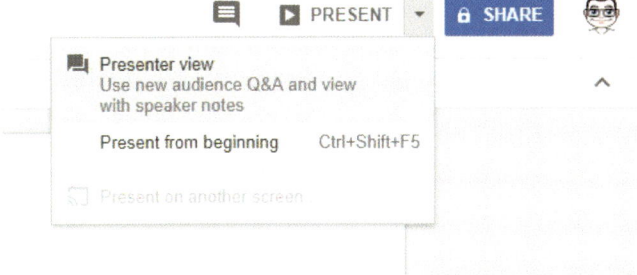

Presenter View is the one I want to look at in more detail with the ability to offer audience Q&A from within your Google Slides presentation as well as viewing your speaker notes. Once you click this button you get a new menu pop up as well as your presentation.

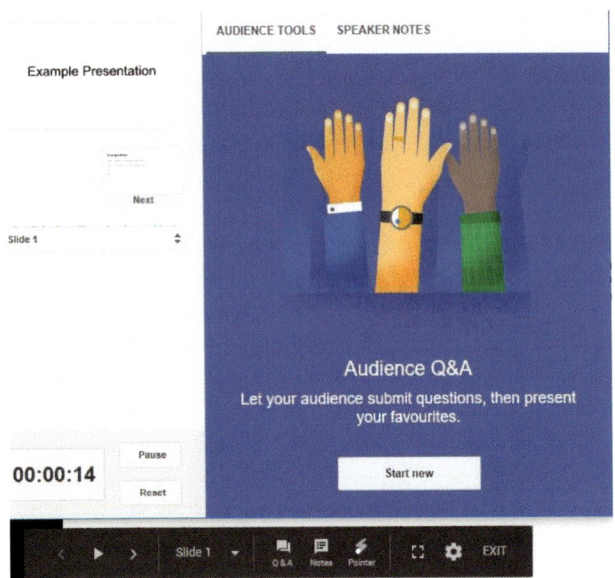

Here you have two sections to choose from, Audience Tools and Speaker Notes. This handy window allows you to control your presentation questions as well as letting you easily read your speaker notes. This does rely on you being able to keep your presentation on one screen and this window on another for you to look at.

Once you press 'Start now' as shown here you will turn on questions and an automatic link will be generated and displayed as a header on your presentation allowing the audience to visit the question page and submit them.

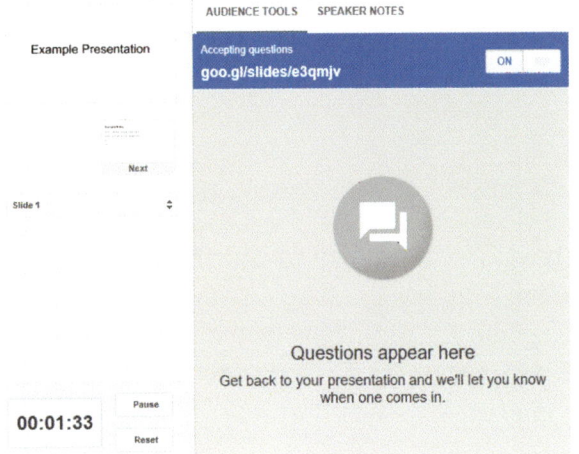

Ask a question at **goo.gl/slides/e3qmjv**

Example Presentation

Once the audience visits the link displayed in the presentation they can submit questions as shown on the next page. They can also choose to do this anonymously and have up to 300 characters to ask their question.

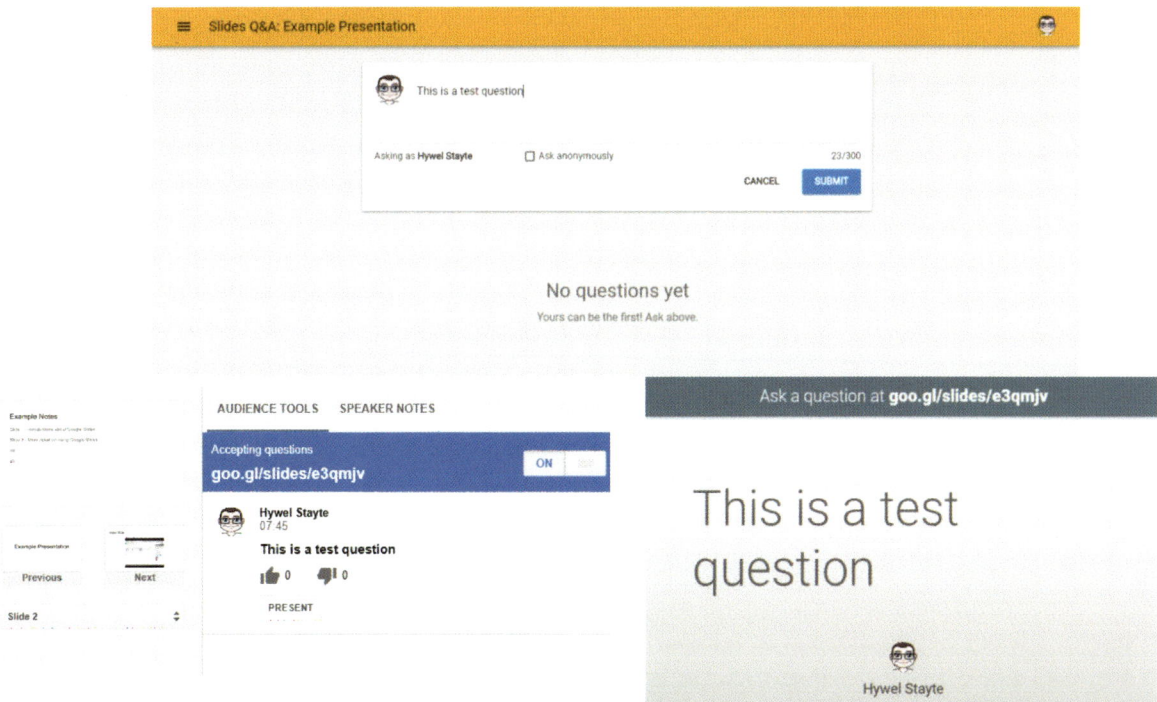

Questions will appear on both the presenters window as shown above and on the submit a question screen. The audience can then vote up or down question that have already been asked to make the most important question to the most people appear at the top of the list. The presenter can then also choose to 'Present' the question to the audience and Google Slides will take over the presentation with a new slide displaying the question that has been asked which allows the presenter to tackle the question within the presentation and move on when required back to the original slide.

As with everything Google all of the questions asked are stored and saved within the Google Slides presentation and can be accessed via the Tools menu shown here.

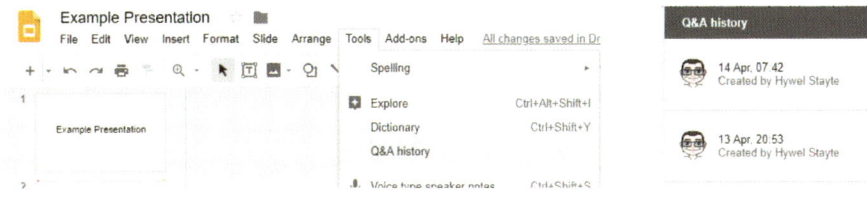

Get more out of Google Slides

There are many uses of presentations within your school environment and in your professional role and what I will attempt to do below is list some ways that using Google Slides might be of benefit to you.

Teacher - Student Use

- Teaching presentation alternative to an installed program

This does have some advantages and most of the options are available in Google Slides that you will find on any local presentation package however the online saving and automatic saving is a huge advantage. I would always argue that it is important to teach both a locally installed presentation package and a cloud based one so that students can see the differences between them but I am finding more and more that students prefer the cloud based packages.

When using Google Slides instead of a local presentation package you also have the advantage that when you need to share the presentation with the teacher to show back the student can simply share via Google. This way the teacher can have full access whereas in the past we would have had to use email or alternatively a memory stick in order to view the presentation.

- Creation of group presentations

This is where Google Slides is hands down vastly superior to a locally installed presentation package. Students are able to work in groups on the same presentation and where in the past they would have all had to have worked on sections and had one person put the whole thing together at the end using Google Slides they can collaborate in real time and work on the presentation together. The ability to chat while working on a document or presentation also has a massive advantage as the students can be working on these presentations from home and collaborating at the same time.

The first time I really saw the power of Google Slides was when I set a group task for students to complete and they automatically opened Google Slides and shared it with each other without me instructing them to do so. The students recognise the advantages of Google Slides straight away and can use it to their advantage.

- All about me presentations (Class activity)

This is an activity that I still do when I'm introducing young students to the power of Google Slides. First I set up a presentation with 25 slides or however many there are in my class and I give each student a number and tell them that they are allowed to edit that one slide only. Then I share the presentation with all the students and they complete their slide of the presentation and in probably about 15 to 20 minutes we have a full 25 slide presentation about the entire class.

This task is really good for showing students both the functionality of Google Slides but also the collaboration element to it. Students quickly grasp the fact that they could then use this to help them in any presentation they have in the future. With all of the Google Apps it is important to make the students understand and recognise the advantages of using a online cloud based software instead of a locally saved piece of software and the built in advantages of collaboration that Google Apps offer.

- Creation of lesson resource presentations

If like me you're a teacher who likes to have a presentation for every lesson you teach, then using Google Slides can help you here as well. Firstly, all you have to do is upload all of your existing presentations to Google Drive in order to just use them within your classroom and within Google Classroom. Once all of your presentations are uploaded to Google Drive you can choose to use them within a lesson and present directly from Google Slides or you can insert them into Google Classroom to allow your students have access to the resources you've created. Also by having your Google Slides presentations on Google Drive you have access to them whenever you want and wherever you are.

Teacher - Admin Use

- Creation of presentations to staff

Along with any proposals you may create using Google Docs you may also be required to create a presentation using Google Slides. Similar to using Google Docs and collaborating with colleagues on them you can do the same thing with your Google Slides presentation and allow colleagues to edit and change the presentation as well as adding their own notes etc. Another advantage of using Google Slides in this way is instead of having to use a memory stick or access your own network area when you arrive to do your presentation all you need to do is log into your Google account via Chrome and you all of your files will be there and ready to access.

Google Forms

I do not know where I would be without my Google Forms! This G Suite tool is so useful and practical in so many ways within an educational environment and in this section of the book I have been able to identify quite a substantial number of ways in which you can all use Google Forms. I will give a little more of a demonstration in how to use and setup a Google Form as this is the first app that is not like a locally installed program most of us have been using for years.

Google Forms

Elements of a new Google Form

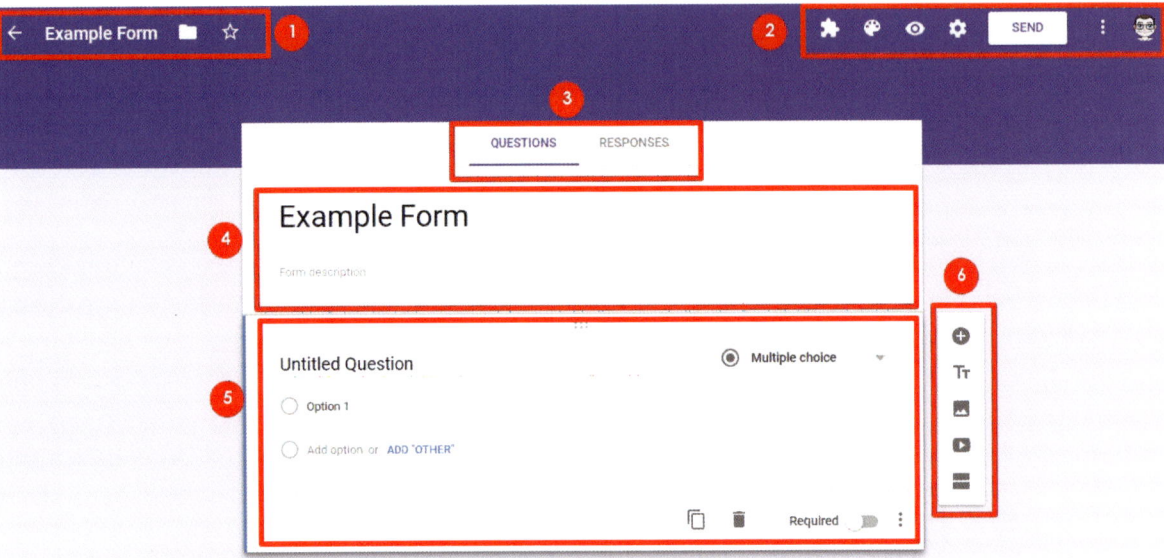

1. Name and Drive controls
2. Options and Settings controls
3. Questions and Responses
4. Name and Description displayed on form
5. Question controls
6. Add item controls

Name and Drive controls

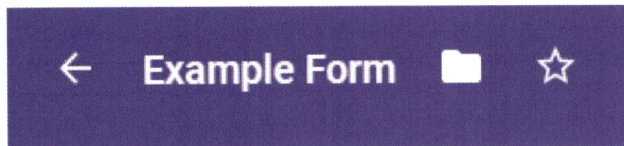

The arrow here takes you back to 'Forms Home' which is an alternative viewing version to Google Drive where only the forms you have created are displayed. The next section is the name of your form as it is stored in Google Drive. The folder icon allows you to organise where the form will be saved in your Google Drive and finally the star allows you to star this form for easy finding within Drive.

Options and Settings controls

1. This is the add-on icon allowing you to connect apps to your form
2. This is the colour palette allowing you to adjust the colours of your form or upload an image
3. This is the preview button so you can see what your form will look like (This actually takes you to the live version of your form as it is at that time)
4. This is the settings menu button of your form and how it works

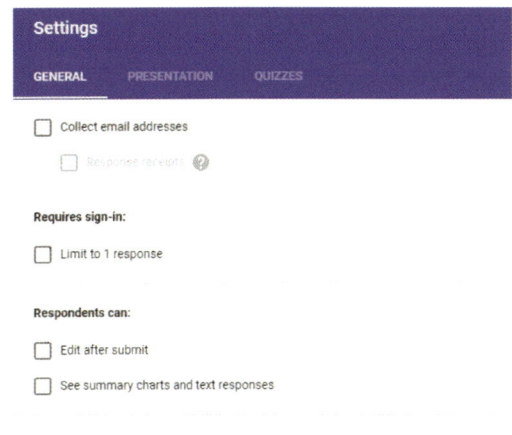

The tab of 'General' settings is shown here.

The first checkbox allows you to select to collect email addresses. If you have a Google for Education domain and are using this within your organisation, then the email addresses will be automatically collected when you tick this box. If you are using it outside of your domain then this will automatically add a question asking for email address and makes this a required field with validation that it must be a correct email address.

If you are collecting email addresses within your domain and people are required to sign in in order to complete your form, then you can also click to limit the responses to 1 meaning that you can only complete the form once. This is a very handy option when using Google Forms for voting purposes as one example when this is required.

The final options allow you to decide if a person can edit their responses after they have submitted and also whether or not they should get to see what the results have been so far after submitting their form.

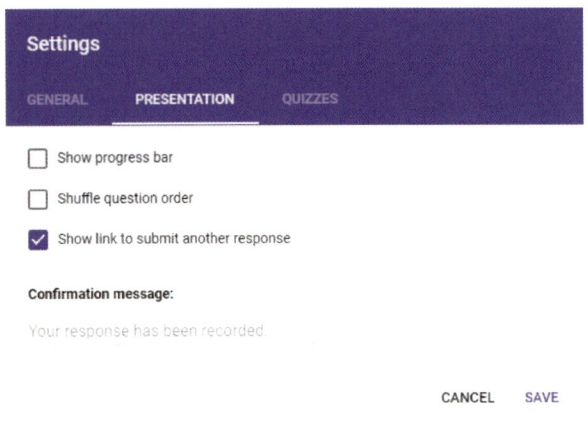

The second tab called Presentation simply gives you a few extra options of how your Google Form works and looks. The progress bar is useful if you have sectioned up your form into multiple pages and shows the user how much more they must complete. If you have all your questions on one page, then there is no need to have a progress bar.

Shuffle question order does exactly what it says and will randomise the order of questions for each user. This can be very useful if you have students taking an assessment and you do not want them to all be working on the same questions at the same time and can just help a little with reducing the chances of cheating in the test.

Finally, you have a checkbox to show a link to submit another response however this option is not available if you have already selected that the users can only submit 1 response. The confirmation message is what will appear at the end of a Google Form once the responses have been submitted and this can be personalised here. Along with changing the message to a more personal one you can also add links in this box to the next classroom task for example and turn the form into a springboard for the next activity.

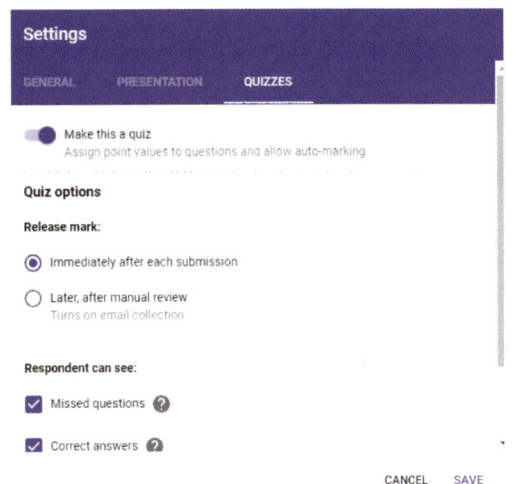

The final third tab is the Quizzes tab which allows you to turn any Google Form into a self-marking quiz built into Google Forms. Simply press the slider button to turn the quiz feature on and then review the options available to you.

Please see page 53 for a more detailed review of how to use Google Form Quizzes.

5. This is the sharing button which gives you 6 options of ways to share your form via email, link, embedding or through social media.

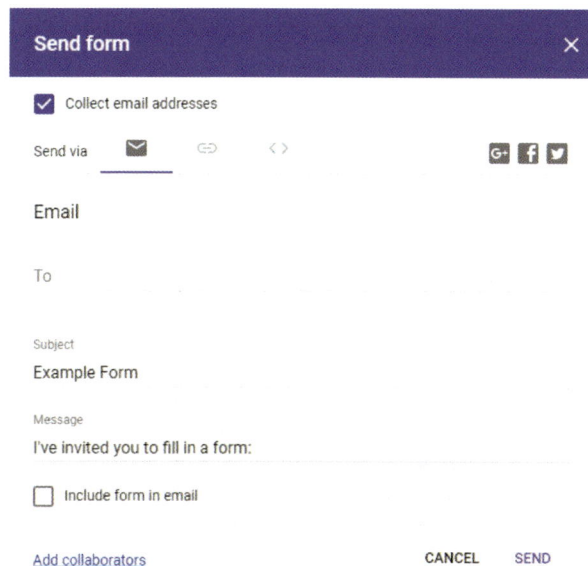

As you can see here from the menu box the default way to send your completed form out to people is via email. This box allows you to enter email addresses and if you start typing you will automatically search the directory. You can also email out to groups that you have setup on your domain.

You can then personalise the email using the subject and message boxes. You can also include the email in the form so the receiver doesn't even need to click a link but can complete straight in their inbox.

You also have an 'Add collaborators' button if you would like to invite people to help design and create your Google Form.

Using the buttons across the top of this menu you can change the way in which you are sharing the Google Form. If you click on the link button, you can copy and paste a link to your Google Form (this is the same link that the preview button opens). The next icon along is the embed code, which allows you to get the code to embed the form in your website. Lastly, the next three are quick links to sharing on social media allowing you to quickly share to Google+, Facebook or Twitter.

6. This is the settings button for the editing of your form

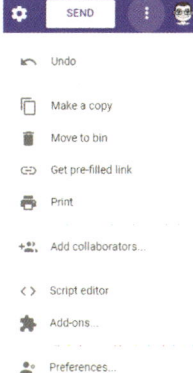

The majority of these options are self-explanatory and similar to the other G Suite applications such as 'Make a copy', 'Move to bin', 'Add collaborators', 'Script editor' and 'Add-ons'.

Print allows you to print off you Google Form in a format that can be completed on paper if you need to.

I will go through 'Get pre-filled link' and 'Preferences' in a little more detail.

⊂⊃ Get pre-filled link

This is an incredible useful tool that enables you to partially/fully complete the Google Form in advance for the users you are going to send it to. This means that you can save them all time by having the form already filled in and completed and the users can simply review and press submit giving their responses.

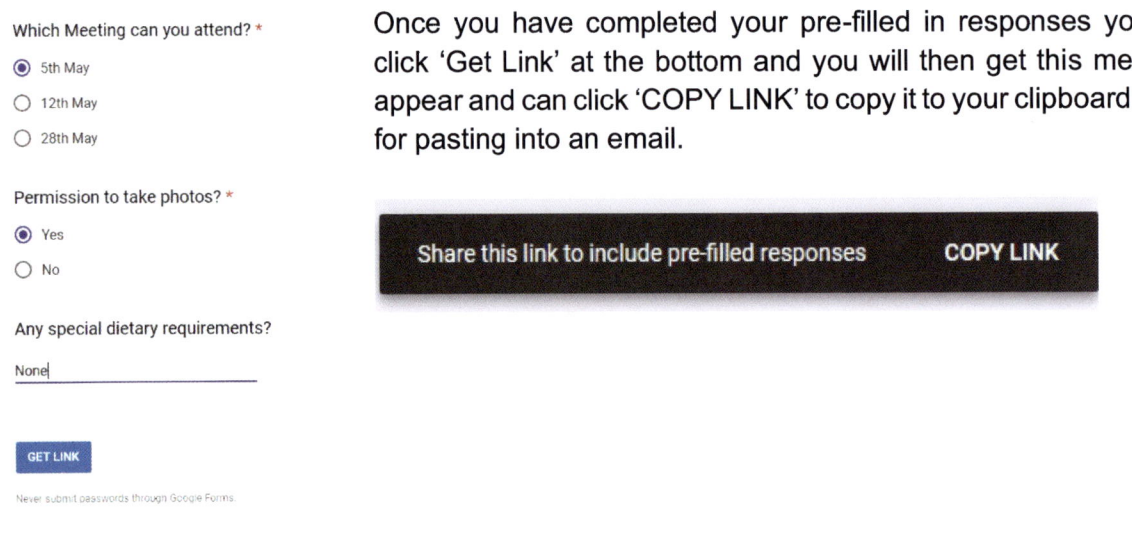

Once you have completed your pre-filled in responses you can click 'Get Link' at the bottom and you will then get this message appear and can click 'COPY LINK' to copy it to your clipboard ready for pasting into an email.

●⚙ Preferences...

The preferences option will load up this menu:

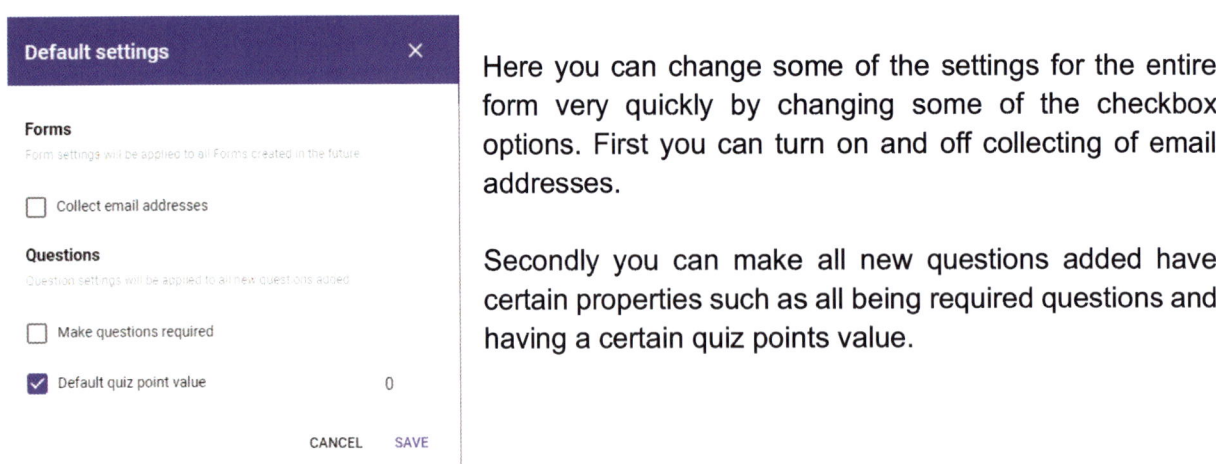

Here you can change some of the settings for the entire form very quickly by changing some of the checkbox options. First you can turn on and off collecting of email addresses.

Secondly you can make all new questions added have certain properties such as all being required questions and having a certain quiz points value.

7. This is your account button which allows you to switch users if required

Questions and Responses

This option allows you to switch between the Questions view allowing you to add and edit the questions and the Responses view allowing you to view the results of anyone who has completed you form already. Shown here you can see no one has completed the form yet.

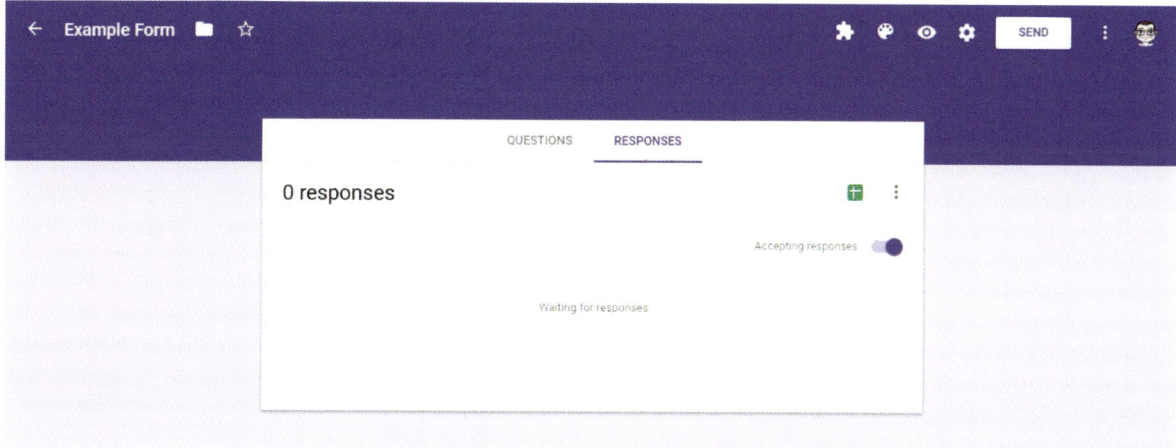

Now you can see the view once 3 people have completed the form and the graphs automatically generated from the responses.

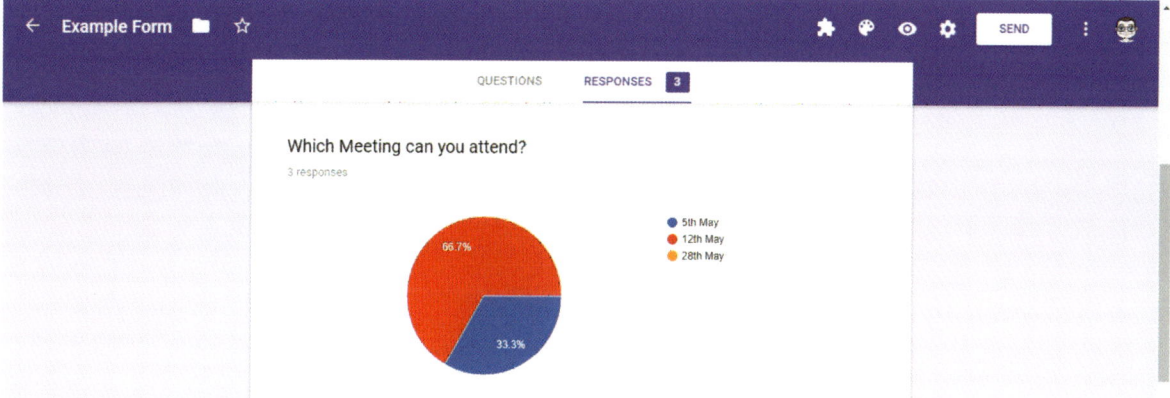

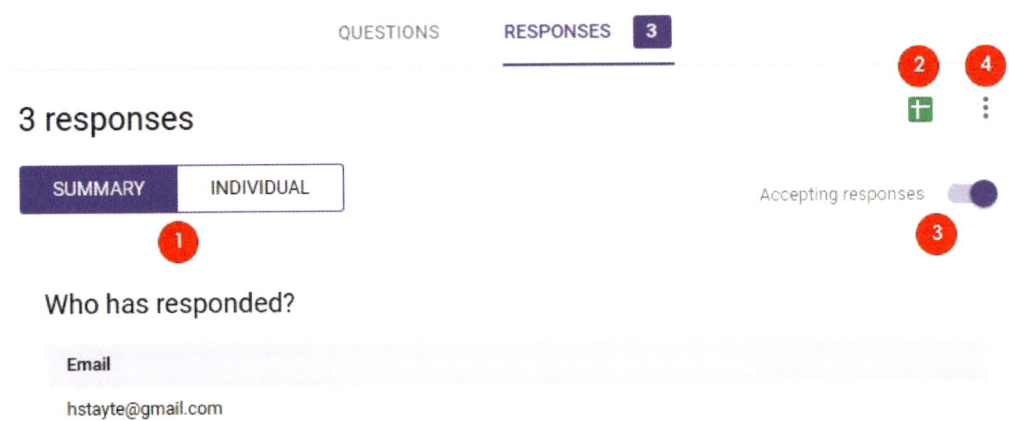

1. These buttons allow you to switch the responses view from the summary of all responses to the individual responses meaning you can review individual answers if required
2. This is a very important option that creates a linked Google Sheet with the Google Form meaning that all responses and future responses are also stored in the Google Sheet and not just the form
3. Here you can turn off the form from accepting new responses meaning that no one else can fill in the form
4. These are the extra option and settings available

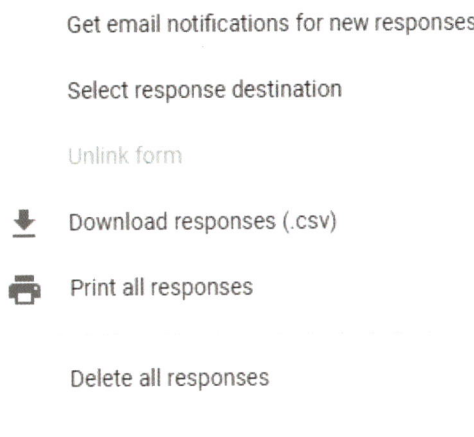

If you want to receive notifications when someone completes a form you can manage that here. You can also select to create a Google Sheet to store the results or link to an existing Google Sheet. Once you have linked the form to a Google Sheet you could also unlink the form using these options.

Download responses(.csv) allows you to download the results in a spreadsheet format that you can open locally on your computer. Print all responses does exactly that and allows you to print the responses in a viewable format. Delete all responses means that you can delete all of the data captured in a Google Form and start again which is very handy if you have been testing out your form before sending out.

Name and Description displayed on form

This is straightforward and is the information that is going to be displayed to the user when they are completing the Google Form. Simply change the text to suit your form and as with all Google products the form will automatically save.

Question controls

The following question controls do alter slightly depending on the type of question you have selected but there are many similarities in controls between questions which I will go through first.

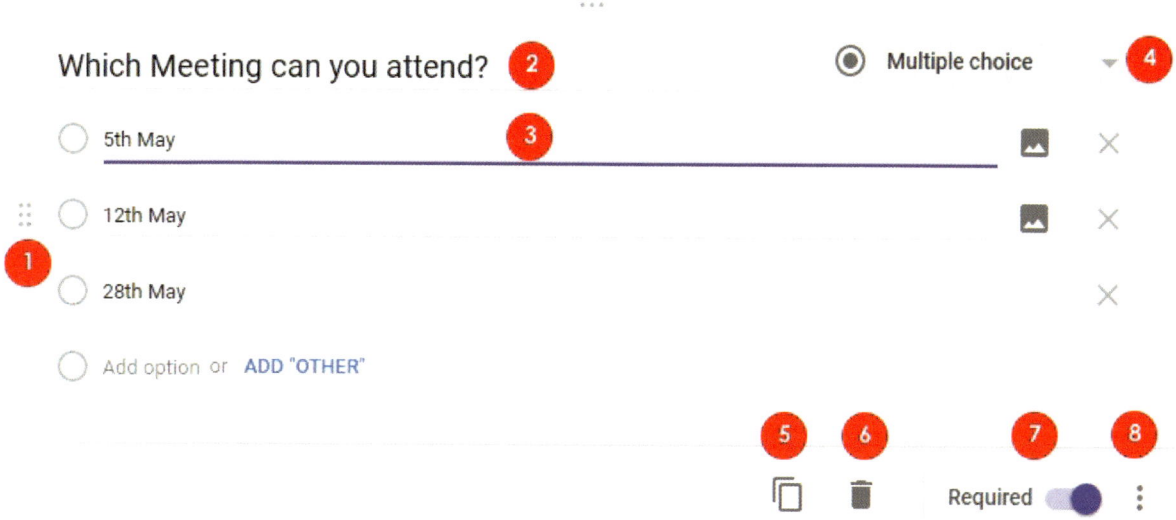

1. These 6 dots allow you to move the position of the question within your Google Form and simply click here and drag up or down
2. This is the title of the question
3. Here are the controls for the multiple choice question where you can add options, change to a picture or delete the option
4. This drop down menu allows you to quickly change the type of question being used
5. This is a tool for duplicating the question. This is very useful if you have the same options repeatedly as you can just duplicate the question and change the question title
6. This deletes the current question
7. This makes the question a required question
8. Here are some extra question controls that you can select

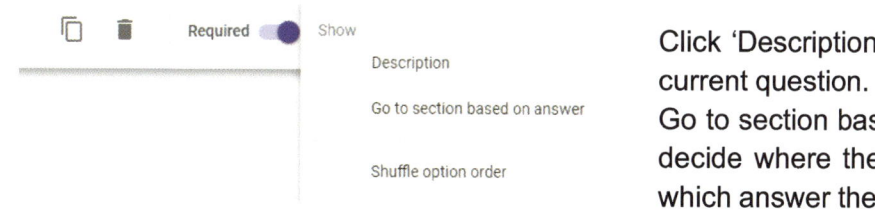

Click 'Description' to add a description to the current question.

Go to section based on answer allows you to decide where the user will go depending on which answer they select.

Shuffle option order will randomise the order of the options every time a user loads the form.

Types of Google Form Questions

1. **Short answer** — 1. This is a short free typed answer

2. **Paragraph** — 2. This allows for a longer typed answer

3. **Multiple choice / Checkboxes / Dropdown** — 3. All three of these options allow for you to setup choices for the user to select. Multiple choice and Drop-down only allow one answer whereas Checkboxes allow for multiple answer to be selected

4. **File upload** — 4. File upload allows the user to upload files and they are automatically stored in the Google Drive of the owner of the form

5. **Linear scale** — 5. Linear scale allows you to select a scale from 1-10 for example

6. **Multiple choice grid / Checkbox grid** — 6. These next two are like multiple choice and checkboxes but allow you to have a grid of choices with rows and columns

7. **Date / Time** — 7. You can add a date and time question. This is useful for the user to select a date and time however you do not need to have this for when they completed the form as a timestamp is automatically collected when the user completed a form

Add item controls

1. This is the button to add a new question to your form

2. This button allows you to re-use questions from other forms which is great for building end of year assessments from form topic tests

3. This button allows you to add an extra title and description (Useful for sectioning out parts of your form)

4. This is to add an image to your form. This can be very useful for assessments because you could add exam questions from papers as images as one example

5. This button is to add a YouTube video to your Google Form. A nice simple idea here is to have a video for the students to watch and then have focus questions they can answer after. This can also work really well as a Homework task

6. This button adds a new section (page) to your Google Form allowing you to distribute the questions better over pages. This is also what you need to use if you want users to go to different questions based on different answers.

Creating Quizzes in Google Forms

I want to dedicate this next section to using the relatively new quiz feature that has been built into Google Forms and will allow you to create self-marking quizzes. When I first began using Google Forms for assessments this feature did not exist which is why I always use Flubaroo add-on for Sheets however the easiest thing to do for the new Google user is Form Quizzes.

If you want your quiz to be self-marking and assign a points score depending on how well the students do, then you need to use questions which have an exact correct answer and not a subjective mark. Multiple choice questions are ideal for this as you can select which option is the correct answer but you can also use the other types of questions as well and as long as the answer key matches then the marks will be awarded.

The first thing you need to do is to create a quiz in Google Forms as shown here:

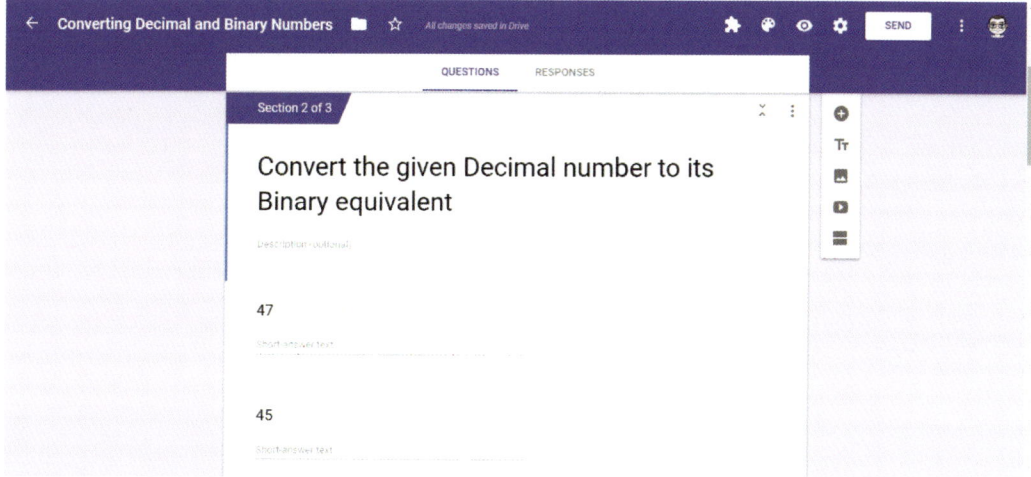

Next you need to go to the settings menu and the 'Quizzes' tab to turn your form into a Quiz as shown here.

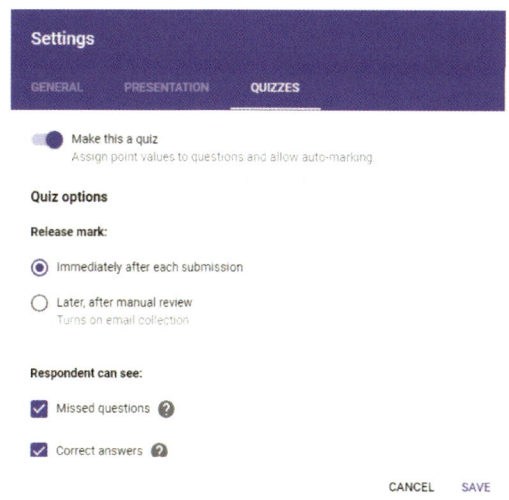

In this example I will be using short text answer questions and I want the quiz to self-mark and give the students their mark at the end of the quiz.

Now I can go back to the questions to edit them and a new option appears at the bottom of each question called 'ANSWER KEY' which is a link to add the correct answer.

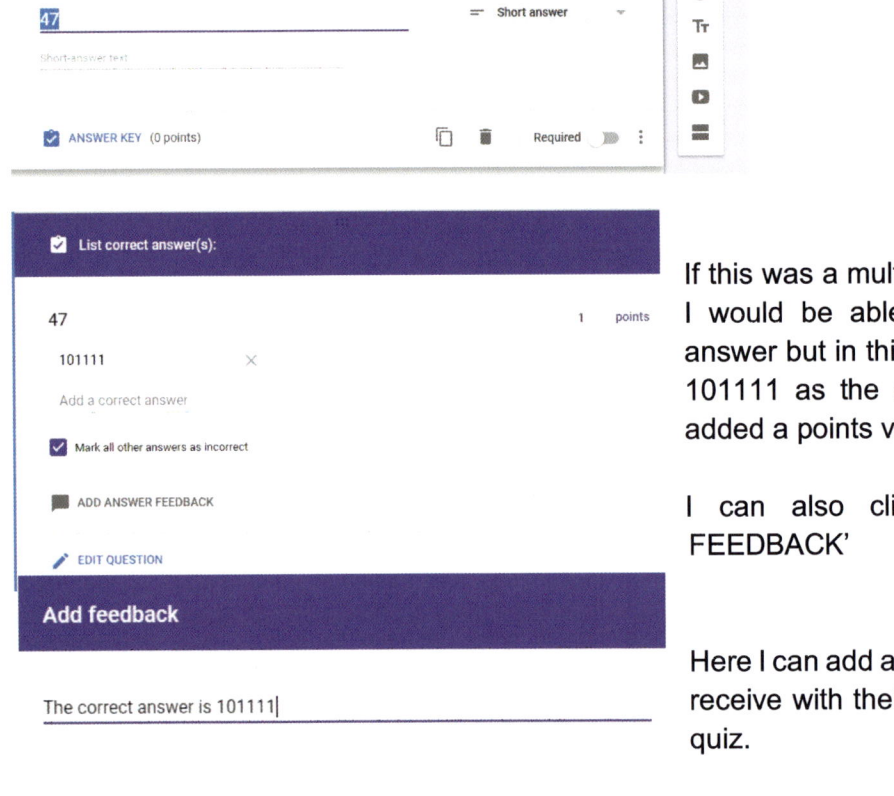

If this was a multiple choice question, then I would be able to click on the correct answer but in this example I have typed in 101111 as the correct answer and have added a points value for this question of 1.

I can also click on 'ADD ANSWER FEEDBACK'

Here I can add a message that the user will receive with their results at the end of the quiz.

You can now go through each question and add the answer and the number of marks each question is worth. Once you have done this you can preview what your quiz will look like.

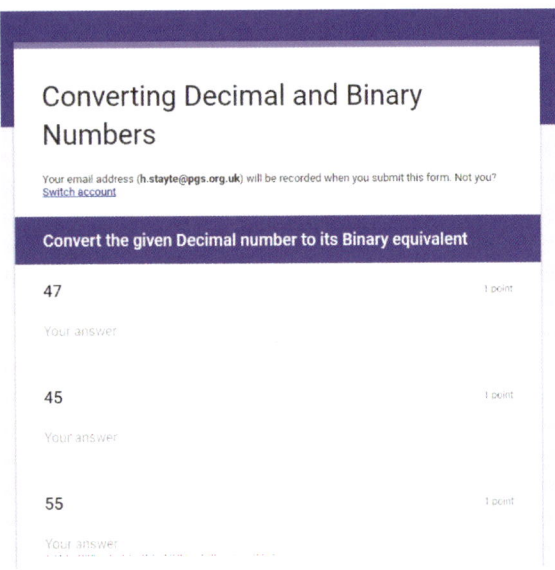

You can also insert this Google Form quiz into Google Classroom which has some extra advantages as well.

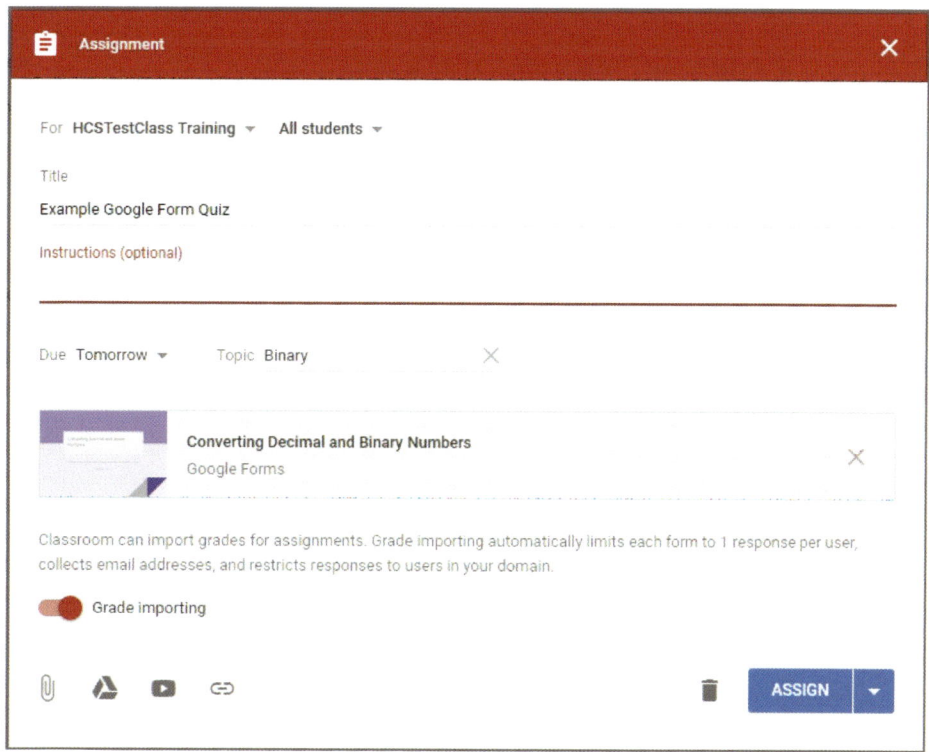

Because this is a Google Form quiz once you have added it to Google Classroom as an assignment you are given the extra 'Grade importing' option. This means that once the students have taken the quiz their scores can be automatically imported into Google Classroom mark book.

Another clever trick with inserting Google Forms into Classroom is that once a student has submitted the Google Form the assignment will automatically be marked as done providing there are no other files listed in the assignment.

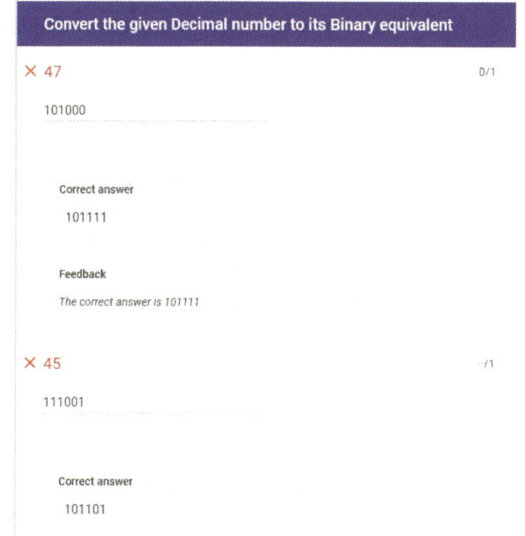

Here you can see the students view after they have taken the quiz and the different information that is displayed.

The correct answer is displayed but also the feedback text. You can use the feedback text in many ways and it may be more useful to the student to have links to model answers or helpful resources if it is an area they are struggling with.

Here is the teacher view of the Google Classroom assignment once one student has completed the Google Form. As you can see it has automatically marked the assignment as completed for that one student and also now loaded an extra option button at the top right called 'Import Grades'.

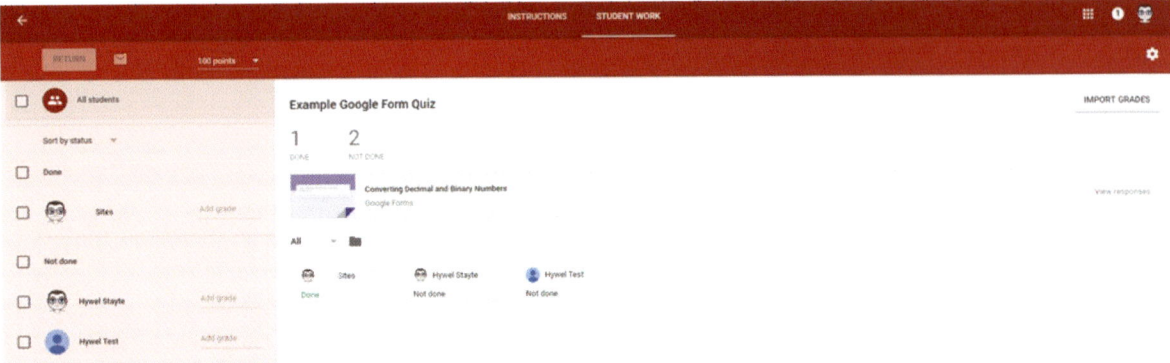

Once you click Import Grades the following warning message will appear.

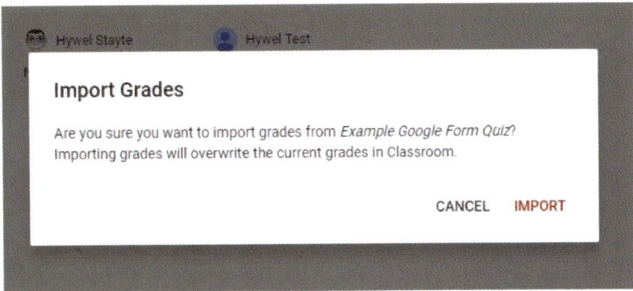

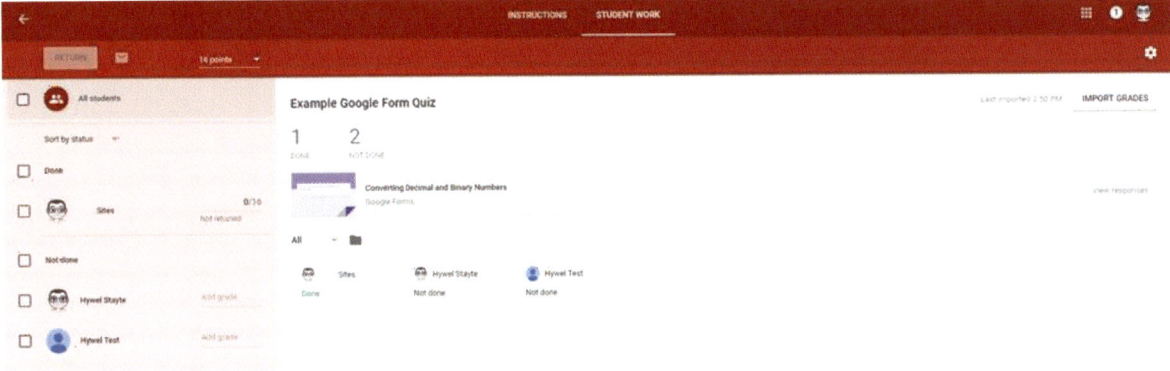

Once the grades have been imported you can still Import Grades again but the total points value has been updated to 16 in this example and also the user who has completed the task has got their score in Classroom. This particular user as you can see did not do very well getting 0 on the quiz! These grades can then be returned to the students with private comments if required.

Get more out of Google Forms

Google Forms has to be one of the most useful and powerful Google Apps that is available for you to use. Once you combine the use of Google Forms with Google Sheets you can create powerful systems and if you start using Google App Script as well you can create very bespoke systems however Google Forms on their own has a large variety of possibilities in how you can use them as a teacher or organisation.

I'm going to go through some possible ways in which you can use Google Forms in an educational setting and hopefully some of these will give you ideas of things you would like to do. The Google Forms listed below are simply ideas and uses of forms however I am sure there are many more uses of Google Forms and actually once you've read these you may be able to easily identify how Google Forms can help you and your organisation. The use of forms has really revolutionised the way I work and has saved large amounts of time both in my own job and the job of others around me.

Teacher - Student Use

- Assessments

Using Google Forms, you can build your own bespoke assessments that can contain just multiple choice questions or a mixture of scaled questions, paragraph and short answer questions. There are several options to you in terms of how you can assess this once your students have completed the assessment. There are systems available such as Flubaroo that can speed up the process and you can read more about how Flubaroo works later on in the book. Alternatives to Flubaroo are simply using the responses you've received in the Google Sheet and marking the answers manually yourself which is fine to do but can take longer than using an add-on to help you. There are of course other add-ons that you can also use to help you and I would always encourage you to search through the add-on store looking for Google Sheet add-ons.

Using a Google Form for an assessment is very useful because the assessment can be completed within a computer suite, on a tablet/latop or as a homework task. Some of the beautiful things about using Google Forms in this way is once you have finished your assessment you can make copies of it for each class. Alternatively, you can just have all of your classes in the same Google Form and the same Google Sheet but that is down to personal preference. If you do start using Google Forms for assessments and want to use a new form for each class, then please look at Magic Make Copies, also featured later in the book, as a quick way to make lots of copies of the same Google file.

- Quizzes

One of the more recent developments in G Suite has been the use of Google Forms as quizzes and the ability to turn any Google Form into a built-in quiz as shown earlier. This was a fantastic addition to Google Forms and actually allows you to add your answer key into your form as well as leave detailed feedback on incorrect answers. Using built in quizzes in Google Forms you can also have paragraph answers which you will mark later and you can then add a grade and release the scores after. This functionality of Forms is really good for reviewing paragraph answers from within Forms without the need to generate a Google Sheet as you can easily click through the individual responses and grade as you go.

- Lesson Progress Checks

Lesson progress checks are really powerful use of Google Forms within the classroom and so easy to set up. Quite simply all you need is a few questions at the end of the lesson and these can be yes or no answers. It could be your lesson objectives and the students can indicate yes or no to whether or not they have completed them. Once all of your results are in you can see clearly how many students achieved all the objectives and how far they got. These don't have to be objectives these could be actual lesson tasks so the end of the lesson you will know exactly how far every single student has progressed with their assignment or work.

The only limitation is obviously you are relying on the student to answer correctly and not to lie however my experience of this is that students are generally pretty honest with how far they've got and you will spot any obvious embellishments of their progress.

- Student Surveys

This may seem like a simple use of Google Forms but there are many times when you want to survey the students and find out their thoughts and opinions. Using Google Forms instead of other systems can save you money if your school has a paid subscription for these as obviously G Suite for Education is free and the Google Form tools are just as good in my opinion but with more advantages due to the integration with Google Drive and Sheets after the form has been completed.

The great thing about using Google Forms for student surveys is when all of the responses are in, Google Forms will automatically generate graphs for you so you can see the responses straight away. All of these charts and graphs can then easily be copied and pasted into Google Docs to produce a report which you can then share with other people in your organisation. Also because Google Forms feeds directly into Google Sheets analysis can be made on the responses using spreadsheet formula.

- Option Choices

For me this was one of the first things I did once we got Google Forms up and running in my school. Many schools spend a lot of time and effort producing booklets on paper for option choices and actually the first thing we did was remove this entirely and make it an electronic booklet. Secondly a lot of schools are also using paper based systems to collect the results of the student option choices and some poor person would then have to manually enter all of these choices into a spreadsheet.

By using Google Forms for the options process you can eliminate the use of paper and you also have all of the results directly into a Google Sheet and there is no need for somebody to copy the responses in. Another way you can improve this and build on this is using Google Apps Script where you can actually get the system to automatically highlight any obvious errors like a student choosing the same subject twice for example.

- Dropping/Changing Subject Choices

Creating your own bespoke system such as dropping or changing the subject choices is a big task but actually anything when there's a paper based form you can simply convert it to a Google Form. If in this case, you simply want students to complete a form and then a member of staff can action then a Google Form with a Google Sheet is enough and a quick email notification whenever a form is completed.

- Prefect Voting System

This idea is based on an old system where students and staff would cast their votes for the prefect from the year group. The problem was that admin staff would then have to count and correlate the results often using a spreadsheet to do it. This is a good example of a complete 'waste of everyone's time' and how Google Forms can replace this system.

One of the great advantages of Google Forms is the fact that you can limit the number of responses to only one and therefore works really well for voting such as this. Another linked advantage here is the fact that you can also limit the responses to only those in your domain even when you do not collect email addresses and find out who they are meaning that only members of your school community could vote. Then because all of the results feed directly into a Google Sheet a couple of countif formula and quick sorts in seconds you have your ranked vote list.

- PE Games Options

PE and Games options are just another example of where students need to select an option choice and you can use Google Forms to help you with this. Simply create the form you would like the students to complete on Google Forms and email or post on Google Classroom the link and then all of the students complete it for you. This Google Form was created because in my school the way Games and PE options we gathered was through all of the tutors. This meant that the tutors had to ask all of the students what their choice was and send the results back to one central person to correlate. This obviously created a lot of work for all of the members of staff involved whereas by creating a Google Form students were responsible for entering their own options. This also means that the member of staff co-ordinating the options process automatically has a spreadsheet produced with the results that they could use and sort as required.

- Activity springboard

As previously mentioned you could use Google Forms as an activity springboard to lead the students from one tasks to another very easily. An example of this could be a starter activity with a few questions and then the next section could be a link to a website with another activity with new sections for after a student has finished one. You could use forms to manage the progress of your students for the entire lesson however a note of caution with making the form too long as currently Google Forms does not save as they go and only saves once the form is submitted. One consideration here of course is that this would only work in a computer suite or if every student had a device which they could complete the Google Form on. This task could also be done in groups if you had one device between a selection of students.

With this in mind you could split up the activities into different forms and in the submission message there could be a link to the next form and therefore all the different sections are saved as the students' progress through. With a task like this there is a large amount of setup to do in advance however it could lead to a lesson where not one minute of time is wasted explaining the next task as the Google Form can do that for you and the students can progress at their own pace. Although there is a lot of setup required, because you would not want to do this type of lesson all the time anyway it may be worth planning a lesson that fits this kind of process and trying it out.

- Video and focus questions

Inserting of YouTube videos is built into Google Forms meaning that it is very easy to get a video relevant to your subject or topic and have it on your Google Form. This could be part of your form or in fact be what the entire form is about. A good task here is having a video and then some focus questions to complete during or after the video. These questions could be multiple choice or more free text answers depending on what is required and this can also be done as a classwork task or even a homework task.

Teacher - Admin Use

- Staff Surveys

If you were ever required to survey the staff, then creating a new Google Form to do it saves you lots of time. In the past where you may have asked staff their opinions during certain staff meetings or smaller groups if you wanted to survey the entire staff then using Google Forms is the most effective way to gather a large number of opinions very quickly. Obviously as shown earlier some of the different types of questions you can have in a Google Form makes it very efficient and much easier to get results. There are obviously a lot of advantages of electronic forms such as not getting lost, being able to complete at a convenient time etc.

- Work Scrutiny

Work scrutiny is another way in which you can use Google Forms to speed up a process. You can have a Google Form setup that will capture the required details every time a member of staff does a work scrutiny on a students' work. These can include multiple choice questions about how many times the teachers have marked the work for example or you can have free text comments where the moderator or person doing the work scrutiny can enter their thoughts and opinions. And with the new feature of Google Forms allowing you to add attachments what you can also do is take photos of the work especially if you want to highlight good practice in marking or feedback. Once you have taken a picture and submitted it with the form it will be automatically saved in the owner of the forms Google Drive.

There are several ways you can do this where you would fill in one Google Form per student's book or in fact you could do it so that you are able to add multiple students' entries into one Google Form and this would be something you would have to determine with your organisation and what is best for your school.

- Leave of Absence Requests

Schools will have procedures in how a member of staff can request time out of school for a trip or a CPD opportunity or even a leave of absence for a special personal reason. With this in mind often what happens in schools is a paper-based form is completed and handed to the relevant person (Head/SLT) for signing off and checking. By having a Google Form for this process you can streamline it and make it much easier for staff to request the leave of absence and also makes it much easier for the member of staff who has to authorise to collect all of the data. Similar to some of the other forms you can use Google Apps Script to automate some of this process such as sending emails to the relevant people and generally speeding up the process but in essence just having a electronic form for the initial completion will improve things as well.

- Sixth Formers Gained Time Tracker

This is an idea for when a sixth former gives up their one of their subjects and has extra free time. The idea of this form is that the sixth former would complete it every time they had a lesson free. They would be logging what activity they were doing, for example being at the library or revision workshops. With this kind of system you could have it set up to automatically email the student's tutor a summary of what they have been doing that day or that week and you can really make it bespoke to what your school needs are. Without making it to technical and without adding Google App Script having the log that the sixth formers are expected to fill in could help in making sure that they are using their time effectively.

- Personal Action Plans

Personal action plans are another method where a tutor could be having a discussion with a tutee and they have a certain action plan that they must fill in and this could be a Google Form. It could be related to whether they have met their objectives for that week with potential yes or no questions. This could quickly form a weekly log or daily log even of what progress that student has made.

- Visitor Forms

This is a really good way that Google Forms can help in the school environment because often the receptionist will be pulling their hair out when a member of staff hasn't let them know there is a visitor coming. Having a quick and easy Google Form accessible from home or from any computer or device which allows a member of staff to let reception know they have a visitor coming can be very helpful for all involved. You can cleverly use Google Sheets so it sorts out and puts the next visitor at the top of the Google Sheet so that the receptionist can always have it open and ready.

- Catering Requests

Catering requests are something that I've seen a need for because most catering requests are all filled in on paper or in some cases will be a electronic document you have to fill in and email. Using Google Forms for this process has its advantages as you can then have a spreadsheet that the catering department could use to fill the orders for that day. By having it in the spreadsheet they can easily have it sorted and arranged by the date. You can also use an add-on like autoCrat so that after a Google Form is completed an automatic Google Doc will be created with the details of the catering request and shared with the relevant person or persons. This is especially useful if it needs to be kept for paper filing purposes as it will be really easy to print out the completed Google Doc request.

- Any paper based system used in schools

As I have mentioned at the start of this section, you can use Google Forms for any kind of paper-based survey and any kind of paper based questionnaire that needs to be filled. Therefore, everything I've come up with I'm sure that you can come up with lots more ways in which you can use Google Forms in your school. Anytime you see something on paper you can always think is there a better way that this could this be done on a Google Form and so many times the answer will be yes.

Google Drawings

Google Drawings are a nice addition to G Suite and it gives you some more functionality and help in creating images that can be used across the G Suite applications. Google Drawings reminds me of painting programs in its simplicity however along with it allowing you to create very quick drawings it actually has a lot more uses within G Suite if you get deeper into what it can do.

The tool bar main menu is much the same as the other G Suite applications I have gone through so I will not do these again but mainly focus on the secondary toolbar underneath.

1. Undo and Redo buttons
2. Print
3. Format Painter
4. Zoom controls
5. Cursor
6. Line
7. Shape
8. Textbox
9. Image
10. Comment

The majority of these tools should be familiar to most users and the ones that have extra options I will explore in more detail.

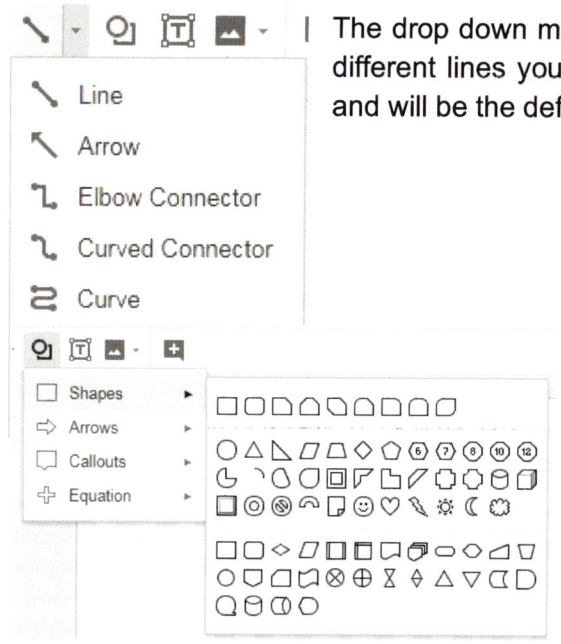

The drop down menu on the Line tools gives you these options of the different lines you can draw. Scribble is handy for matching activities and will be the default if a student is using a tablet.

Shapes has even more options available for the user to select premade shapes that can be easily drawn into their Google Drawing.

Standard Flowchart shapes are found here also.

There is not much more to say in terms of how to use Google Drawings and I would hope that you are able to explore and play around with designing and creating images using it with not too much assistance. Remember that because this is a Google Drive application Google Drawings can also be shared with collaborators so that multiple users can all edit and contribute to a drawing at the same time simply by pressing the Share button.

When you have completed a Google Drawing it will be automatically saved into your Google Drive but in order to use it as a completed image you will need to download and save the Google Drawing as a picture file. In order to do this simply go to 'File' and 'Download as' and I would recommend you select a .png file as this is higher quality. If file size and space are an issue then you can choose the .jpg option.

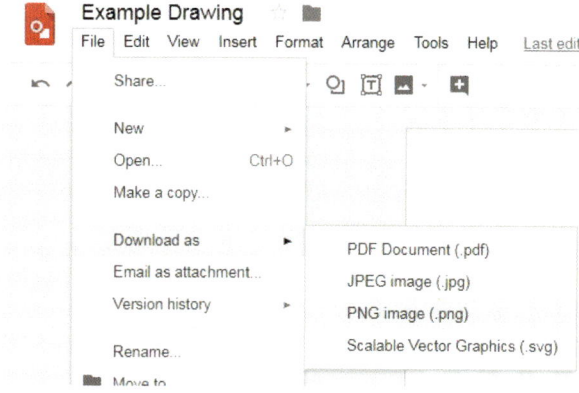

This will download the file onto your computer which you can then insert and use in any document you would like to. It can of course be uploaded to Google Drive as an image file and then inserted from Drive into any of the G Suite applications.

Get more out of Google Drawings

Teacher - Student Use

Matching Activities

The first thing that you may not realise that you can do with Google Drawings is you can insert them directly into Google Classroom assignments and 'Make a copy' for each student. This means that you can create interactive worksheets using Google Drawings and for example a simple line matching activity can be created in Google Drawings so that when a student completes this task on a tablet they can actually use their finger and draw the lines in. This task can also be completed on computers and the user can use the line tools to create the matching lines.

Diamond 9 Activities

Related to this you also have the opportunity to create activities of dragging and dropping so for example if you have a similar matching activity but this time instead of having to draw a line you have boxes that you drag into the right place or the right order you can use Google Drawings for this. One limitation of this is on a tablet device you can't use the dragging and dropping a box like you can if you use a desktop computer so you do need to be aware of this.

A little side note here is that a dragging and dropping activity could easily be made in Google Slides that would work on a tablet device which you can use as an alternative to Google Drawing drag and drop activities. You can use Google Drawings in a related way and in the example shown here of a Diamond 9 activity grid with the students being required to make judgements and decisions about which option they consider to be the most important and placing this at the top of the diamond.

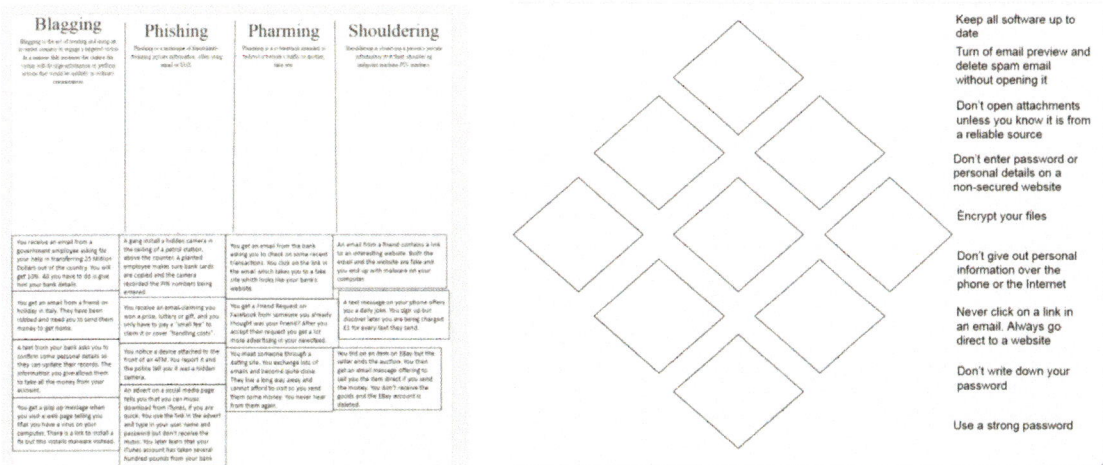

Flowcharts

Another use of Google Drawings is for creating flowcharts. There are other options available on other websites which will save directly into Drive and some are much better however if you want a very basic quick program to be able to create a flowchart then Google Drawings works well. If you are a Computer Science teacher then a website like https://www.draw.io/ maybe a much more efficient flowchart creator than Google Drawings but will also save the creations in the student's Google Drive.

Teacher - Admin Use

Google Classroom Banners

One good use of Google Drawings is the ability to use them to make bespoke headers for your Google Classrooms. All you need to know is the standard size for a Google Classroom header and then you can use Google Drawings to create your masterpiece. You need to setup the size of the image to 1600x400 pixels as shown here.

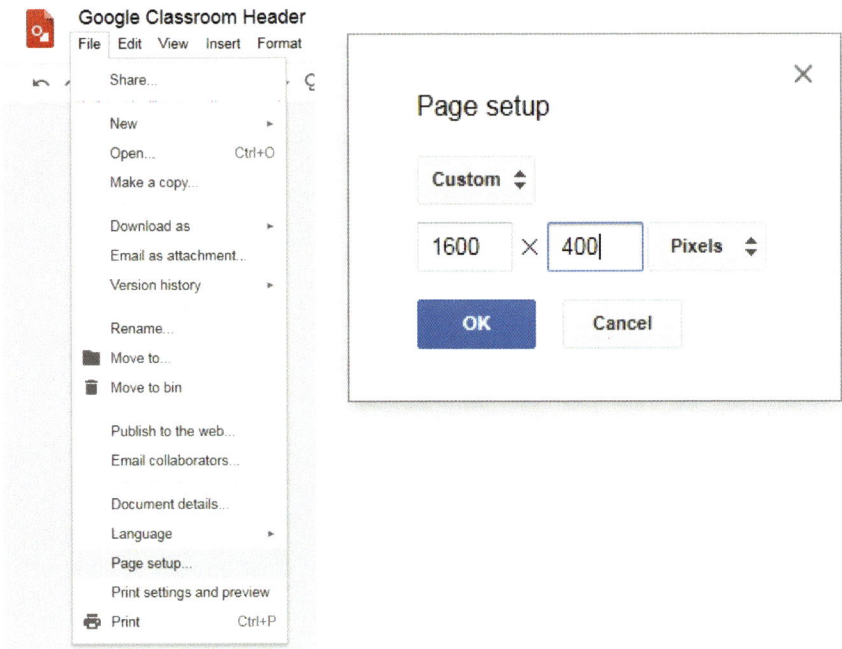

Use a Shape to draw a solid colour background like this:

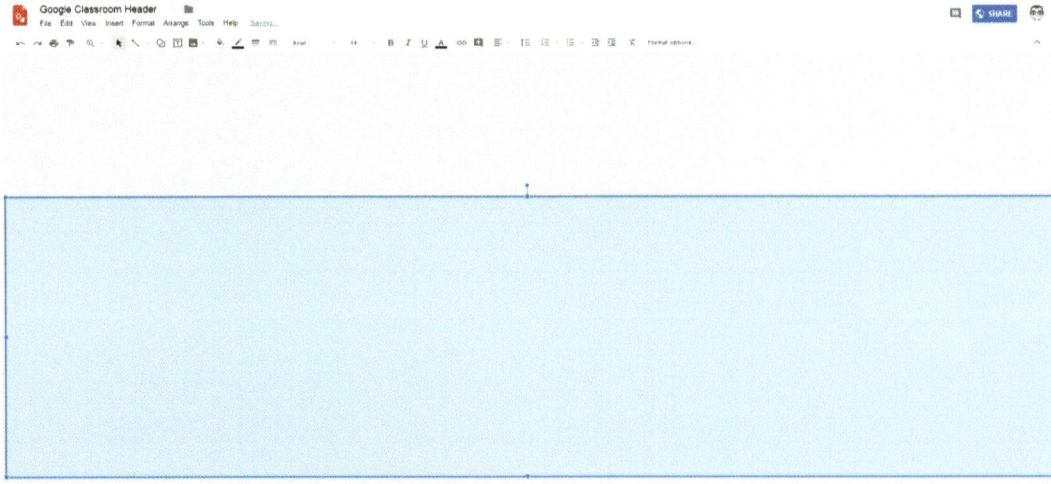

You can also insert images you have such as your school's logo and make that form part of the header. You can even insert your own Bitmoji like I have and also a textbox to state the name of the class. Obviously yours will look much better than this!

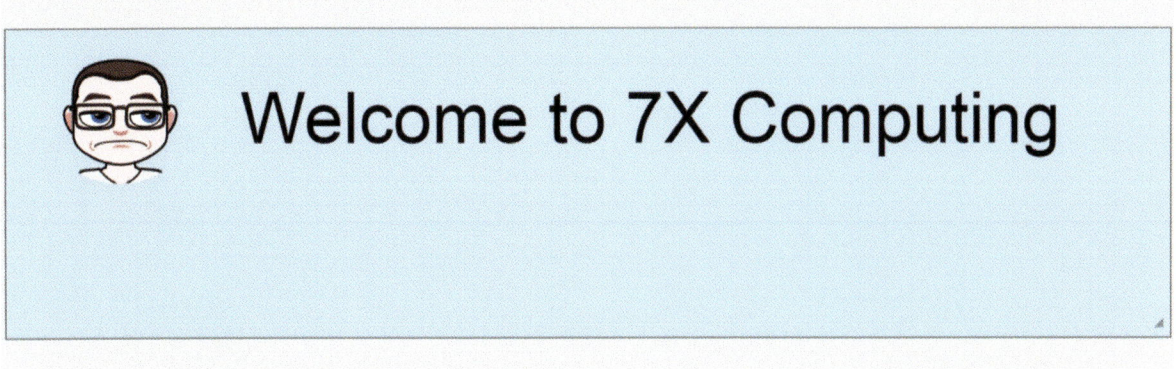

You can then add more images and elements to make the header more appealing to the eye but simple functionality will not take very long to achieve. Once you have completed your drawing you can use the file menu to download as an image file ready for uploading to Google Classroom. You will notice that a little of the image is lost at the bottom so you will need to keep your design to the top of your Google Drawing to ensure you do not lose anything.

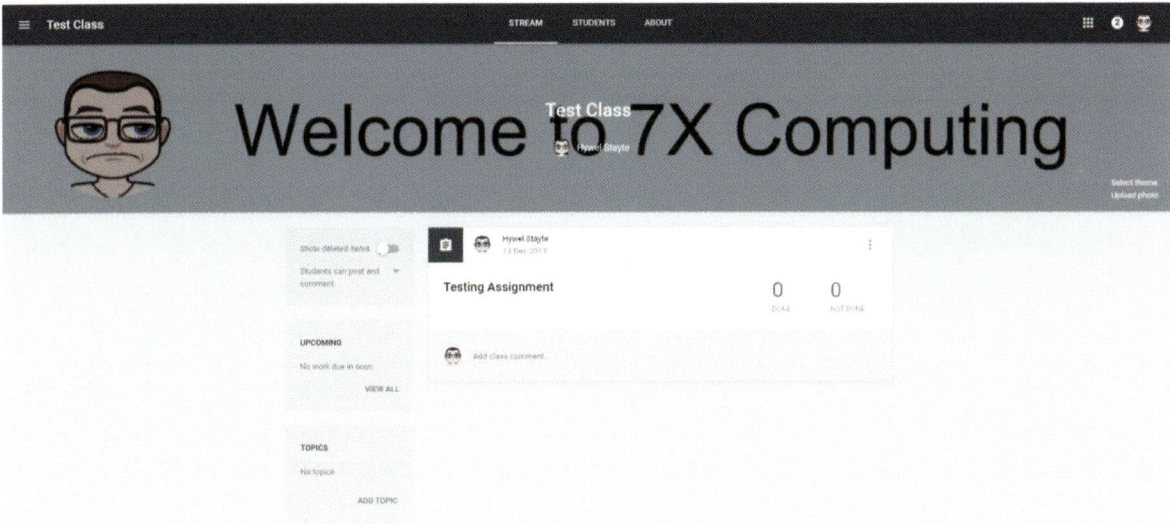

Google Sites Banners

In the same way you can create a banner for Google Classroom you can also use Google Drawings to create your page banners for Google Sites. Simply set up a new blank Google Drawing in Drive and create a rectangle shape roughly in the middle of the screen but slightly further down.

Just like with the Google Classroom banner you can insert any text and images you like and as long as you keep it within the middle area then that should form your Google Site banner. When you have completed your banner you can simply download the file and insert it into Google Sites.

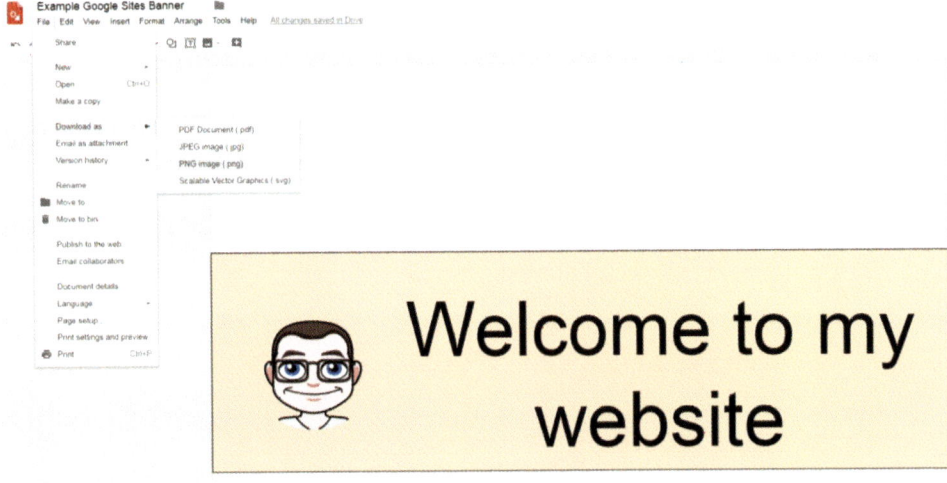

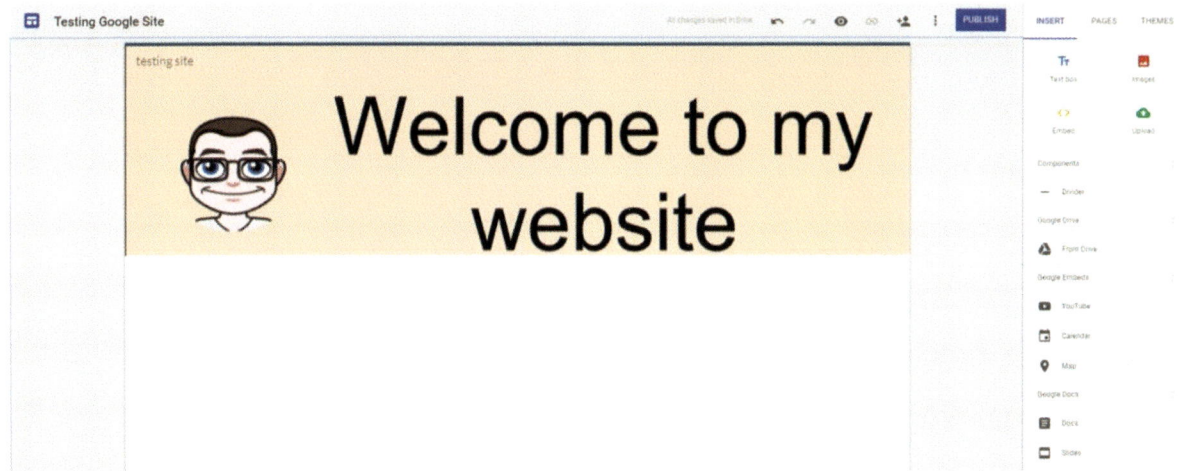

Google Jamboard

Google Jamboard is an excellent new addition to G Suite. Being relatively new it is still under development and there is a lot that is still to be done however I can already clearly see that this has great potential as a core app on a tablet device.

How to use Jamboard on a Tablet

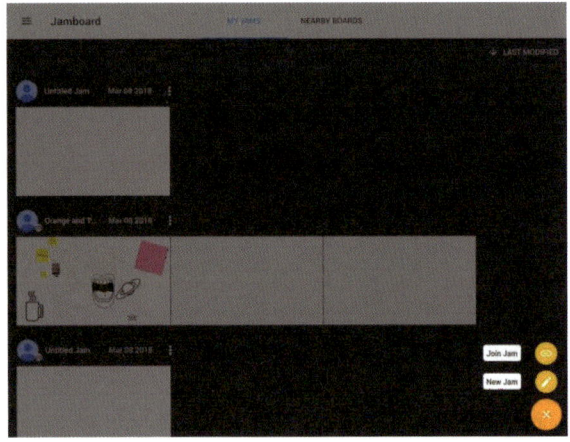

The first screen will load and just like with other Google products you have a small + button at the bottom right of the screen. You only have two options here with Jamboard, one to 'Join Jam' and the other to create a 'New Jam'.

Joining an existing Jam means you need to type in a special code just like joining a Google Classroom. Once entered you will join the existing Jam with other users.

If you select to create a new Jam, then you will get the following blank screen appear.

Pen Tools

This first button is your pen tool that allows you to select the different thicknesses and types of pen you would like to use and the first four options here are different types of pen.

The Aa button is the handwriting recognition button to allow the user to write using their finger into the Jam and then Jamboard automatically converts the images into digital text.

The next tool is the shape recognition tool which you can use in the same way as the handwriting recognition to attempt to draw a shape and Jamboard will convert it into a digital perfect shape.

The final tool is the AutoDraw function that has now been built in to Jamboard. When using this tool, you can simply attempt to draw something and Google will search its database to try and match it allowing you to use a pre-made image.

Using AutoDraw

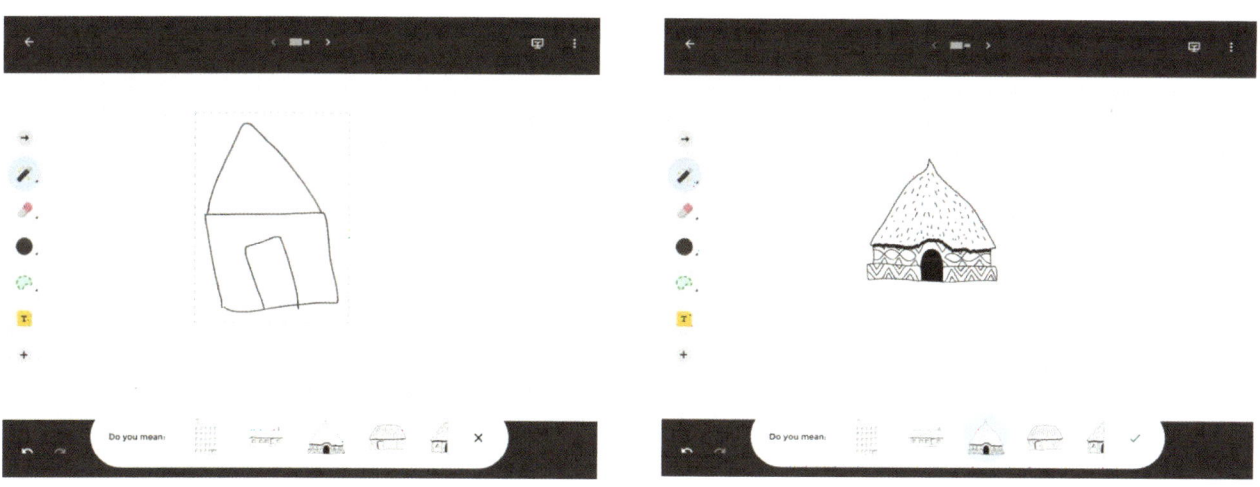

Eraser Tool

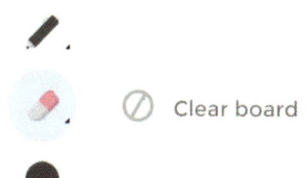

This is a straight forward button that allows the user to rub out any drawing that has been created. There is a very nice fall away feature that looks like you are rubbing of the lines from the screen and it is very satisfying to rub out! If you press the small arrow on this tool as well you are given the option to 'Clear board' to erase everything created so far.

Change Colour

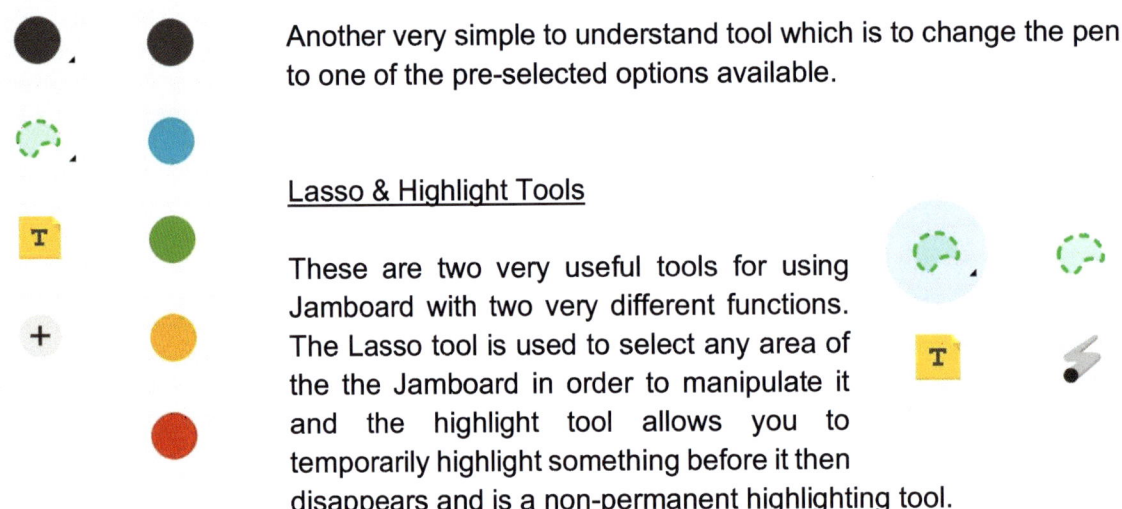

Another very simple to understand tool which is to change the pen colour to one of the pre-selected options available.

Lasso & Highlight Tools

These are two very useful tools for using Jamboard with two very different functions. The Lasso tool is used to select any area of the the Jamboard in order to manipulate it and the highlight tool allows you to temporarily highlight something before it then disappears and is a non-permanent highlighting tool.

Using Lasso

In order to use the Lasso, you first select it from the left hand side menu and then using your finger draw around any part of your Jam. Once you have drawn around an object you can then use pinching to adjust the size of the selection. This is useful for lots of purposes including making everything smaller to move it out of the way. Once selected you can also drag around the selection to any new location on the screen.

Post-it Note

This is a useful tool for making notes and longer pieces of text required in your Jam. You can change the colour of your post-it notes using the little circle button at the bottom right of the post-it notes tool. After you have written one note and pressed 'return' you will automatically get another note that you can choose to write on if you require multiple notes. This is useful for quickly brainstorming notes onto the Jam and then allowing the users to move around and sort all of the post-it note ideas.

Additional Menu

 This button allows you to insert Google Drive files into your Jam

 This button allows you to search the internet from within Jamboard and take a screenshot

 This button allows you to insert an image from a Google Images search from within Jamboard

 This is a sticker button

 This allows you to create Post-it notes with Jamboard

 Here you can select an image from your device or even take a picture using the camera and insert it directly into the Jam

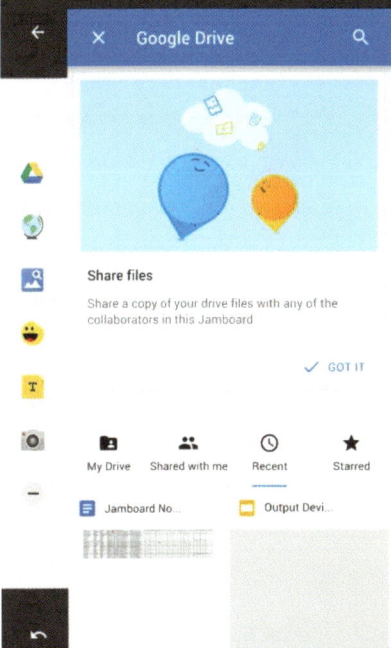

Inserting from Drive

Here is the window that will appear when you first select to insert files into Jamboard. As you can see the message that the files you insert into Jamboard will be shared with the collaborators of the Jam.

You can then browse your Google Drive files and insert any of the them into the Jam. The way this works is a copy of the file is inserted into the Jam and the user is able to scroll through the pages or slides for example and select what they would like to insert into the Jam.

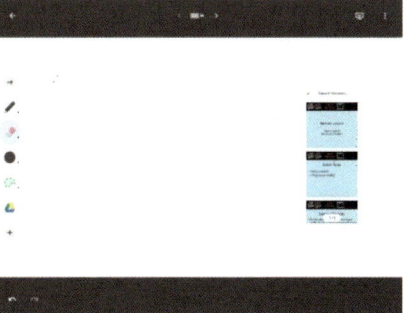

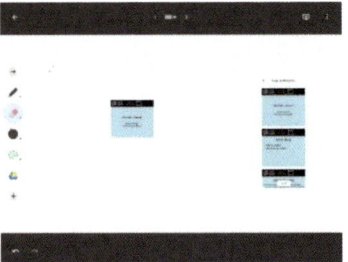

Once you have dragged your slide or part of the file into Jamboard you can then manipulate it like a object and resize and move. You can also of course use all of the other Jamboard tools to highlight areas and annotate for example.

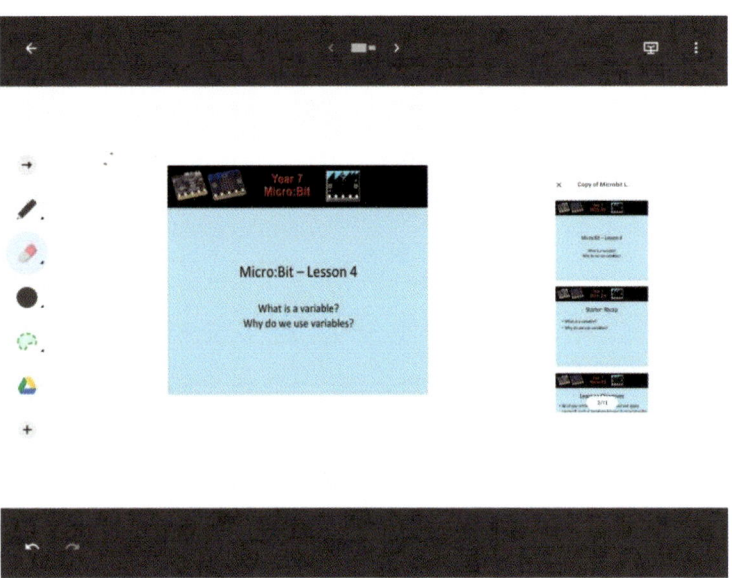

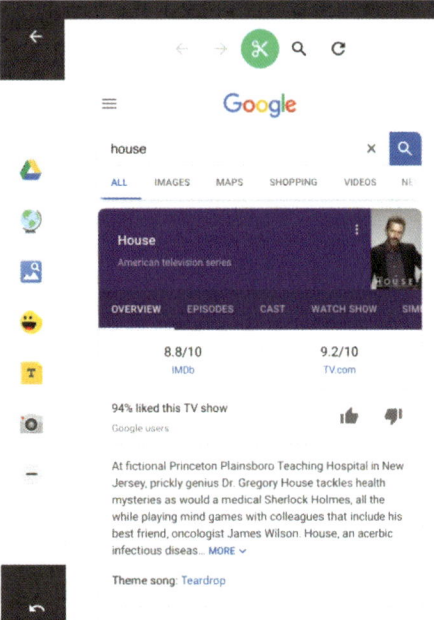

Searching the Web

As you can see you can search the web from within Jamboard and use the 'Cut' tool (Green Scissors at the top) to take a screenshot of anything you find.

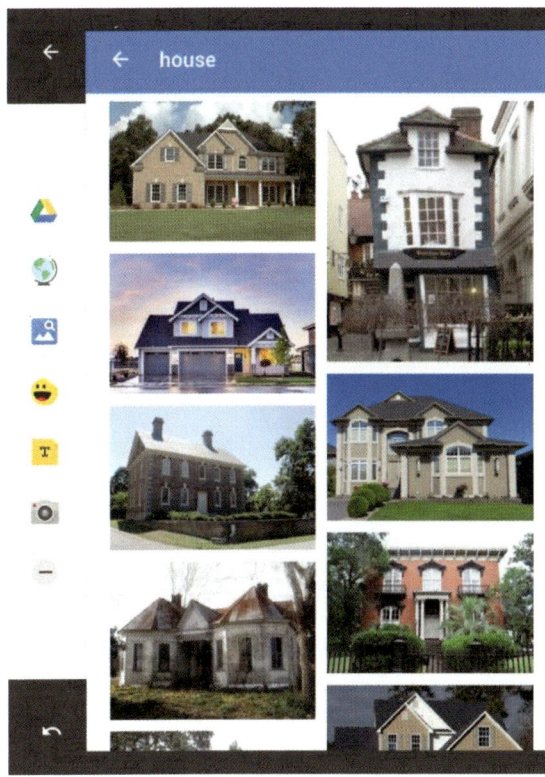

Insert Image

Using the powerful Google Image search you can search from within Jamboard and find an image that you would like to use.

Once found you can tap on the image and it will automatically be inserted into your Jam.

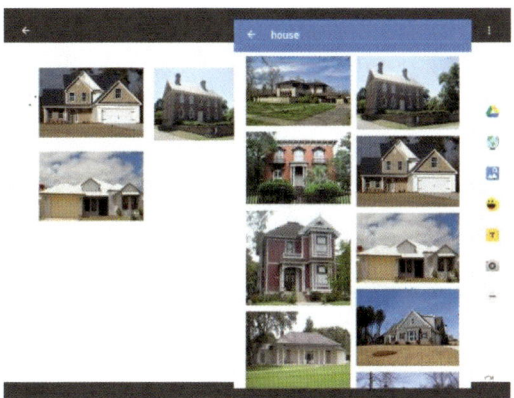

Insert Stickers

Much like modern day apps for messaging you also have option to use stickers within your Jams which has some advantages as a teacher. If you are marking a series of work that has been completed using Jamboard as the platform you can use the stickers to indicate correct answers or pleasing responses. Much like using a traditional stamp you can use these stickers for praise and reward for the students.

Using the Camera

The next available option is the Camera function that allows you to insert an image directly from your device. As you can see it will look through your images and also give you the camera option at the top right of the menu. You can multi select images using this tool and insert as many images as you would like into the Jam.

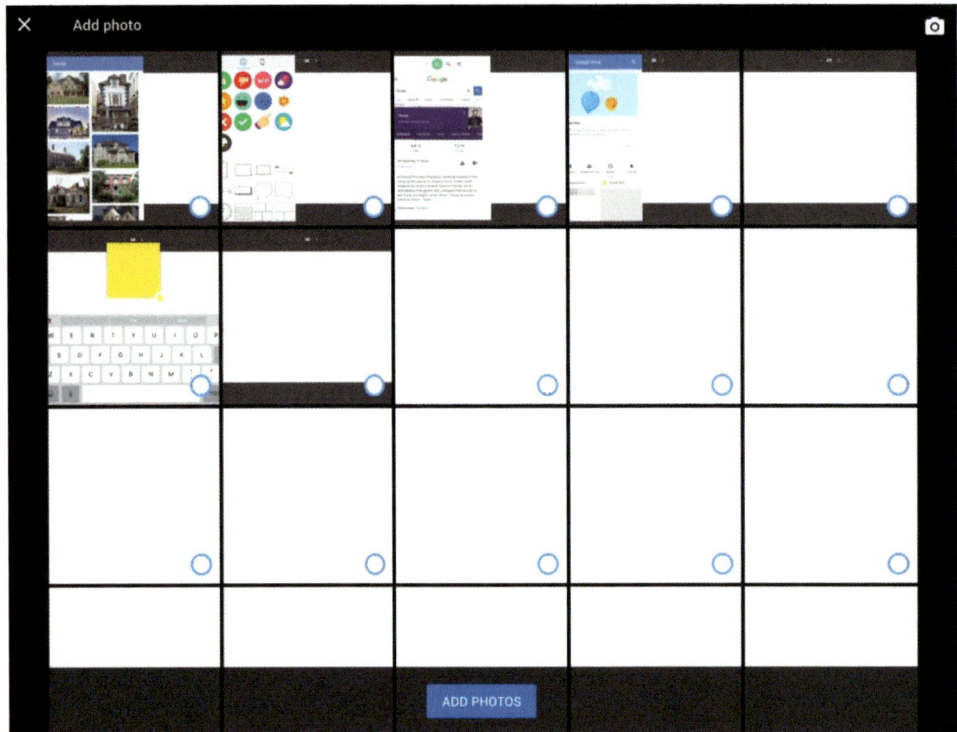

Two Finger Select

Now this is the one thing that I do not think is that easy to figure out for yourself unlike lots of the other elements of the Jamboard. Google are pretty good at making their products easy to navigate and usually you can find exactly what you want and how to do things without too much trouble however the Jamboard app can become very frustrating if you do not know about two finger select.

Once you have inserted any object into Jamboard you can use the Lasso tool to select it again and move it around however the Lasso tool is not designed to help you select existing objects but more to select whole groups of objects and manipulate together. In order to select an individual object again in Jamboard so that you can move it around the screen, resize it or even make a duplicate of it you need to use two finger select.

So instead of trying to tap on an object using one finger within Jamboard you use two fingers to tap on the object. This will then reselect the one object and allow you to move and resize using pinching. It will also display this icon in the top right of the object allowing you to make a duplicate of what you have selected.

Adding Pages

In order to add pages to your Jam all you have to do is click on the arrow here at the top of the screen that you would use to navigate the pages. If there is not a page it will automatically add one once clicked.

Push to Jamboard

If you are lucky enough to have an actual physical Jamboard then this button at the top right of the screen allows you to push your creation on the Jamboard App to the Jamboard screen.

After pressing the App will look for a nearby Jamboard which it can send its Jam to.

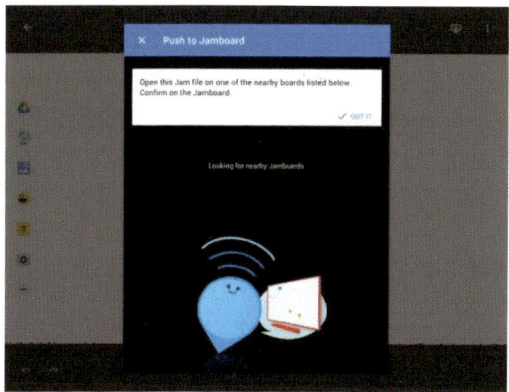

Additional Options

Always look for the 3 dots! With all Google products you will get additional options available by clicking on the three dots at the top right hand side of the screen.

✏ Rename

🗑 Remove

➕👤 Add people

🎥 Connect to a meeting

< Share Jam as PDF

< Share this frame as an image

Here you can see the three dot menu is pretty self-explanatory and you should be familiar with rename, remove and add people.

Connect to a meeting is used for setting up a meeting with different users through the Jamboard app.

Share Jam as PDF and Share this frame as an image allows you to export you whole Jam as a PDF or just the screen you are on as an image. You can then share in the normal methods and ways such as email and social media.

Main Menu Additional Controls

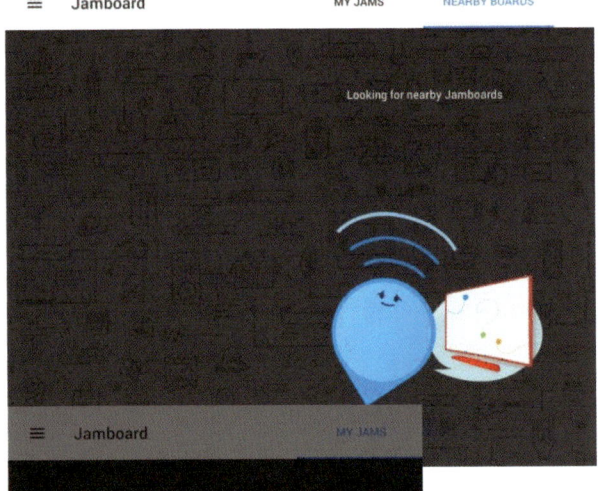

Back on the main menu controls which load when you first open the Jamboard App you can click on 'Nearby boards' at the top of the screen.

This is the feature similar to 'Push to Jamboard' and will look for a physical Jamboard in the vicinity. If found you will be able to connect to the Jam or start a new Jam on the board.

The three dots next to the Jams have all the normal options as shown here and only has missing the save as an image option as from this view you are looking at the entire Jam and not just one page of it.

Get more out of Google Jamboard

Jamboard is now integrated fully with Google Drive and therefore Google Classroom meaning that any Jams that you create on Jamboard also appear in Google Drive. This means that you can insert them into Google Classroom Assignments for students to view, edit or make a copy of. This is why it is going to be as good as other similar paid for apps and hopefully better for G Suite users as you will be able to drag things from your Drive into your Jam. This also means that as a teacher you can set up template files for students to use within Google Classroom Assignments that everyone will get their own copy of.

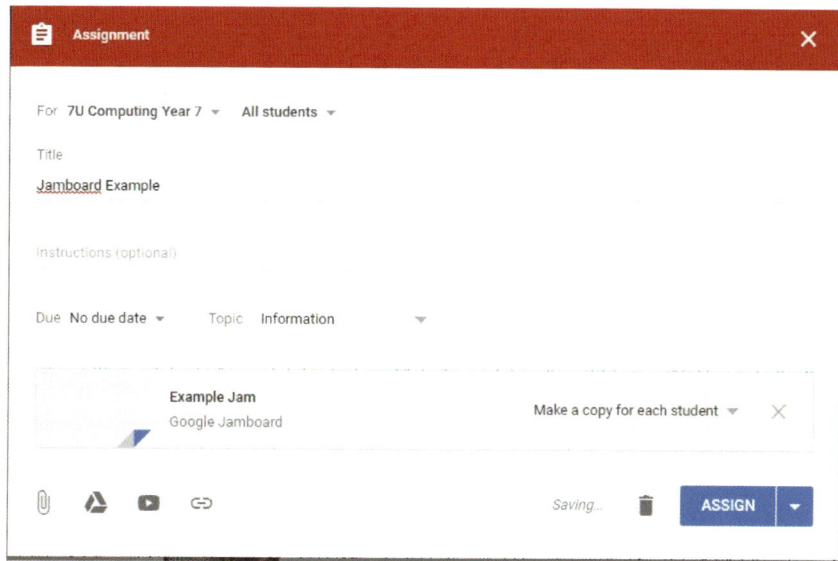

You can buy a Jamboard which is essentially a much more modern interactive whiteboard however these are very expensive and you do not need the interactive whiteboard side of it to use the Jamboard App and in fact in a Google for Education setting I think it's far more likely you will use the Jamboard App to do your collaborating rather than needing the physical board.

As a teacher I can get on a Chrome browser and I can have the Jam open and I could see live students editing it so we could still display it for the whole class. The functionality to edit a Jam from the Chrome browser is now available which only enhances the ability to use it within a classroom.

Due to Jamboard being so new to G Suite it has been hard to identify all of the ways in which it can be used in the classroom and I hope that the above will give you some ideas in which you can use Jamboard. It definitely has potential to create hyperjams (hyperdocs are Google Docs that takes the student through a series of tasks within the document) and of course useful for mind mapping tasks and collaborative Jams.

Google MyMaps

Google MyMaps is an interesting app and there are a few features that I would like to go through with you to show you things you might not realise you can do in MyMaps. I think this this is a definitely a useful tool for the Geography department and any kind of lesson where there is a worldview taken.

With all G Suite applications, the use of MyMaps allows you to share your creations with other specific people or indeed the world using the same Google Sharing methods identified in the earlier applications. To get started with MyMaps from the screen shown here all you need to do is click on the red button 'Create a new map'.

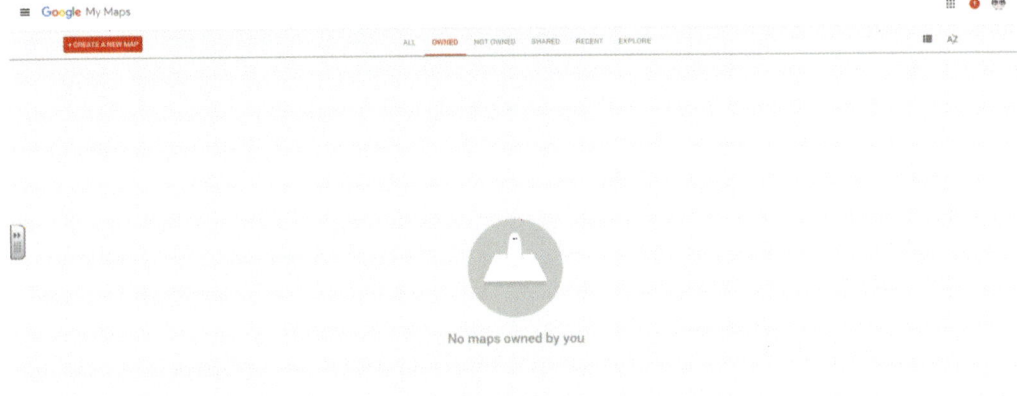

Creating your own map

The first thing you need to do is to give your new map a name and this can be done by using the top left menu options where it states 'untitled map'. Next you can enter the title and description for your new map.

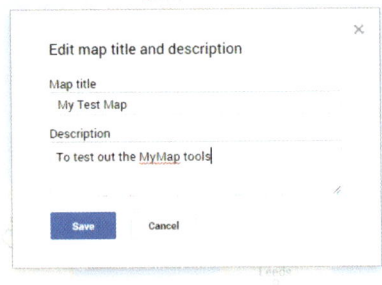

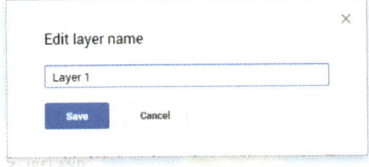

You can have multiple layers in Google MyMaps and your new map will start with the first layer already created and you must give this a name also.

Main Tools and Controls

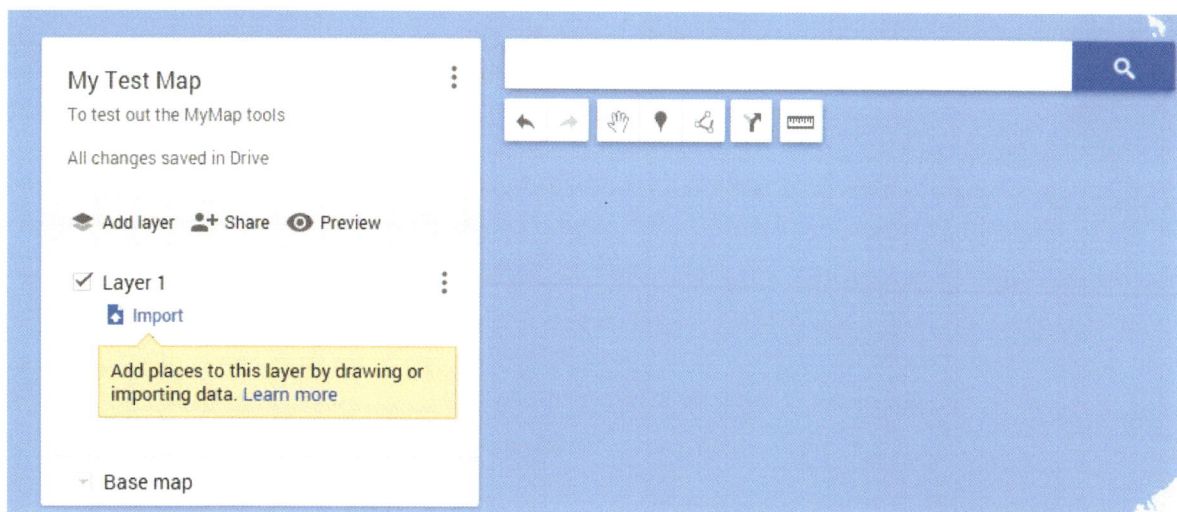

My Test Map

To test out the MyMap tools
2 views

All changes saved in Drive

✓ Layer 1

You would have already changed the details in this menu of the map name and then the first layer name.

The extra options you have here are to 'Add layer' which allows you to have unrelated layers within the same MyMap.

You also have the 'Share' button so you can share you MyMap with others as collaborators or viewers just like in a Google Doc.

The 'Preview' button allows you to see how your map would look to the viewer.

Individual styles

These are the next main controls that you have available to you in Google MyMaps. The first two are common controls of Undo and Redo allowing you to manage any errors and mistakes you make on your map.

The next control is the hand control which many of you will be used to using in lots of other applications and this allows you to drag your view of the map. There are zoom in and out controls at the bottom right of MyMaps just like on Google Maps however you can use the scrolling wheel on the mouse to zoom in and out along with the hand tool leading to easy manipulation and control of the map.

Add a Marker

The next tool is 'Add Marker' which is going to be one of the most commonly used features for anyone who is creating their own MyMap. Using this tool you can mark locations onto your Map. You can control how zoomed in you are when you mark your location and in the image below I have taken a wider view and added the marker to 'Portsmouth'. You can of course zoom in and be very exact with where you want to add your marker.

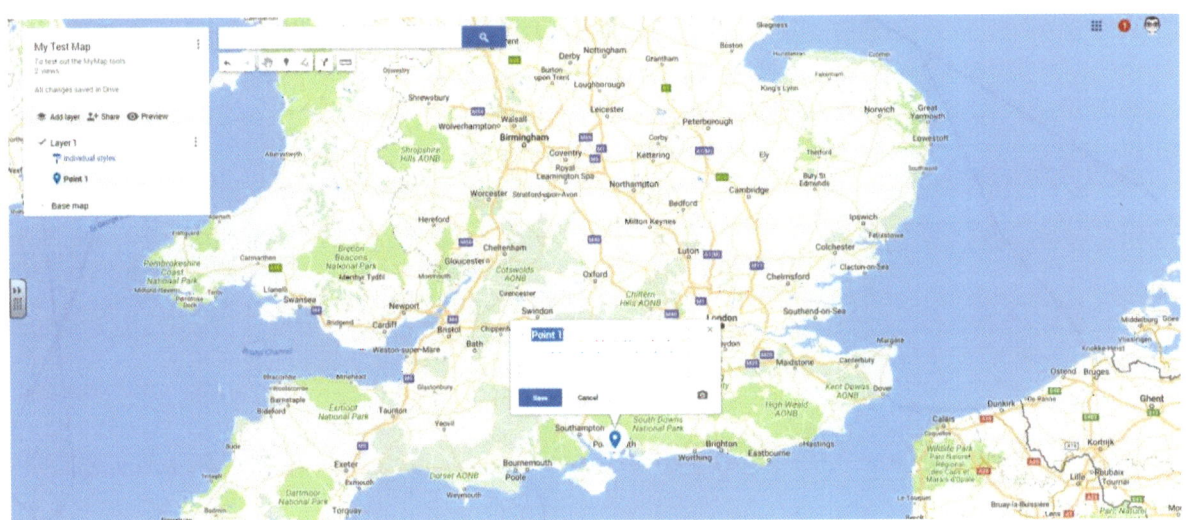

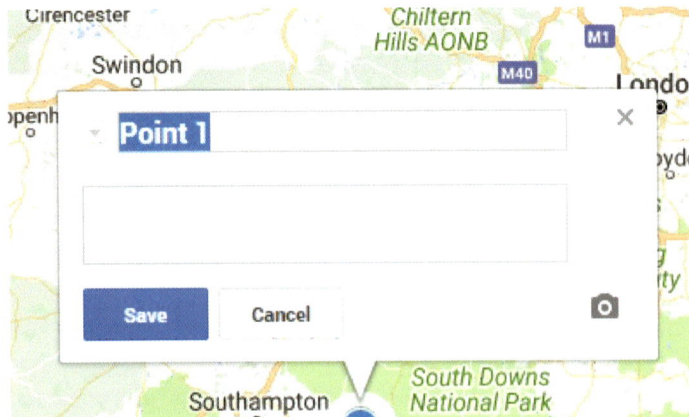

You can now add a title for your maker to this pop up window as well as description. You can also add an image or video to this marker by clicking on the little camera button at the bottom right of the window.

Once you have completed your marker you are given extra options based on the marker. You can first choose to change the colour of the marker by selecting the paint fill button. Edit your marker and add photo/video using the next two options. You can also get directions to this marker simply by clicking on the next button and finally you can delete the marker altogether with the bin button.

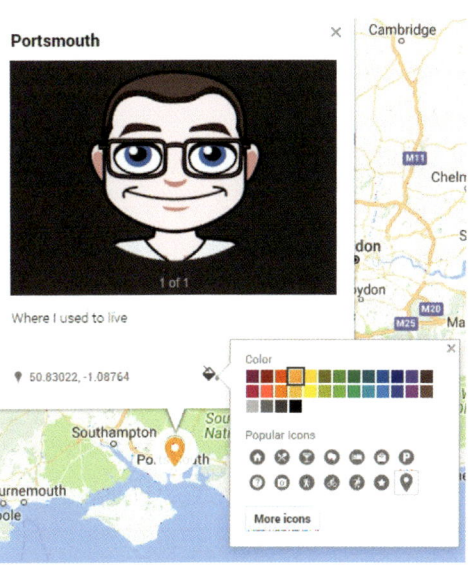

Another option you have when you select to change the colour of the marker is that you can also change the icon displayed.

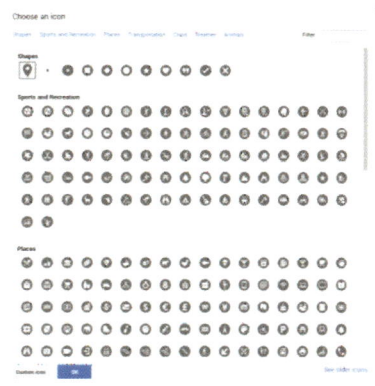

You can also use images to create your own custom icons that can be used on your MyMaps.

Add a Line or Shape

This tool allows you first of all to draw connecting lines between points and add them to your map. Once completed it will also record the distance on the pop up.

This tool can also be used to create and draw out shapes or areas on your map. Again once it is completed it will record the circumference and also the squared area you have selected in Km.

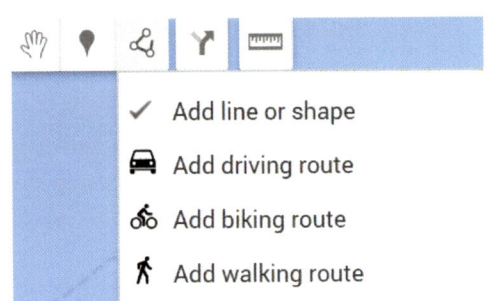

You can also choose other options when using this tool to allow you to create driving, biking and walking routes on your MyMaps.

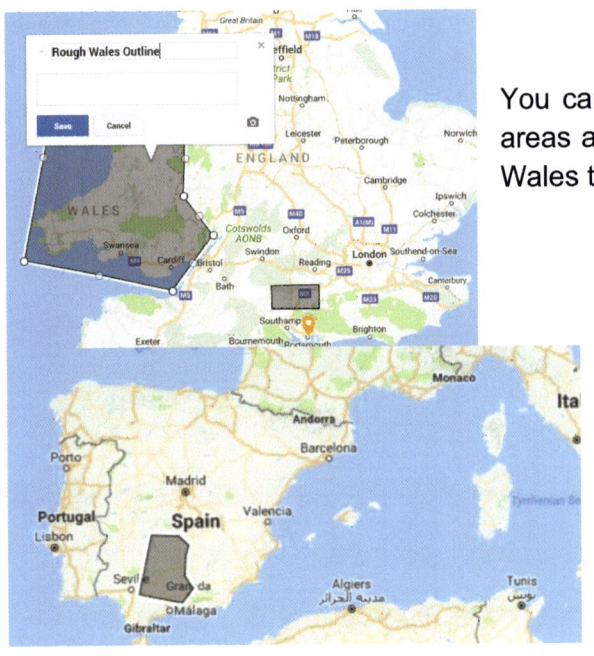

You can also use the shape tool to draw around large areas and in this example I have drawn roughly around Wales to compare the size to other parts of the world.

Here is the shape placed on Spain and notice the size is smaller than when compared with the original and also when placed over Sweden.

This is because Google MyMaps adjusts the polygon to the curvature of the Earth and therefore as you drag around the map it will automatically adjust for you.

A very useful tool for Geography lessons and demonstrating the differences in land mass of different areas of the world.

Directions

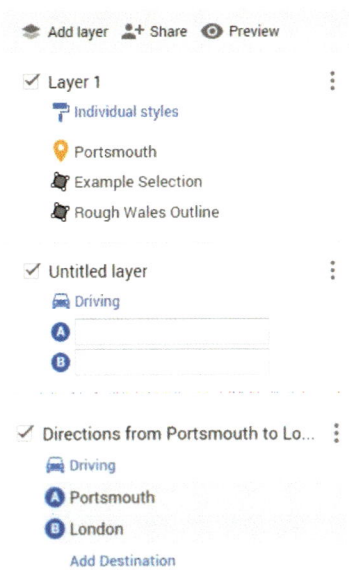

This tool allows you to create a layer of directions on your map. Once you have selected this button from the main menu a new 'untitled layer' of directions will be added as shown here.

This layer can be renamed and the two starting points can be added and adjusted. You can also change the transportation method as required by clicking on the icon or blue text.

Just like in Google Maps you can add more destinations and create longer route maps that can be added to your MyMap with ease.

Ruler

The final tool across this main menu is the Ruler tool that allows you to measure distances from one point to the next in a very similar way to the line tool. This ruler tool is also fantastic for again demonstrating to students the curvature of the Earth as shown in the image below

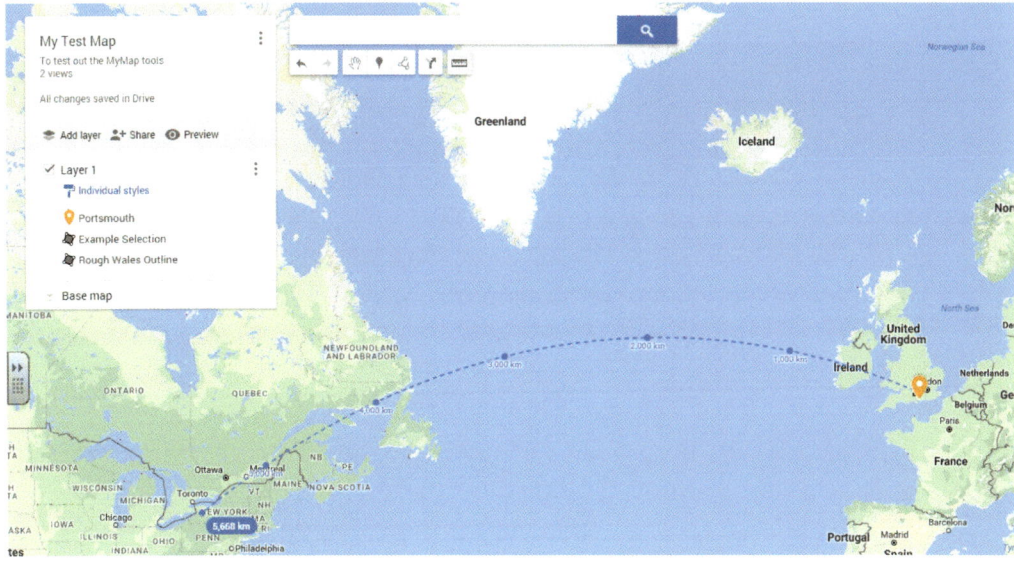

Get more out of Google MyMaps

Explore existing maps shared publicly

From the main MyMaps menu you can also Explore maps that have been created by other users and shared with the community. There are thousands of maps to use and choose from and many with good educational value. Make sure you explore these maps to find ones already made!

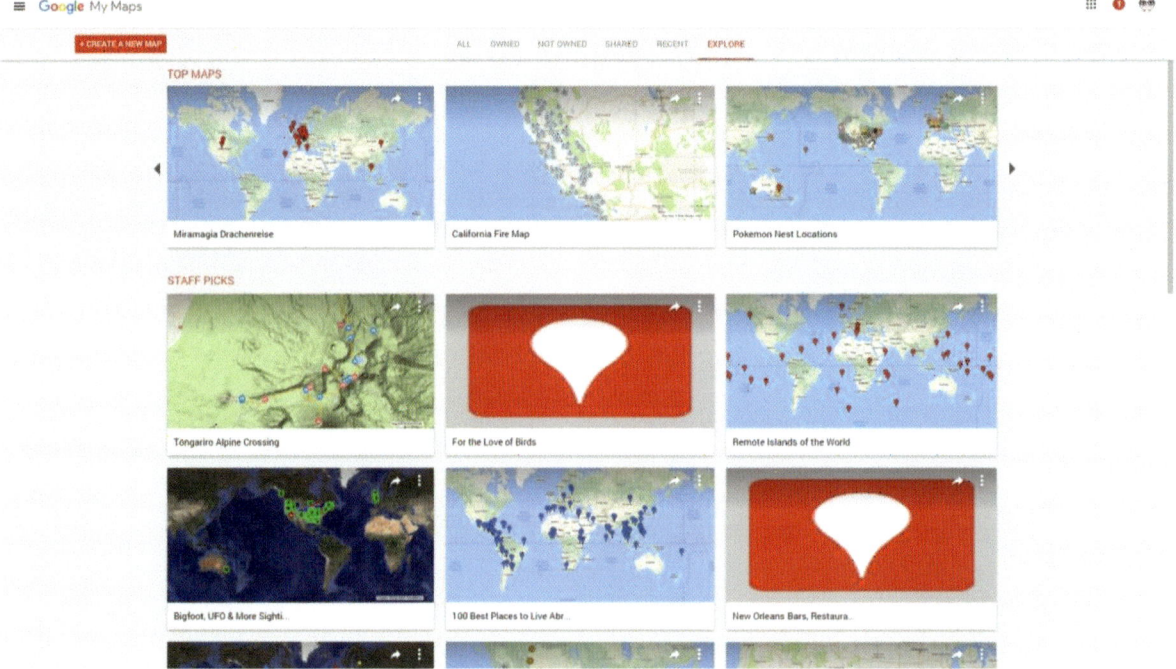

Route Planning

You can use Google MyMaps for any kind of route planning for trips or expeditions such as Duke of Edinburgh. MyMaps gives you the ability to add markers and checkpoints to anywhere on a Google Map meaning it is perfect for this activity. Public viewers or collaborators of the map can help to create it or have access to it for safety reasons etc. You can also create more custom route planning as well with directions for on foot or transportation.

Customized City or Area Maps

I have seen this used commercially on a caravan holiday park where the owners of several caravans used MyMaps to draw a shape around their caravans and add details about the different ones they owned. This could be applied to an educational setting if you have a particularly large campus that has different buildings noticeable on Google MyMaps that you could label. A university campus, especially one within a city, could also work very well for this purpose and function.

Mapping places of interest for a project

This is quite a broad heading as the types of mapping could be anything from meteorite locations to archaeological dig sites. I am sure there are many examples you could think of yourself here as to how you could use MyMaps for your own special projects but basically anything where items or locations are logged can have customized maps created.

Mapping school trip locations

If you are planning a multi-day trip or a residential trip, especially abroad, then marking on your own map all of the locations where you will be visiting and staying could be very useful for parents' peace of minds and also just giving everyone the extra information they need.

Mapping Geocaches or Rock finding

Many of you will have clubs in your organisations or indeed in your personal lives where you take part in Geocaching or Rock finding and these could be great things to also map where you find them on your own MyMaps.

Google Classroom

Even before Google Classroom came along I was very much a supporter and passionate in using G Suite tools in the classroom. The use of Google Drive and collaborative Docs, Sheets and Slides was enough for me however, with the introduction of Google Classroom, Google have really taken it up a step and the ease you are able to distribute, collect and even mark work online is amazing.

In my school we are lucky enough that all the students have their own device which they can use in the classroom and this means that using Google Classroom across all subjects and across all year groups is very practical. Even if you don't have this in your school using Google Classroom for homework for example is really beneficial. I would always say that in Computing and ICT the use of Google Classroom should be standard practice in all lessons however when your students do not have access to a device this is not always possible in classrooms.

In this section of the book I will go over some of the basic functionality of Google Classroom simply because it is the bread and butter of everything you're going to do if you have Google for Education. If you have never used Google Classroom before then you need to understand how it works and see all of the possible posts you can create on it.

There are now four main sections of any Google Classroom:

Stream   Classwork   People   Marks

Stream is where all the work you set will appear and it is like a blog where the most recent posts appear at the top and the older ones get pushed down. All Announcements, Assignments, Questions and Materials will be posted in the Stream.

Classwork is the section that allows you to create Assignments, Questions and Materials which not only appear on the Steam but can be organised under Classwork.

People tab will display all the people who have access to the particularly Google Classroom. It will first display teachers and below that will be all the students who are members of the classroom. You have the option to invite more colleagues or students to join the classroom as well as communication options.

Marks tab is where you will find the built in Gradebook for each Google Classroom. You can see assignment marks, student overviews and even return work.

Stream - Announcements

Announcements are the simplest thing you can do using Google Classroom and allow you to post information quickly to all of your students in your classroom. You can add attachments and files by uploading or from Google Drive. You can also add links or a YouTube video.

You can only create Announcements in the Stream and you do this by clicking in this box shown below that will appear at the top.

Once clicked the box will expand and allow you to add the detail, files and links required.

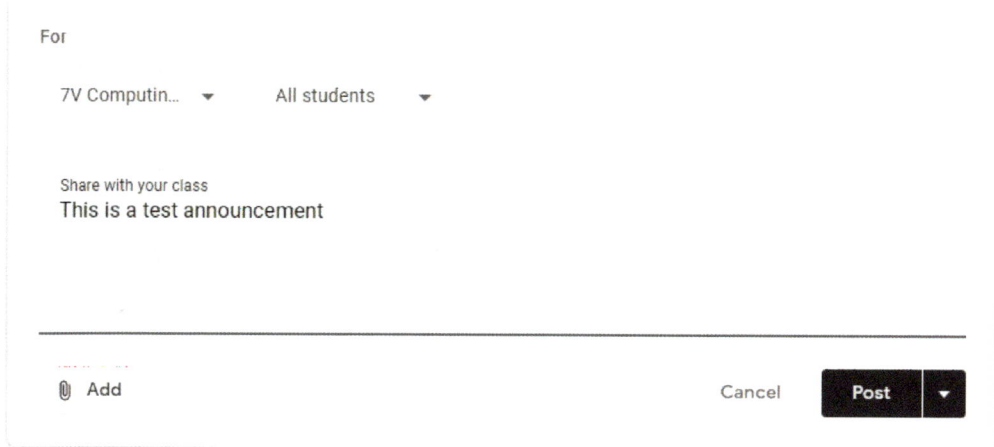

Another thing you can do with Announcements is you can decide to post them to all students within your classroom or to specific students. Similar to an Assignment which will look at next you can also post Announcements to more than one class and if you use this method you can post the same Announcement to all of the classes you select within your Google Classroom. If you are posting to multiple classes, you cannot post to individual students and you must post to all students. Rather than go over everything twice I will go through some of the details of how to do things in the Assignment section as this is very similar to both Announcements and Questions with the main difference being you cannot set a due date or collect work using an Announcement.

Stream - Reuse Post

 You can use this button to re-use an Announcement that you have posted previously in the class or any of your other Google Classrooms.

Classwork

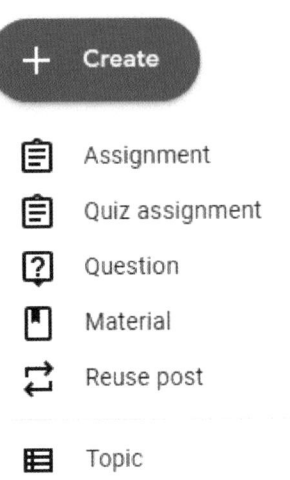

At the top of the Classwork page you will find the Create button that will allow you to produce all of the items you would like to for your Google Classroom. Once clicked you are given the following options which we will go through now.

Classwork - Assignments

Shown below is a standard Assignment created in Google Classroom labelled with some of the features you can do which I will be explaining in more detail.

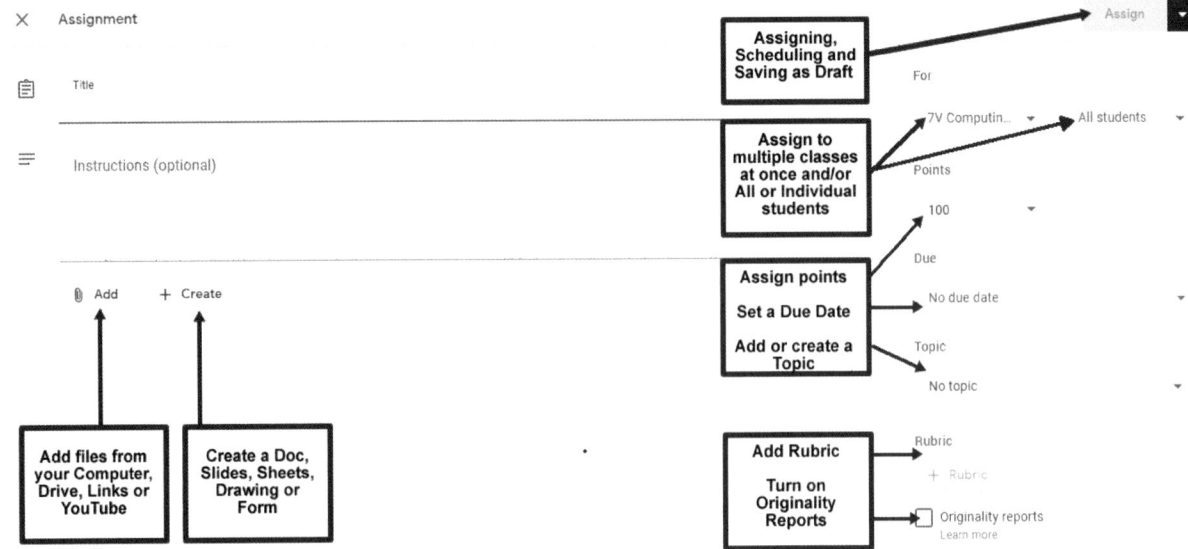

Assign to Multiple Classes

Click on the drop down menu as shown in the screenshot on the previous page and you will be given a list shown below of all of your classes in Google Classroom. You can then use the checkboxes to select and deselect as many classes as you would like to allowing you to post the same post to all at the same time.

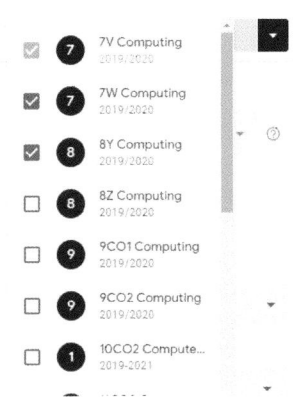

As you can see this assignment will be posted to three classes at once. You can use the drop down menu again to amend this as required. Please note the message stating that posts across classrooms must be shared with all students.

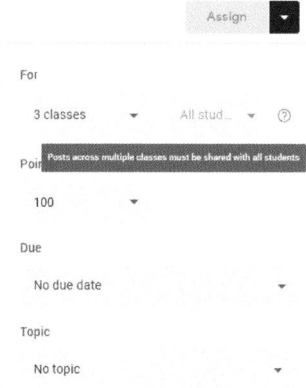

Assign to All or Individual students

Click on the drop down menu as shown in the screenshot above and you will be given a list shown below of all of your students in the classroom selected. You can then use the checkboxes to select and deselect as required.

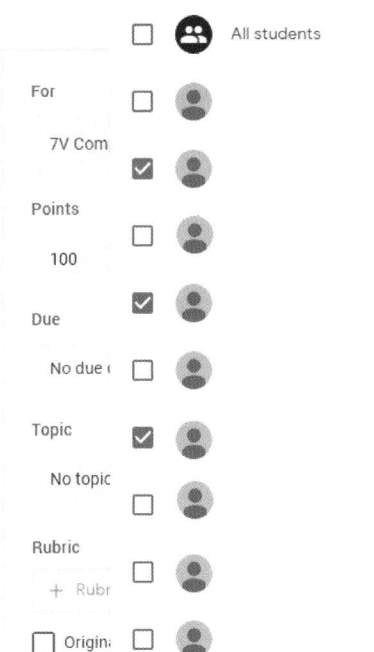

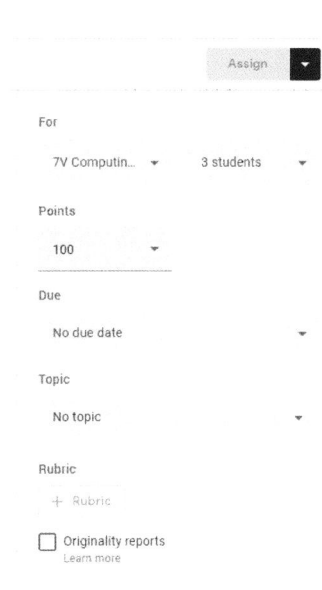

As you can see this assignment will be posted to three students only. You can use the drop down menu again to amend this as required.

Please note that after the assignment has been posted you are able to edit it and add more students. This is very useful for extension work and assigning students to it gradually.

Create Topics for Assignments

Click on the Topics drop down menu shown in the screenshot below in order to select an existing topic or create a new one. Topics are very useful to the students and allow them to filter their Google Classroom Classwork to find work easier. This will become essential during revision and exam preparation time. You can also create Topics from the main 'Create' button menu shown earlier.

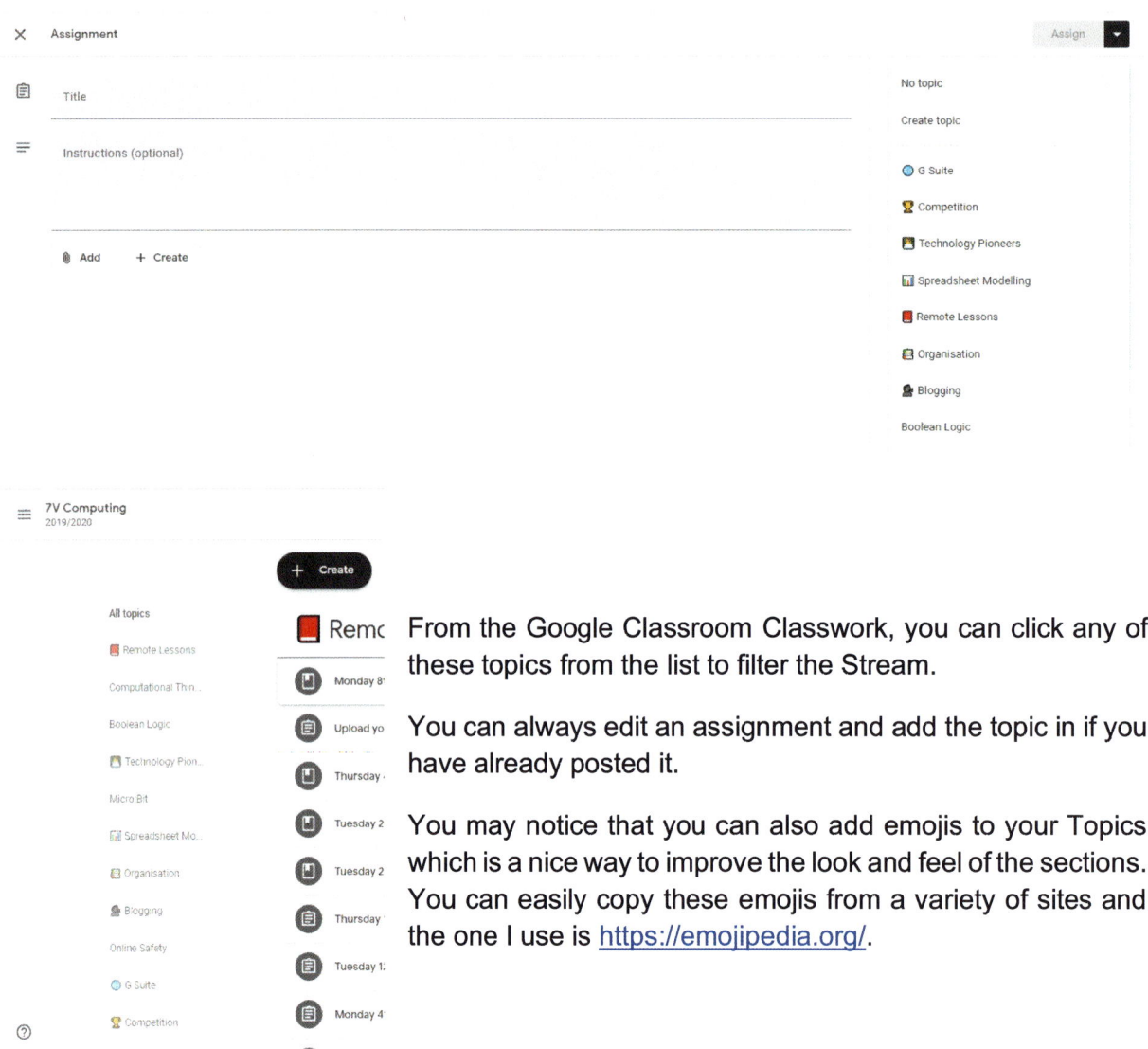

From the Google Classroom Classwork, you can click any of these topics from the list to filter the Stream.

You can always edit an assignment and add the topic in if you have already posted it.

You may notice that you can also add emojis to your Topics which is a nice way to improve the look and feel of the sections. You can easily copy these emojis from a variety of sites and the one I use is https://emojipedia.org/.

Scheduling and Saving as Draft

When you have completed creating your assignment you can then choose to assign it straight away or click on the drop down menu for more options as shown below.

You can choose the option 'Save as draft' ready to be posted later or you can select Schedule allowing you to choose a date and time in the future for the assignment to automatically post.

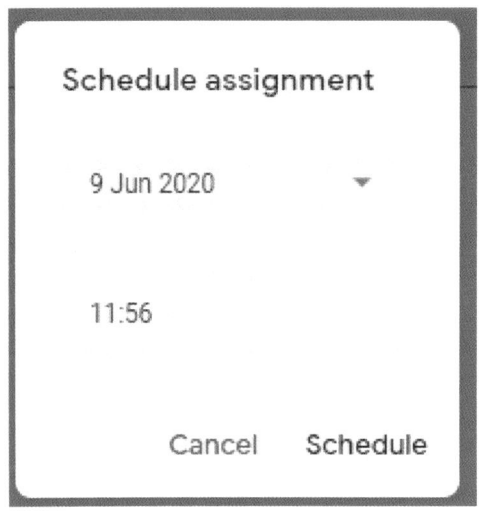

If you select Schedule then this window will load and allow you to enter a date and time

If you have already tried to 'Save as draft' you may have had the post accidently post when you meant to save as a draft or schedule the assignment. This can be very frustrating. If you just want to save the post as a draft, then the best way to ensure that you do not accidently post it to the classroom is to use the Cross at the top left of the Assignment window as this will automatically save the assignment as a Draft.

Benefits of adding due dates

There are benefits for both the teacher and the student of adding due dates to assignments that are created on Google Classroom. Due dates are optional however by adding them it means that the assignment or work will be automatically added to both the teacher and the students Google Calendar. This is extremely useful for the student specially to manage their workload as the assignment is shown on the date it is due and therefore the student can use Google Calendar to see what work they need to be focusing on.

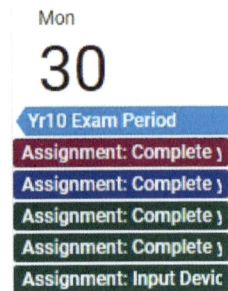

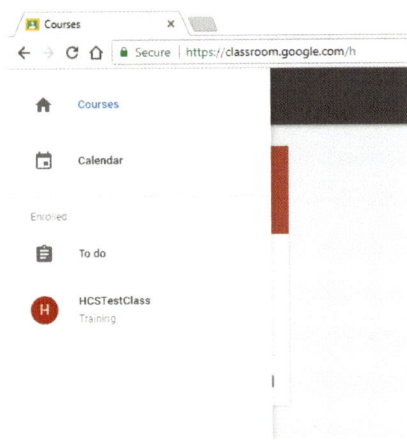

Adding the due date also adds the work to the student's 'To do' list within Google Classroom that can be access from the main three line menu at the top left.

The most urgent work to be completed will appear at the top of this stream meaning that the student can easily manage their workload and complete the tasks in the most appropriate order. This does of course require all teachers to set work as Assignments with due dates and for students to make sure they mark work as complete once they have done it, however it is a very efficient and helpful system when used correctly.

There is also a tab for your 'Done' list as you can see here which lists all of the completed work that you have done.

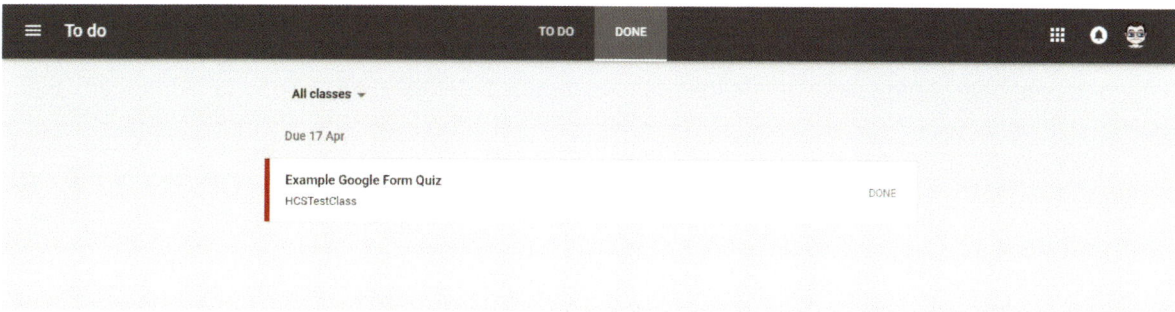

Teachers also have equivalent views in their Google Classrooms of work that has to be reviewed and what has already been reviewed. One problem here at the moment however is you have to manually use the three dots to indicate you have reviewed each piece of work even if you have marked and returned the work it still appears here as needing review. Hopefully Google will update and change this so that once an assignment is returned it is automatically puts it into the 'Reviewed' section.

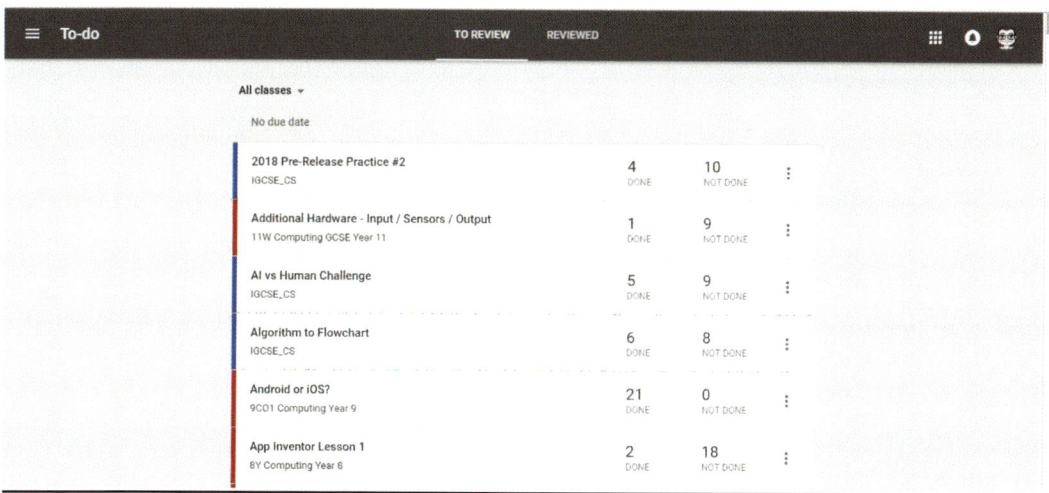

Quiz Assignments

Another additional feature that has now been built into Google Classroom is the ability to create quizzes using Google Forms directly from the create menu in Classroom.

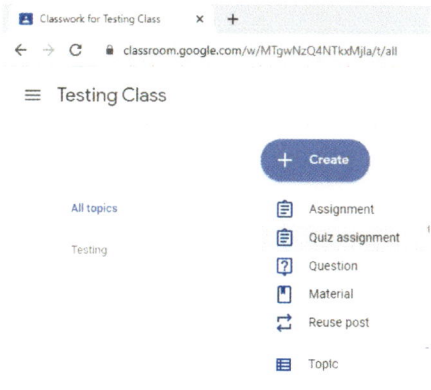

You can see here how now you can easily add a quiz assignment and this button will create you a new assignment and automatically add a Google Form which settings have already been set to a 'Quiz'.

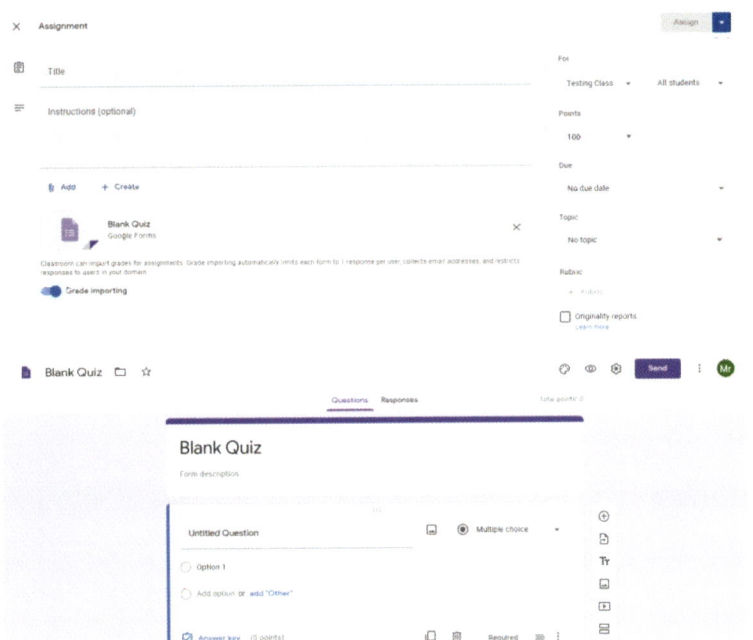

You can see here the blank quiz ready to be edited and you can also see 'Grade importing' has also been turned on.

When you click on the quiz it will open Google Forms ready to be edited and all changed will be linked to the post on Google Classroom

Classwork - Questions

Creating a question in Google Classroom is very similar to creating an Announcement or Assignment but this time you can post a question for the students to answer and they will be given a multiple choice or a written answer box that they can fill in. With a question you can add a due date and topics which means it treats it more like an Assignment therefore you can mark and provide feedback online if you wish to. You also have extra options about whether you would like students to be able to reply to each other and whether students can edit their answer which is really useful if you want to do a collaborative question task or if you want it to be an assessment question you can turn these settings off. With Assignments and Announcements you always have the option of adding attachments, adding from Google Drive, adding a YouTube video or indeed a link to a website.

Example Short Answer Question

Example Multiple Choice

One of the great built in functions of using a Question multiple choice is the fact that Google Classroom will automatically give you a generated bar chart of the results as shown here:

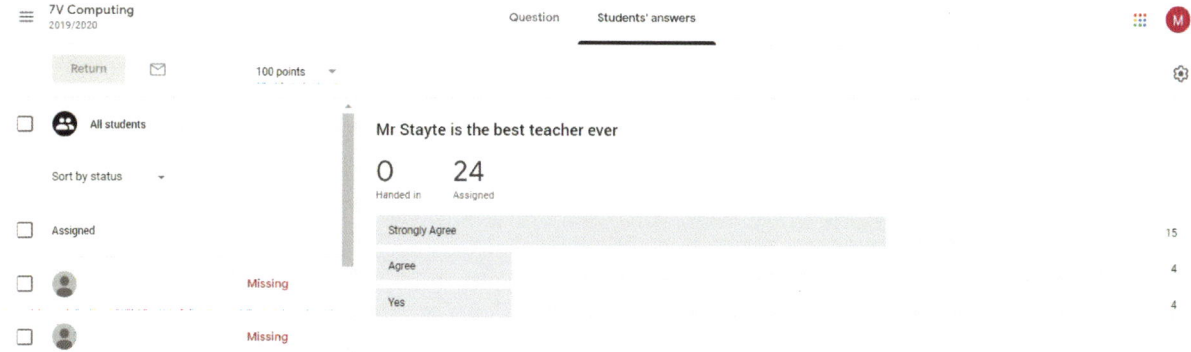

This is a handy little tool especially if you would like to do a quick class poll on a topic or debate as you can show the live results to students.

Classwork - Materials

This option allows you to post materials to the Classwork page that do not require the students to do anything with them. Therefore, they do not have due dates but can have attachments and topics as shown below:

One of the reasons why this is so useful is because Materials will not appear in the student's 'To do' list but can still be found easily by the topic assigned in the classroom.

Classwork - Reuse Post

The reuse post option within Google classroom is very useful especially once you get into year two of using Google Classroom. Reuse post allows you to look back at any classroom you've made, including archived classrooms, and reuse the posts from them. This will save you hours of time in preparation because you have already got your scheme of work from last year bar some tweaks you may need to make for this years class.

Reuse post can also be used to help you if you have forgotten to post to multiple classrooms when creating a post. This has huge benefits for teachers who have same age classes and share resources. As long as the teacher is added to a Classroom they can you reuse the post of another teacher as well which is a huge advantage and very collaborative.

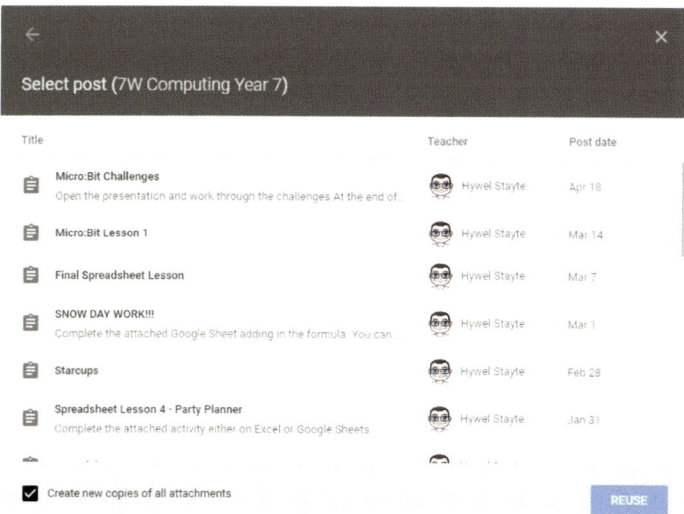

When reusing a post, you can choose whether to make new versions of the attachments or not. It is important to think about this carefully as most of the time it is better not to do so because then you can update the attached Google File in one place. If you make copies you will have multiple versions of the same file buried in your Google Classroom Drive folders and it may cause you problems.

Classroom - Marking

Google Classroom has undergone many updates since its launch and one of the most recent was the improved marking tools built directly into Google Classroom Assignments. In order to make use of this tool you need to set an assignment and then view the assignment where you will see a screen similar to this displaying all of the students' names and files. In the past you would click on the file and it would open directly in Google Docs for example whereas now the new marking tool will load around the file.

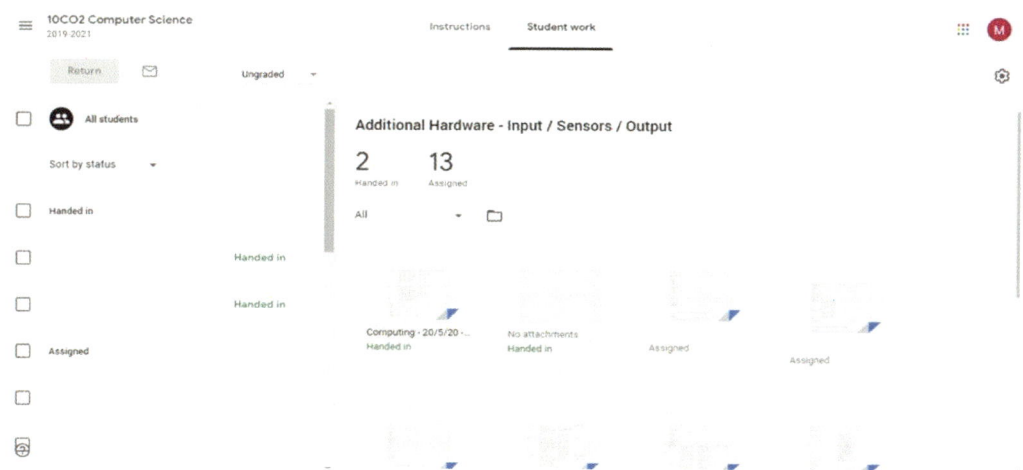

Shown below is the new tool and what it looks like. You can see the students work and surrounding the file are several options and tools for you to use.

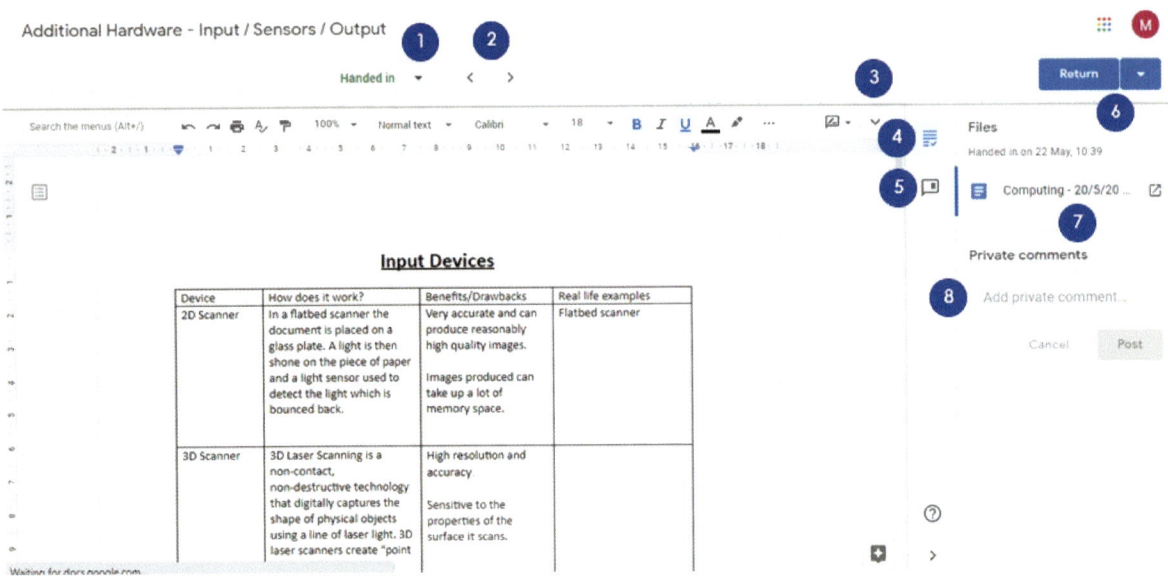

1. Use this drop down tool to change the student that you are currently looking at

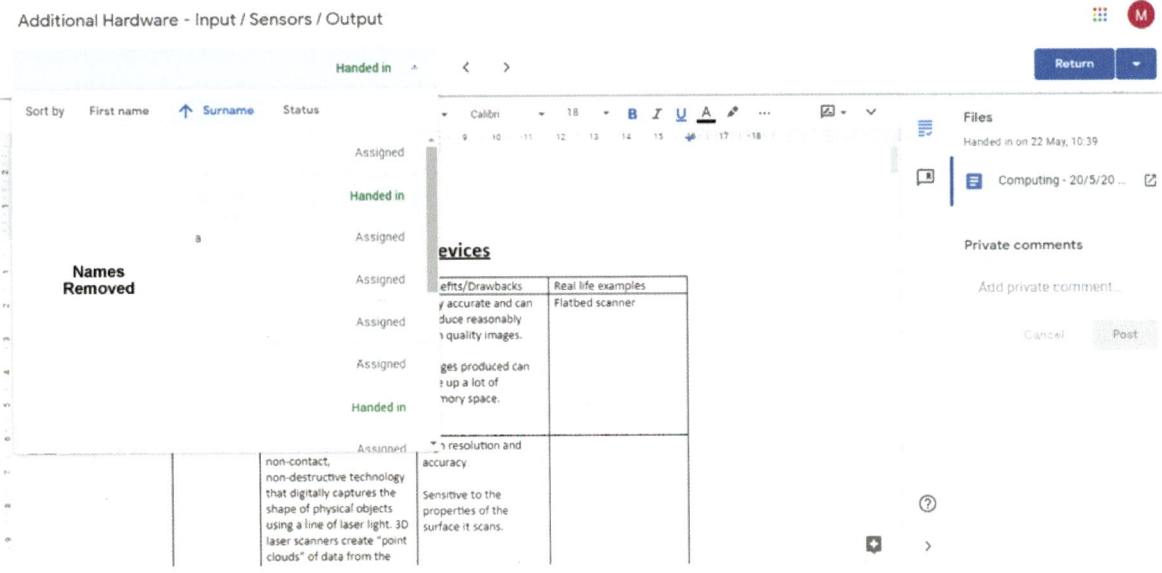

As shown in the image above you can also change the order the students are displayed in this drop down by changing what they are sorted by. Instead of surnames it is sometimes better to sort by status so that all of the ones handed in are first with missing ones at the end.

2. Use this control to navigate through the different students
3. This arrow displays the Google Doc controls for the Google Doc you are currently looking at
4. This is the 'files' tab so you can change between the student's files on the assignment
5. This is the 'comments' tab to allow you to adjust your comment bank

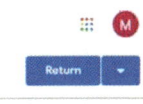

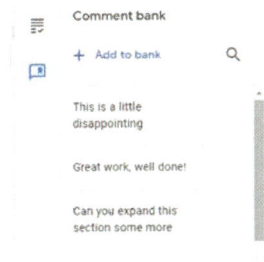

Here you can click to 'Add to bank' in order to populate with your own comment to use within your marking.

You can separate your comments with a line space and enter multiple at once. A great tip here would be to have a shared Google Doc/Sheet where all of your department add comments to which you can all add to your own Google Classroom Comment banks.

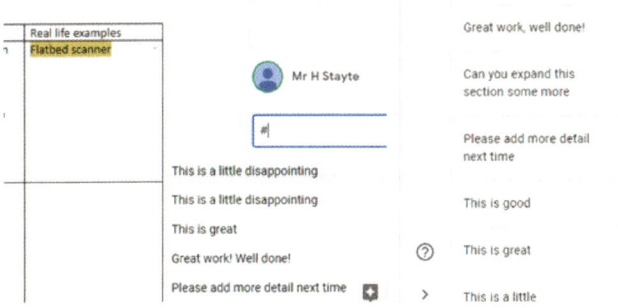

When you are adding comments to your students work (Ctrl+Alt+M) you can access your comment bank quickly by pressing #. If you start typing what you are looking for you will find it quickly.

6. Use this control to Return the current assignment or multiple assignments

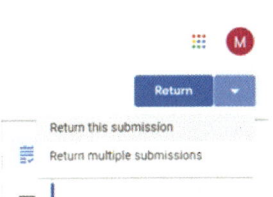

7. These are where the files are listed in the 'files' tab. (Only one file on this assignment but you can have multiple) You can click the pop out button here to open the files in a new window
8. Here you can leave private comments directly to the student

Originality Reports

One of the big updates recently to Google Classroom has been the introduction of Originality Reports on Assignments that allow you to check for plagiarism in the students' work. You can see it here at the bottom right there is a checkbox that you can tick to enable Originality Reports on the assignment.

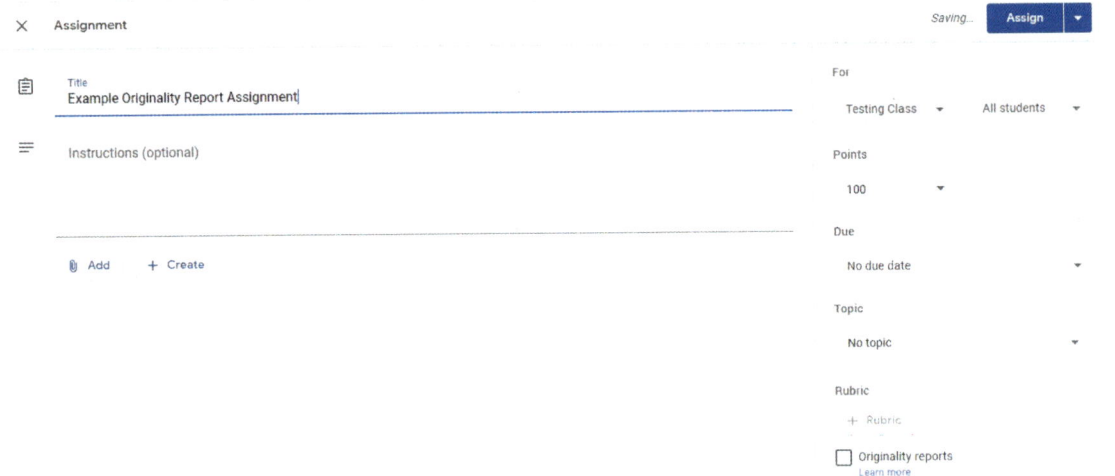

When you click the checkbox to enable the Originality Report you will be greeted with the following message.

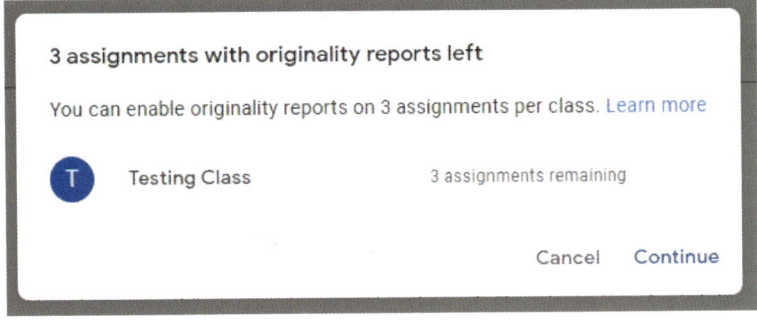

This is because with the standard G Suite for Education you are limited to only three assignments per Google Classroom that you can run Originality Reports on. If you would like to increase this feature then this is part of the Enterprise edition for Education but there is a cost involved here. My advice would be to self limit the use of this feature in your standard Google Classroom to only a couple of assignments and if you are in need of frequent use then what you could do is create an 'Assessment' Google Classroom where you can add your students to. This way you can have three assignments on your assessment Classroom which have Originality Reports and then once you have used your three you can create a brand new 'Assessment' Google Classroom in which you can use three more Originality Reports.

Once enabled Google will scan each of the students' work (Google Doc format only) for copied passages from the internet and produce a report for the student and the teacher upon submission of the work. Shown here is the teacher view from the built in marking tool which now displays an extra option 'Check originality' under the Google Doc file on the right hand side in the files section.

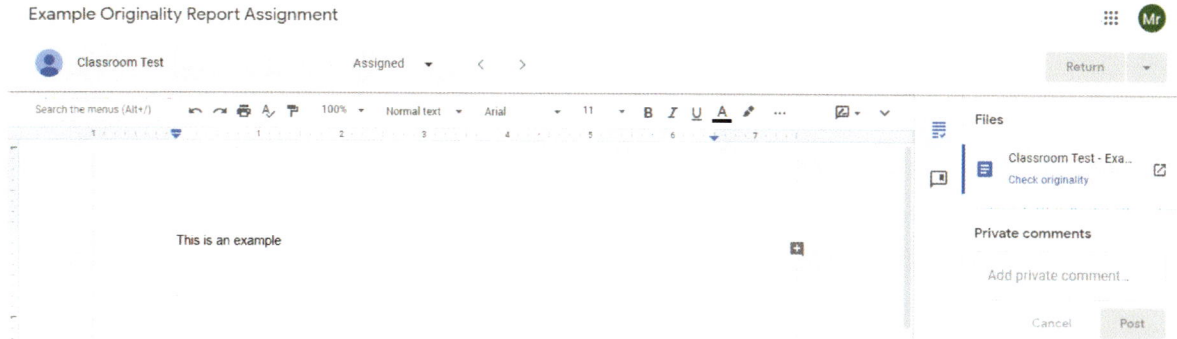

After clicking on this link the Originality Report will run and as you can see here there are no flagged passages of plagiarism present in this piece of work.

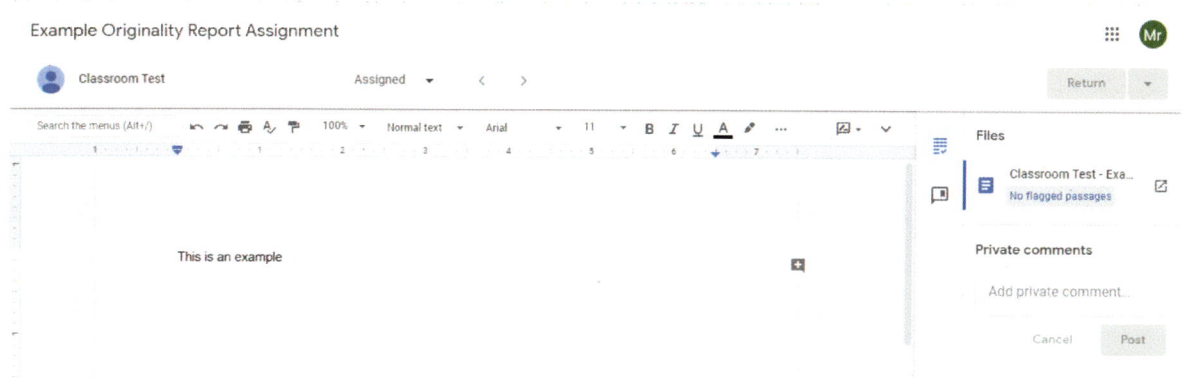

The student can check the Originality of their own work before turning it in up to three times. Here is the view the student would see when viewing their assignment from Google Classroom and they have a new link to 'Run' the Originality Report.

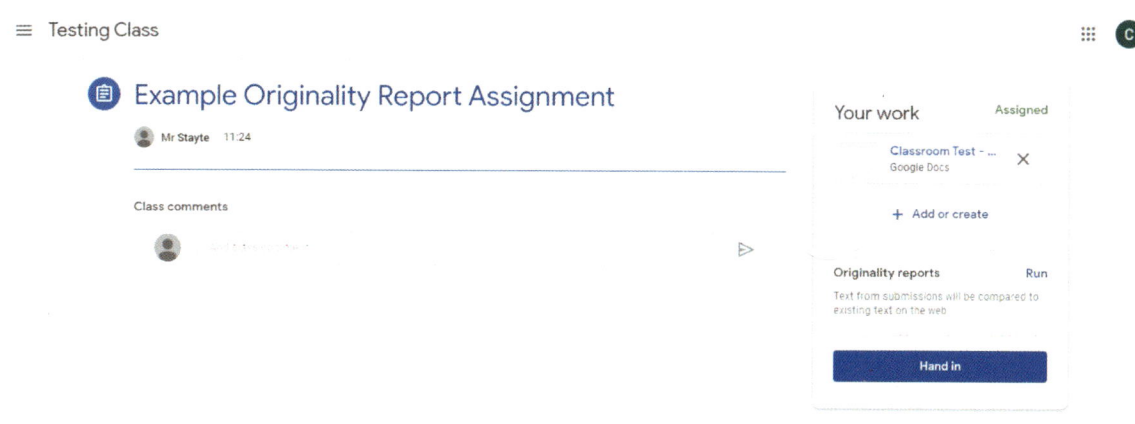

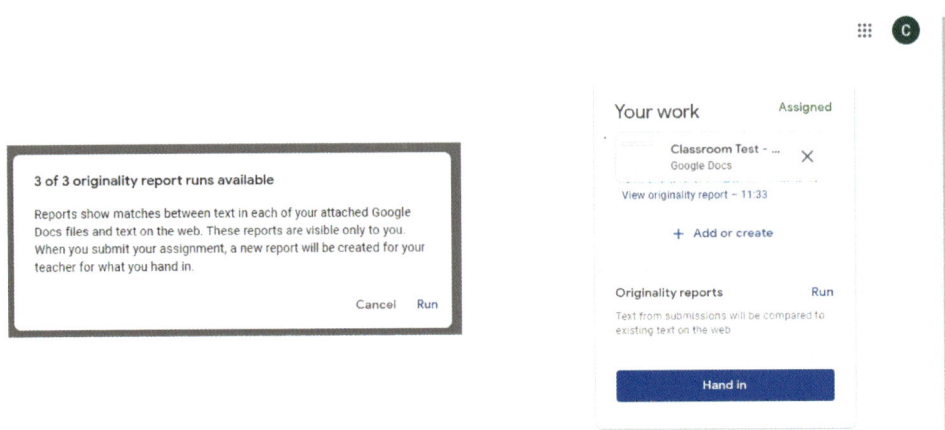

The students are given the warning message limiting them to being able to run the Originality Report three times and then once run they are given a link to view the report generated.

Once handed in the teacher can see this view of their marking tool showing that in this case there is one flagged passage for them to review and it gives the details of the website where it found a match to the text on the Google Doc.

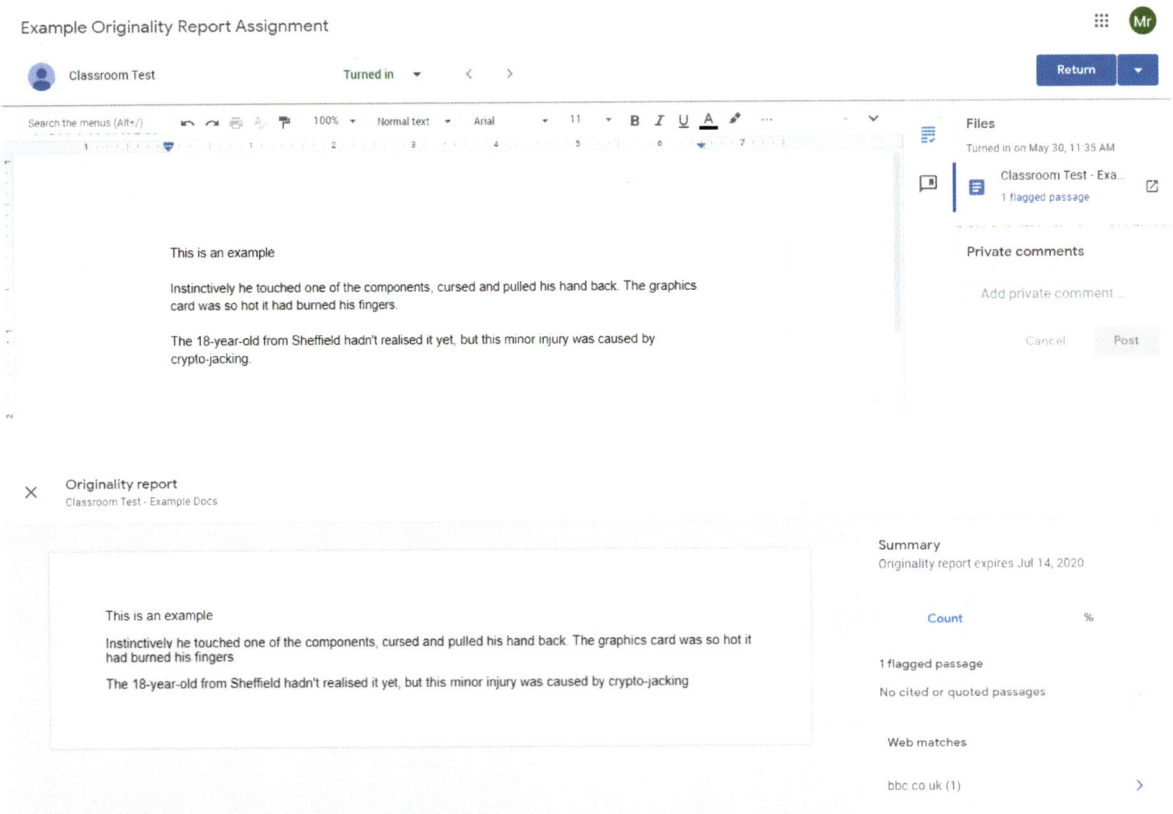

Rubrics

Another large and useful update to Google Classroom has been the addition of Rubrics for marking work built into assignments. When creating your assignment you can choose to add a Rubric that will be used to assess the work on the assignment. You can add this when you create the assignment however you can also edit an already posted assignment and add a Rubric to it. When you select the Rubric button you will be presented with three options for adding your Rubric.

If you select to 'Create rubric' then the built in Rubric creator will load allowing you to customise your marking rubric. You can add a points value and have scoring here if you wish which means that the assignment total points will be adjusted based on the rubric you create however you can also select not to have points associated with the selections.

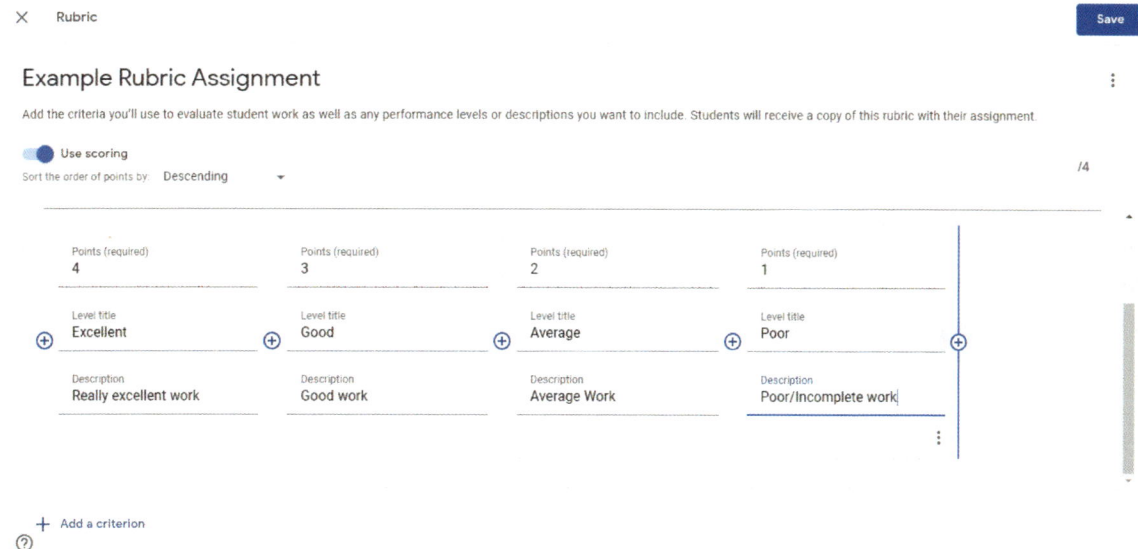

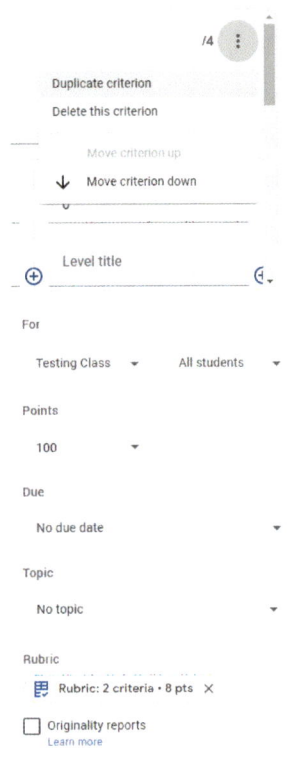

You can use the small + sign at the side in order to add in more options into your rubric. Once you have completed your first criterion you can use the button at the bottom to 'Add criterion' or if you click on the three dots at the top right hand side then you can actually 'Duplicate' your current one in order to save yourself some time. Here you can also delete and re-order your criterions within your rubric.

Once you have completed your rubric and pressed 'Save' at the top right hand side then you will see your rubric appear on your Google Classroom assignment as shown here. You can click on this rubric to see a preview of it within Classroom.

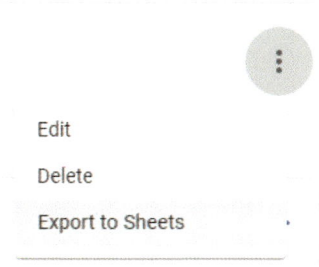

You can use the three dots on this preview in order to Edit, Delete or even Export the current rubric to Google Sheets. Exporting to Sheets can be useful for sharing your rubrics with people who are not co-teachers in your Google Classroom. You can then use the 'Import from Sheets' option to load it back into a Google Classroom.

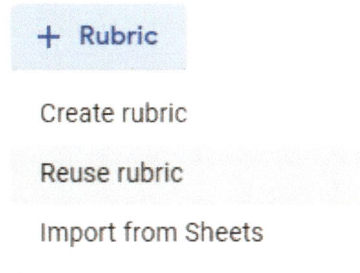

Instead of creating a new rubric each time on Google Classroom you can also select to reuse a rubric you have previously made before. This will allow you to use other teacher's rubrics providing you are a co-teacher in their Classroom.

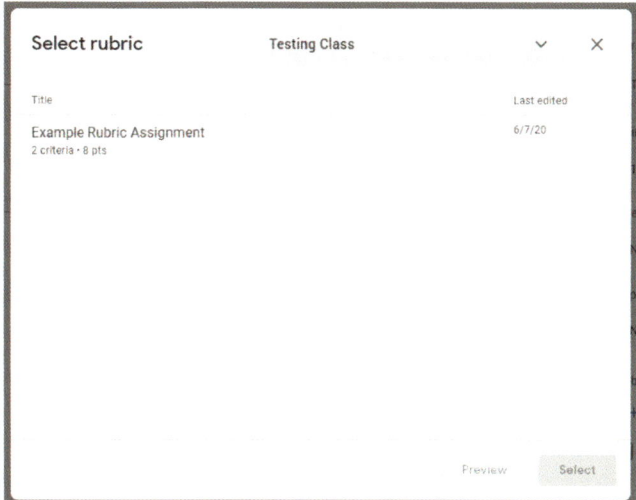

At the top here you can select which Google Classroom you would like to reuse a rubric from.

Listed below are then all of the rubrics from the Classroom and you can select any of them to use.

When using the marking tool in Classroom the rubric will now be available for you to use in order to quickly mark and assess the work you are looking at. Just click on the small rectangles to indicate your selection.

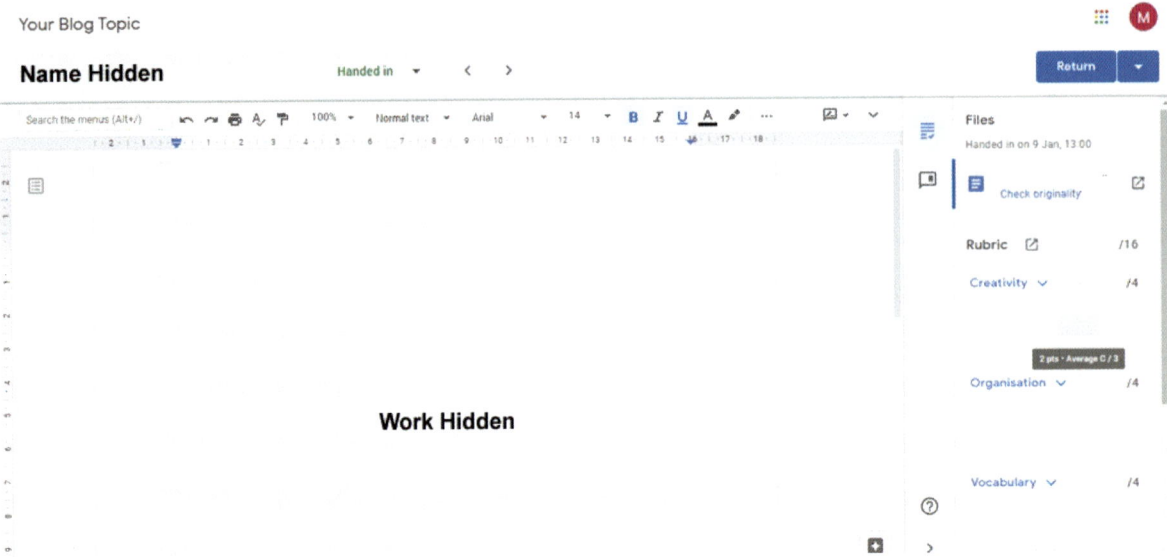

As you click on the rectangles if you have chosen to use points then the score will be automatically added to the boxes and the total added up automatically. You can of course use the marking tool options here to return and/or click through the different students.

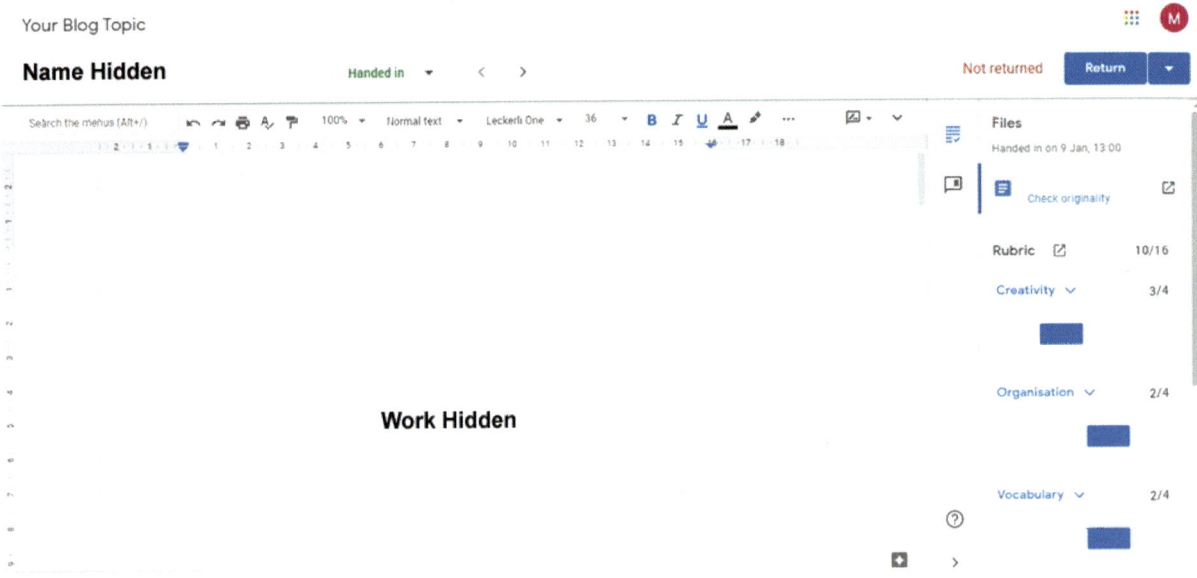

Gradebook

You can access the Gradebook from the 'Marks' tab on Google Classroom and this will load up a screen similar to this one.

Every single assignment that you create on Google Classroom will be added automatically to this gradebook and any results will also be input with the corresponding student. This does give you a nice overview of the work you have set however it can become quite large and there is not currently an option to hide a column or remove it from the gradebook. If you delete the assignment it will be removed from this gradebook.

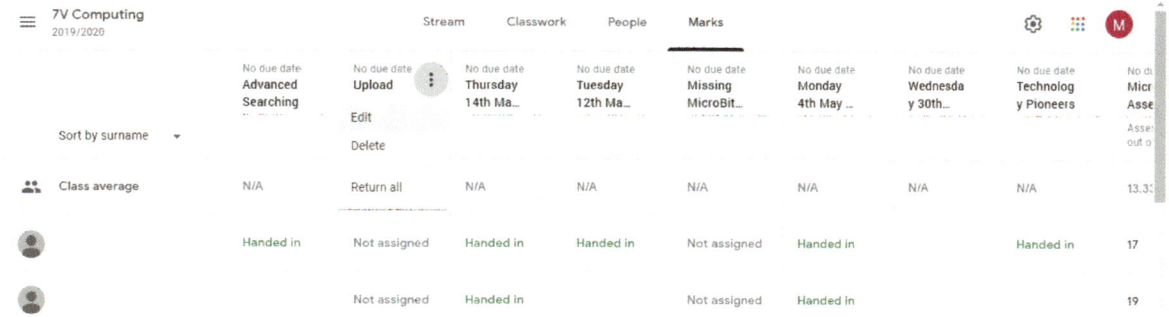

There are a couple of things that you can do here directly from the gradebook that do come in handy. If you click on the three dots on an assignment then you can edit the assignment directly or even delete it from the gradebook. You also have the option to 'Return all' in order to very quickly send an assignment back to all of your students. Additionally you can also click on any of the assignments at the top to go directly to them and also click on any of the students from your gradebook in order to be shown a list of their assignments and their scores/statuses of the work.

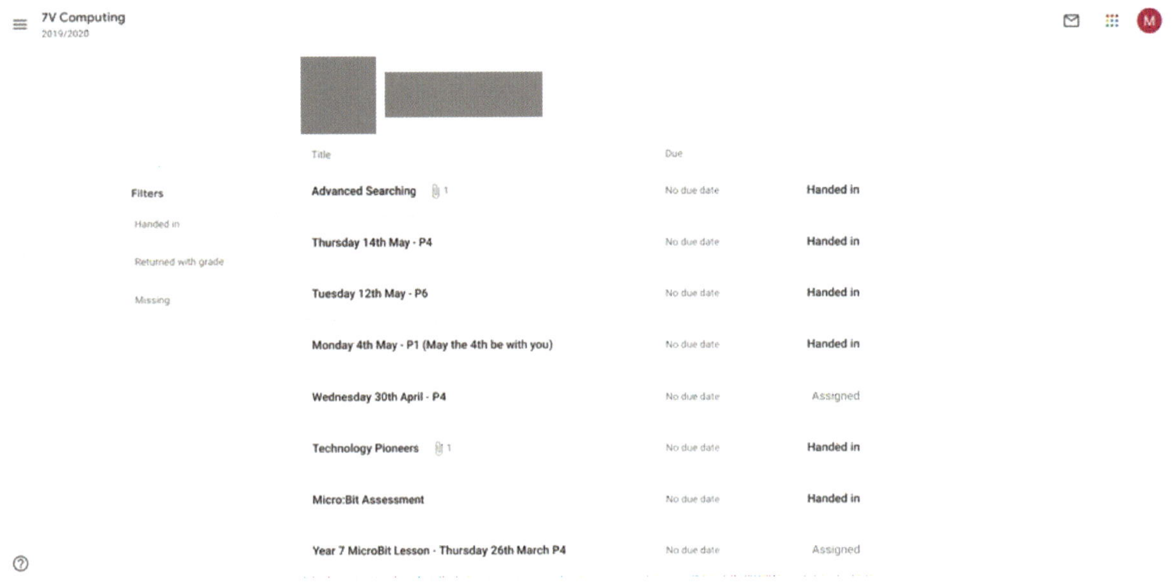

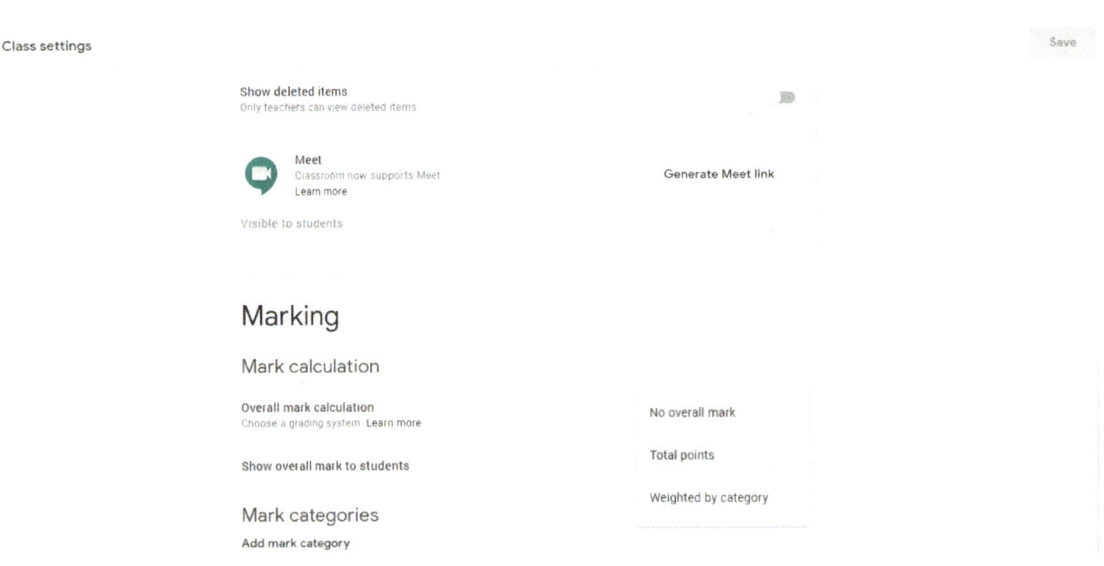

7V Computing 2019/2020		
	Title	Due
Filters	Advanced Searching 📎 1	No due date	Handed in
Handed in	Thursday 14th May - P4	No due date	Handed in
Returned with grade	Tuesday 12th May - P6	No due date	Handed in
Missing	Monday 4th May - P1 (May the 4th be with you)	No due date	Handed in
	Wednesday 30th April - P4	No due date	Assigned
	Technology Pioneers 📎 1	No due date	Handed in
	Micro:Bit Assessment	No due date	Handed in
	Year 7 MicroBit Lesson - Thursday 26th March P4	No due date	Assigned

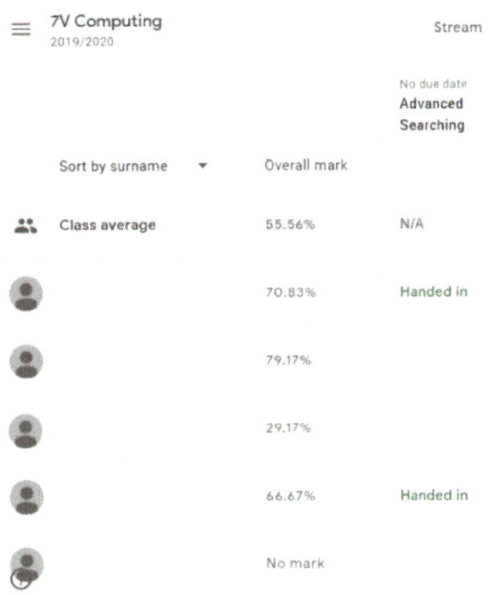

You can also use gradebook in order to calculate an 'Overall mark' based on all of the work set within your Google Classroom which appears at the start of the gradebook in the first column.

In order to calculate an overall mark you will need to press the cog at the top right in order to edit the settings of your Google Classroom and scroll down to the 'Marking' section. Here you can change it from 'No overall mark' to one of the following two options:

7V Computing 2019/2020

Stream

No due date
Advanced
Searching

Sort by surname ▼   Overall mark

👥 Class average   55.56%   N/A

👤   70.83%   Handed in

👤   79.17%

👤   29.17%

👤   66.67%   Handed in

👤   No mark

✕   Class settings   Save

Show deleted items
Only teachers can view deleted items

📹 Meet
Classroom now supports Meet
Learn more   Generate Meet link

Visible to students

Marking

Mark calculation

Overall mark calculation
Choose a grading system Learn more   No overall mark

Show overall mark to students   Total points

Mark categories   Weighted by category

Add mark category

1. Total Points - Uses every assignment that has points associated with it to calculate the overall mark

When using a 'No overall mark' or 'Total points' you can create categories and have default points associated with the different categories which can be useful if you have certain assignments that are always worth a certain number of points.

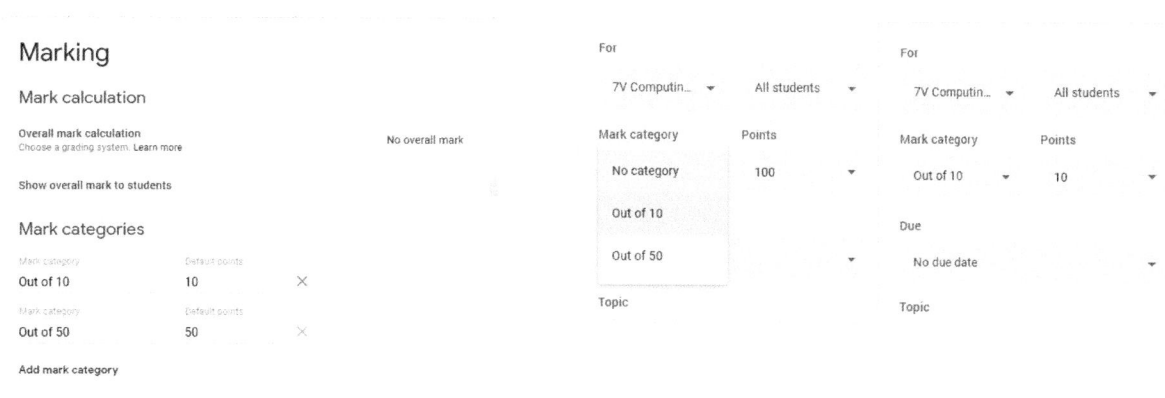

2. Weighted by category - Allows you to <u>only</u> include those assignments that have a category assigned to it.

Before anything under the category

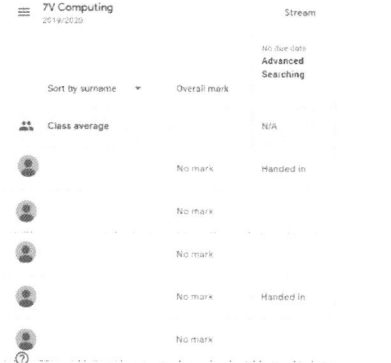

After assignment added with category

Get more out of Google Classroom

Start of Academic Year

At the start of the academic year you often need to tidy up your Google Classroom and remove all of your old classes. Once on your main Google Classroom area you are able to use the 3 dots on each classroom to perform the following functions.

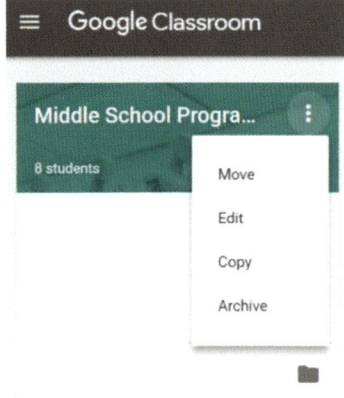

Move - Use this to move your classroom order

Edit – This will allow you to rename an existing classroom and change some of the details. i.e. change a class name from Year 10 to Year 11

Copy - Allows you to make a copy of an existing classroom

Archive – Will hide the classroom away and you will not see it again unless you want to retrieve it

The reason there is no delete is once you have archived you are able to still reuse posts from these classrooms. If you would like to delete a class permanently then you have a delete option once the class is archived.

Use of Google Forms in Classroom

Now that Google have fully integrated Forms with Classroom as explained in the Google Form section of the book you have the ability to import the results from the form directly into Classroom. Another nice little feature about using Google Forms in Classroom is that if you insert the form using the Drive icon rather than posting a link into an Assignment, Google Classroom will automatically mark the Assignment as completed for the student once they have completed the form. This does only work if the only thing in the Assignment is the Google Form but still a very useful function to save that little bit of time for the student and show the teacher easily who has completed the form and who hasn't.

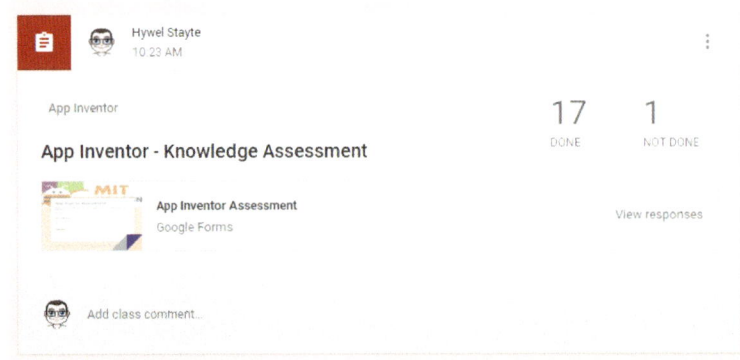

Links to Google Drive folders in Classroom

Another useful tip is that if you have a lot of files that you would like to share with students you may want to add them all to Google Classroom. The only issue here is that when it is a large number of files it can become rather cumbersome to add them all to an Assignment or Announcement so instead just add a link to a Google Drive folder. If you create a folder and add all of the files you want to it you can simply copy the folder link:

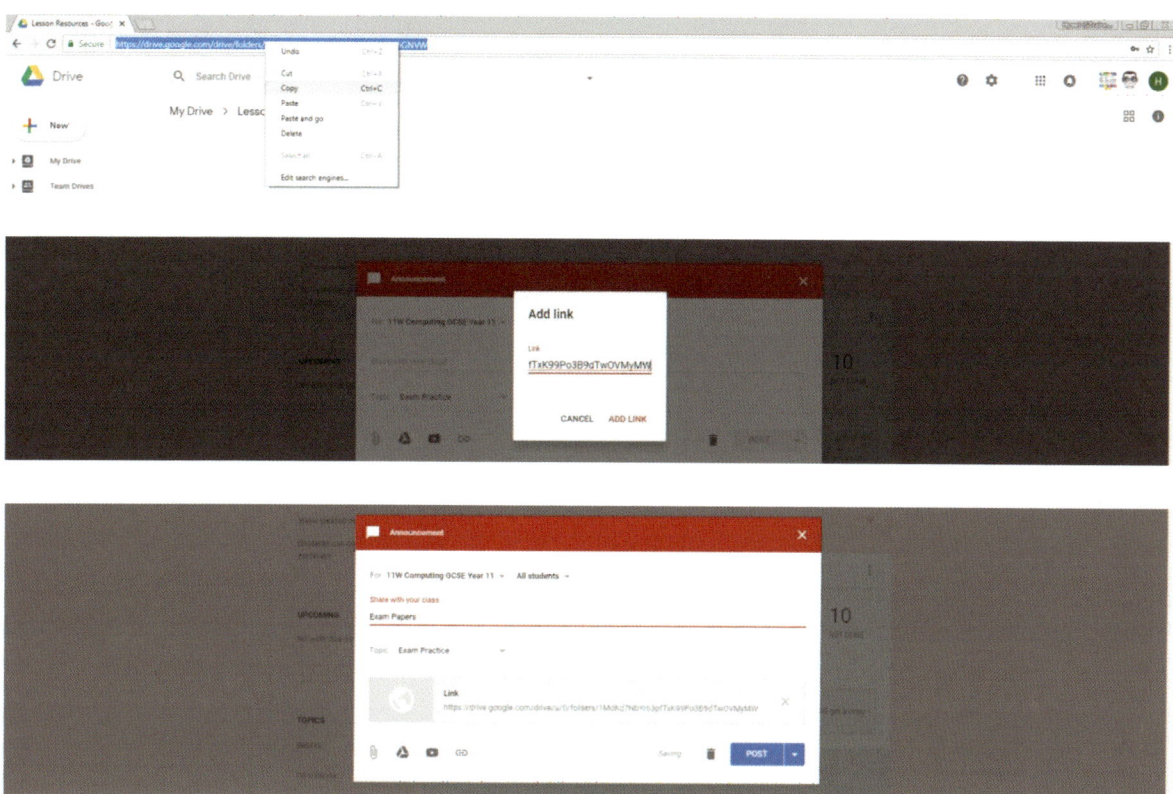

As soon as you post the Announcement or Assignment the Google Drive folder will be automatically shared with the members of the Google Classroom and the link to the folder will work and allow them to access the files.

Display on board

You can use Google Classroom as your teaching aid and sometimes you may not want to have an additional presentation to display on your board and simply the post you have created on Classroom is enough for the students to know what they are doing. One problem with doing this is that for most of us our boards do not always project the largest image.

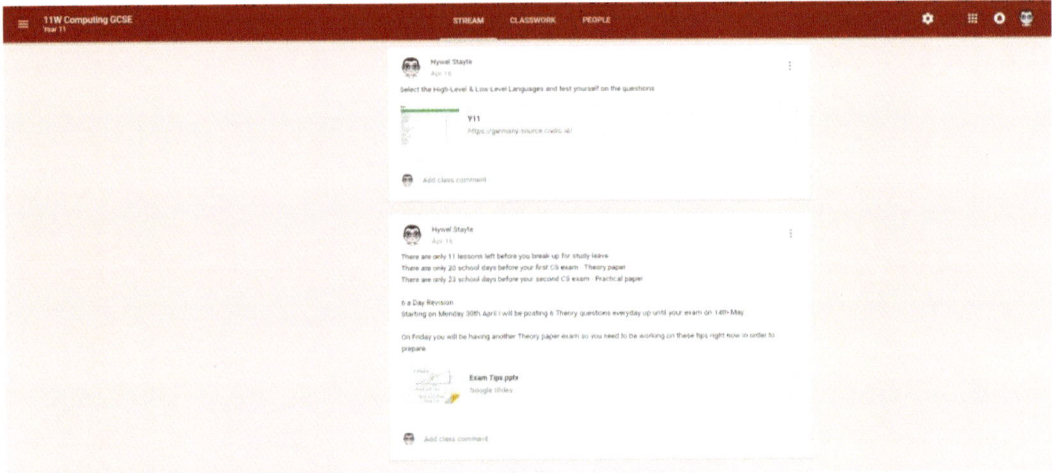

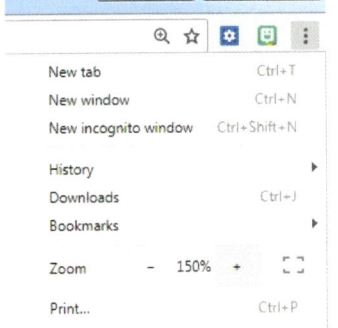

Using Google Chrome, you can click on the 3 dots at the top right of the browser and use the Zoom controls to zoom the screen in. This will then display your Google Classroom post much larger and hopefully big enough to use as your classroom display for that lesson.

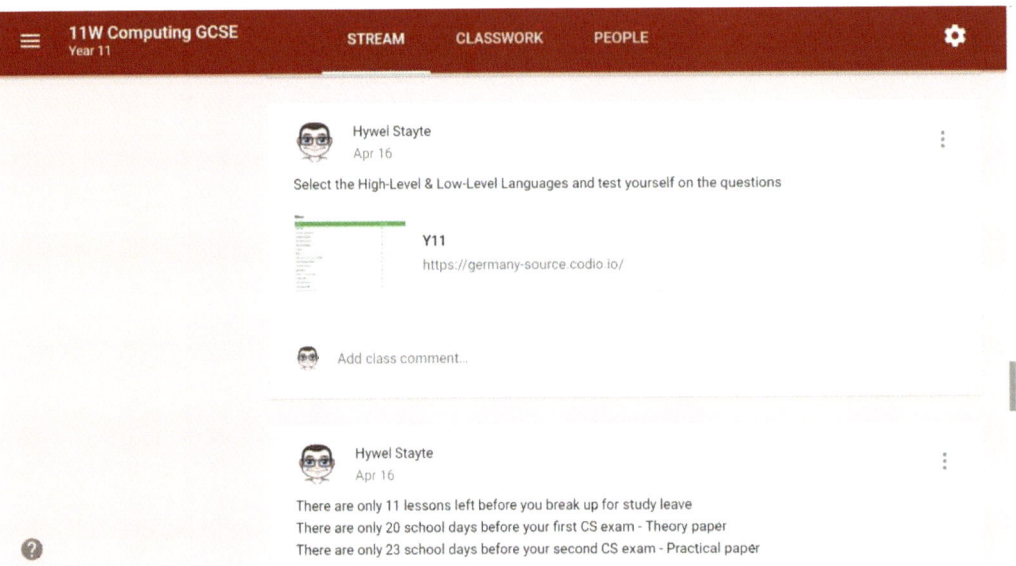

Display class code shortcut

The easiest way to get all of the students in your class to join your Google Classroom has to be to give them all the class code. You can manually add all of the students yourself using their email address and you can also give them all on paper the class code however if they all have a device or are sat in front of a computer then the best thing to do is display the code on the board.

You will find the class code at the top of your Google Classroom on the Stream. If you click on this you are able to select broken square to display the code. You can click the broken square again to display even bigger on the screen. You can also find the class code under the 'Settings' of Google Classroom.

It is possible for your Google Admin to have already created classrooms and added all of the students to them however this would not be something I would expect a standard teacher to do so I will not get into that in this book. If you would like to find out more about this, then please visit techproblems.co.uk

Use of Add-ons with Google Classroom

You cannot add add-ons specifically to Google Classroom however there are many add-ons that can pull information from your Google Classroom for you to use in other G Suite applications such as Google Sheets. Some of these are explored later in the book however it is important to know that they are available so when you are looking through add-ons you can keep an eye out for those useful ones that integrated with Classroom.

Staff Meetings or Staff Groups with Classroom

As a teacher on Google Classroom you can not only create and manage classes but you can also join classes as a student. This is useful if you have a meeting group of staff where you would like to share resources or minutes and agendas electronically and you can make use of Google Classroom to do this.

You may prefer to use Shared Drives for this purpose however Google Classroom may well be an easier alternative for the more less technology savvy staff as the files will be populated to the stream and they will receive an email about them when they are posted. Google Classroom for this purpose has some advantages over Shared Drives and one example could be the use of

Google Forms within Classroom as the link to the form will be added rather than giving staff access to the editing of the form if you were using Shared Drives.

I think again with this use it is up to you to decide which method is most appropriate for your staff but I would suggest that for small working groups Shared Drives would be better however for larger announcement groups Google Classroom would be the one to use.

Year Group or House Group Classrooms

This idea is just like the previous one but this time using Google Classroom with large groups of students in the form of a year group Google Classroom or indeed House group. The advantages of this is that it allows you to get information out to a large number of students very quickly and this would be most suited to Announcements that need to be made. You could of course use Assignments within these classrooms for standardised CVs or documents they all need to produce from a template however mainly I see this being used for getting information out.

Tutor Group Classrooms

There are many types of Google Classroom you could have within your organisation and depending on if you already have year group classrooms you may not have the need for a Tutor Group classroom however I have found this a very useful tool for getting posters and notices to all my tutees. I have used my tutor group classroom as a way of displaying tutor board notices electronically and therefore saving the need to print out and put up within the physical classroom as often these boards are neglected and easily get out of date.

Student Clubs on Classroom

Having a Google Classroom for any clubs that you run in school can be very valuable as it allows you to share information with them easily and post things that they may need for your club or activity. One thing I have posted as a class Material in Google Classroom for these clubs that I run is a Google Form register. In my organisation there is no formal register for our clubs and we are required to keep our own records and the easiest way I have found to do this is via a Google Form. At the start of each club the students are first required to access the Google Classroom and complete the Google Form register providing me with an automatically populated Google Sheet of their attendance.

Classroom Headers

You would have already read about this in the Google Drawing section of the book but personalising your Google Classroom headers is a nice touch and something that can make your Google Classroom stand out from all of the others in the students view. Clearly this is not essential but if you are like me you just like to be different!

Editing Access to Classroom Posts

This can be a useful tool to use depending on how you are using Google Classroom but essentially you may wish to show a Google Classroom post to only a few students who have finished all of their work (extension work) and you can select just these users when making your post. You can 'Edit' any post on Classroom and give additional users access or indeed take access away. I use this a lot if I have students getting ahead and I will release the post to them and gradually and add others as they catch up. I do this as not to confuse them by having posts that are not yet relevant to them yet.

Differentiation through Assignments

The functionality within Google Classroom to assign different posts to different students also allows you to therefore assign different worksheets and activities to different students meaning you can have differentiation through task really easily without them knowing about it so obviously. Of course this requires a little more setup but no more setup than physical differentiated worksheets would be.

Gmail

Gmail is one of my favourite parts about G Suite and is very simple to use so I will not go into too much detail here on how to use the inbox as I am sure the vast majority of you would have been able to figure this out for yourselves. I will highlight some of the advantages of using Gmail for your organisations email system over some of the other products available to you before we look at the more advanced features in the Getting more out of Gmail section.

Before I begin to list the reasons why I believe Gmail is far superior to other email products out there please first know that I am aware that some of these advantages will be available in these other products however I want to give the overview and the advantages as I see them and, in my opinion, are more slick and easier to use.

Firstly you can control your inbox using any web browser on any device and of course there is also a Gmail App available on all platforms and Gmail embraces the web based email system with no local application. The advantage of this is the consistency for the user making use of Gmail without the need to change product or use a reduced service product.

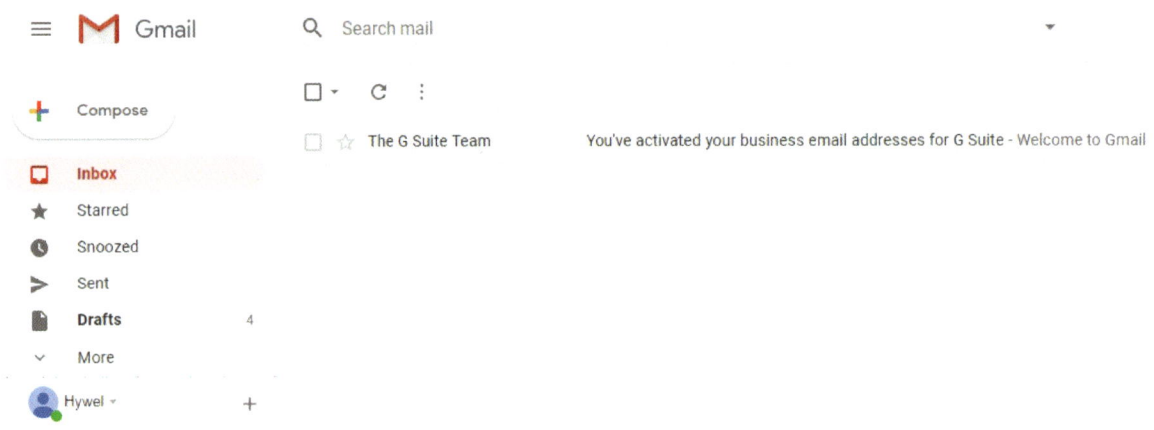

Email creation

The simplest thing to do is compose an email. Despite the fact that the button is the big one labelled Compose I remember when I first used Gmail years ago and it took me a minute to find it! Once you have located the Compose button you can use it to create an email and the following window will appear in your inbox.

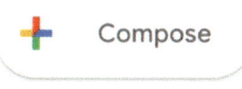

You will see the standard options available to you that you would expect in any email package or software and you are able to insert email addresses in the To, Cc and Bcc boxes. You can add your email subject and then the main body of your email. Any email signature you have will be automatically added at this point as well.

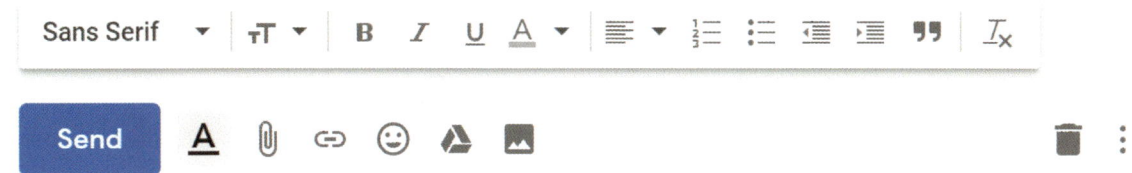

Across the bottom of the email creation window you will find a selection of other options available to you with the first one being to send your email. The next option allows you to customize the text and formatting options of your email.

Most of these options are pretty standard for editing digital text so I will not bore you by going through each one but I will highlight the last two as particularly useful.

The first one here is a 'Quote' button which allows you to format quotes into your email really effectively.

The second is a 'Clear formatting' button which allows you to wipe all of the formatting of the text. This is great for when you have copied and pasted text into your email.

The next main option is pretty standard in email software and it is the paper clip to attach any file you would like to the email you are sending. This will enable you to send any offline file to the recipients of your email and you can upload it directly from your computer or device. You can also insert hyperlinks and emoji's to your emails using the next two option buttons.

The Google Drive icon allows you to insert directly from your Google Drive this also means that you can send Google Drive links if the attachment is too big and therefore despite the standard email attachment size being 25mb using Gmail there is effectively no limit to attachment sizes being sent through Google Drive. You also have the option to insert an image into your email and you can also take an image if you are using a device with a camera. The trash can image is a delete the current email button and the three dots are for more options.

Another advantage of Gmail is the ease in searching global contacts of the entire domain by typing. Students can simply start typing the name of their teacher for their email address to populate and give suggestions. This feature can be controlled by the admin of your domain so it can be turned on and off and altered as required but is an incredible useful feature for everyone.

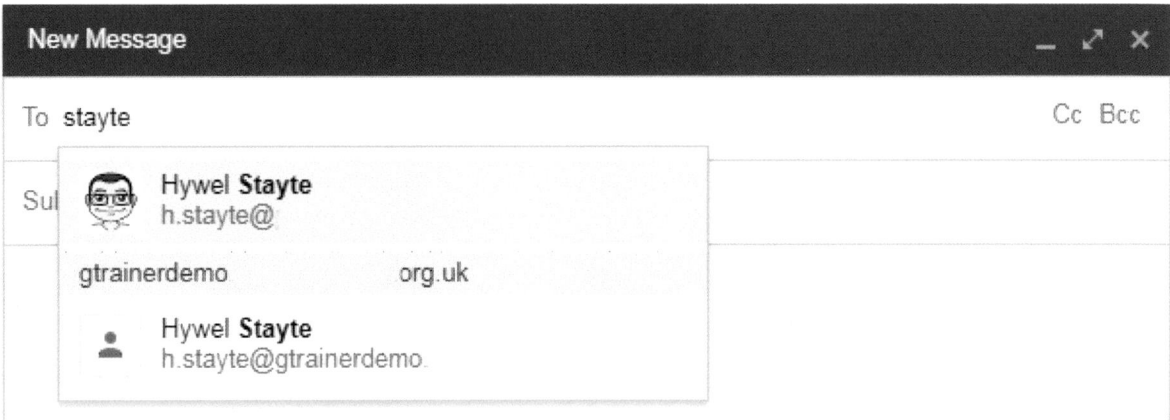

Google Groups also work in this way allowing you to search for groups to send emails to simply by typing in the name of the group.

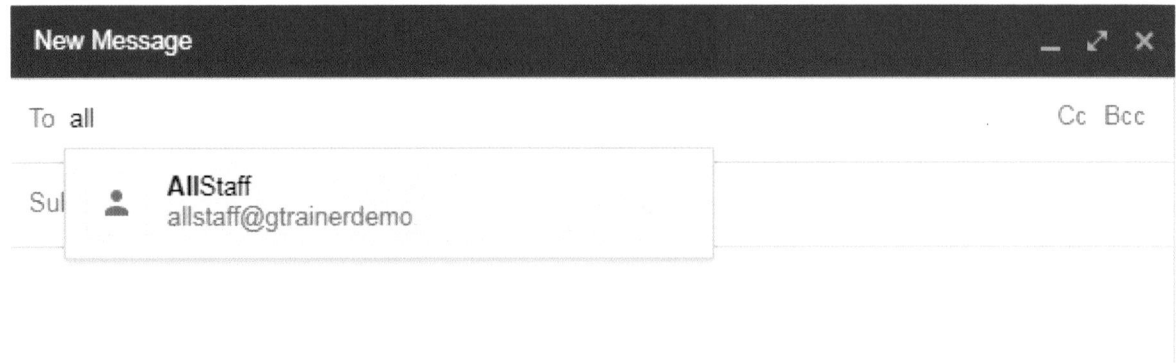

Whilst you are creating your emails you will also notice that Google continually saves your draft emails automatically for you. If you create an email and cross it off by mistake it will have been automatically sent to your drafts ready to use again.

Managing your Inbox

Whilst viewing emails you have these options that appear at the top of Gmail to allow you to control the emails you have received. The first button here is one of the most important and useful which is the Archive button.

 This is a very slick and neat method for managing your inbox and you can say goodbye to large numbers of read emails in your inbox without the need to manually organise or delete your old emails. Google have cleverly built in an archive function into Gmail that allows you to quickly remove emails you have read and no longer need in your inbox.

Simply hit this button whilst reading an email or after you have selected them from your inbox to remove them from view but still have them stored under your all mail section.

   The next three buttons are 'Report spam', 'Delete' and 'Mark as unread'.

A new addition to Gmail is the introduction of the new button 'Snooze'. This button allows you to select an email or indeed a selection of emails and remove them from your inbox for a selected period of time. Once you press the Snooze button you are given the following options to select from.

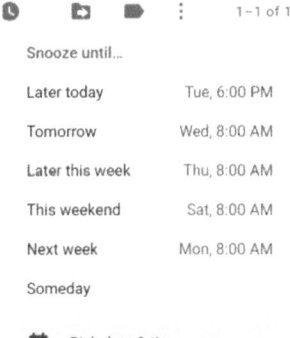

Here you can select one of the predetermined set options to quickly remove the email from your inbox or you can even be more specific on the date and time you would like the email to come back to your inbox.

This is a fantastic addition to Gmail as rather than having an email sitting in your inbox because you cannot deal with it until a certain point in the future you can set it to disappear and reappear when required.

 The next three options are 'Move to', 'Labels' and 'More options'.

You can apply Labels to any of your emails you have received in order to manage and organise them and similar to other email products you can then load up a Label and see all of the emails which have that Label applied. The 'Move to' option allows you to move emails to different sections of your inbox applying Labels to them and removing them from your inbox.

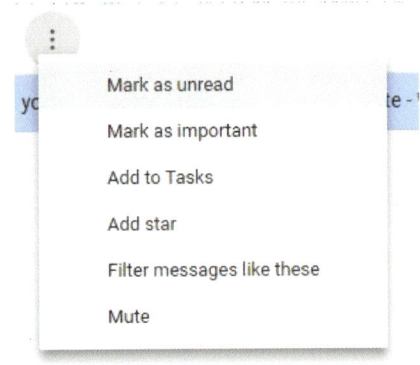 More options give you some extra functionality that you can add to your emails which are shown here. You can set up filters for your emails here and also add an email to your tasks list. I will be explaining Tasks in more detail in the Getting more out of Gmail section.

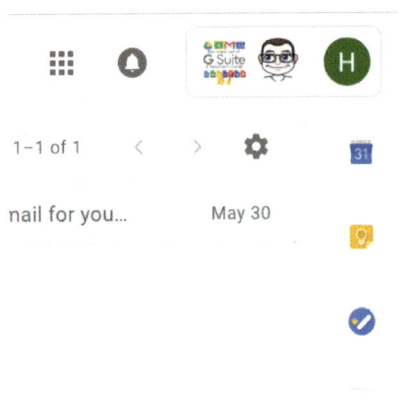 Google have now added some quick links to the right hand side of Gmail that enable you to quickly select Google Calendar, Keep or Tasks. You also now have a quick button to add Gmail Add-ons.

As you can see the standard cog for entering settings is also displayed here and you can use this to create an email signature and adjust all of your Gmail account settings.

Google Search Tools are built into Gmail and I think you will find that the search in Gmail is superior to other providers and much easier to find old emails. You can also use search syntax such as *sent:hstayte@gmail.com* to find all of the emails you have sent to a specific address. There are of course many other search criteria you can use and a link to them is given in the Links & Resources at the end of this book.

If you have a Google for Education account, then there is unlimited storage and no need for you to run your own email server and store all the old emails which is great news for your organisation's infrastructure. There is also easy setup for mobile devices using Gmail as there is no requirement to add server details and the login is managed through your email address and a lot of the difficulties with logging into email on mobile devices is removed and made much simpler.

Threading of emails is much neater than in other packages and it is clear to see the structure of the emails that have been sent without having long trails at the end of every email that is sent. There are of course other advantages to using Gmail but one of the problems with using a separate email provider when your organisation is using G Suite is that many of the integrated features across the different packages do not work, such as the communication section of Google Classroom. Other parts of G Suite still work without Gmail such as emails being sent when you share a Google Doc however having everything integrated can streamline workflow and some of these will be explored in the Getting more out of Gmail section.

Get more out of Gmail

Sidebar Menus

Quickly load Google Calendar, Google Keep and Tasks as a sidebar menu from within your inbox.

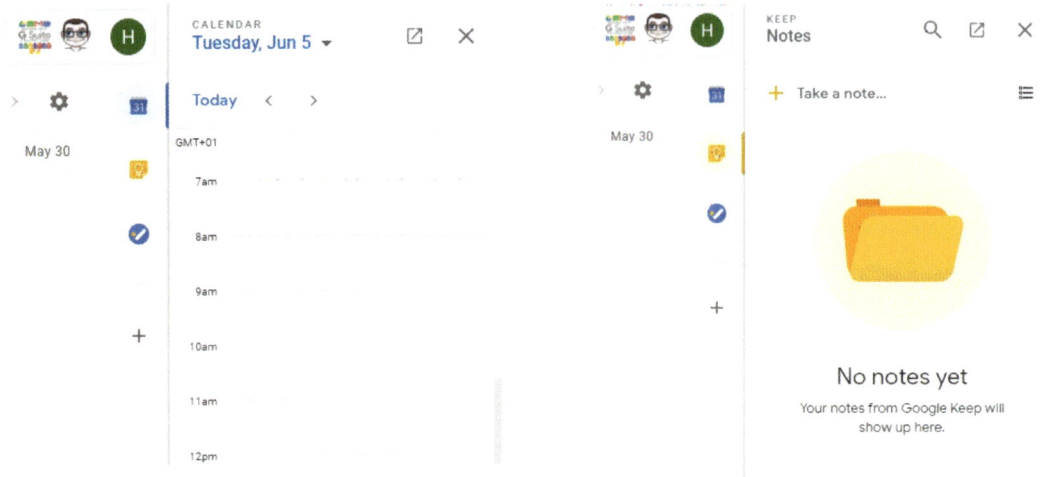

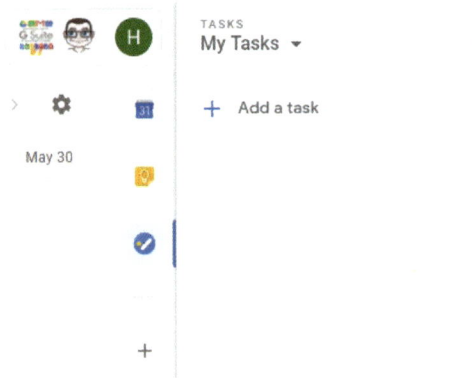

All three of these are ideal for managing your workload whilst you are dealing with emails. You can easily add, edit and delete from your Calendar, Keep or Tasks without having to open separate windows.

Each one of these applications are powerful in their own right and can really benefit your workflow so having them directly in your inbox is fantastic.

This feature has now also been rolled out for Docs and Slides which is great for integrating all the G Suite Apps together.

Add-ons

The next icon available down the right hand side of Gmail is the small plus symbol that stands for add-ons. Press this button to load the add-on store for Gmail and explore the potential options available to you.

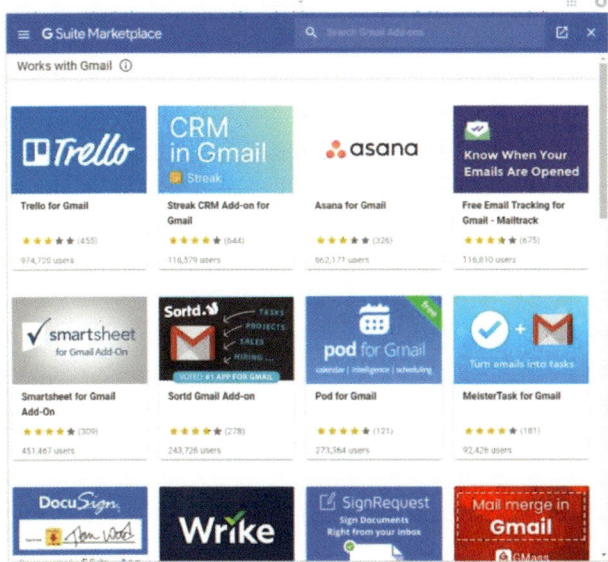

There are not a huge number of add-ons available for Gmail however some of these are very powerful and it is always advisable to explore what is on offer.

Google Calendar

Google Calendar is a fundamental G Suite product that is integrated with so many services it is very useful for your day to day work. I do not know where I would be without my Google Calendar Daily Agenda and emails to remind me about events I have such as meetings and detentions I have set. Google Calendar lets you take control of your organisation and will not allow you to forget anything!

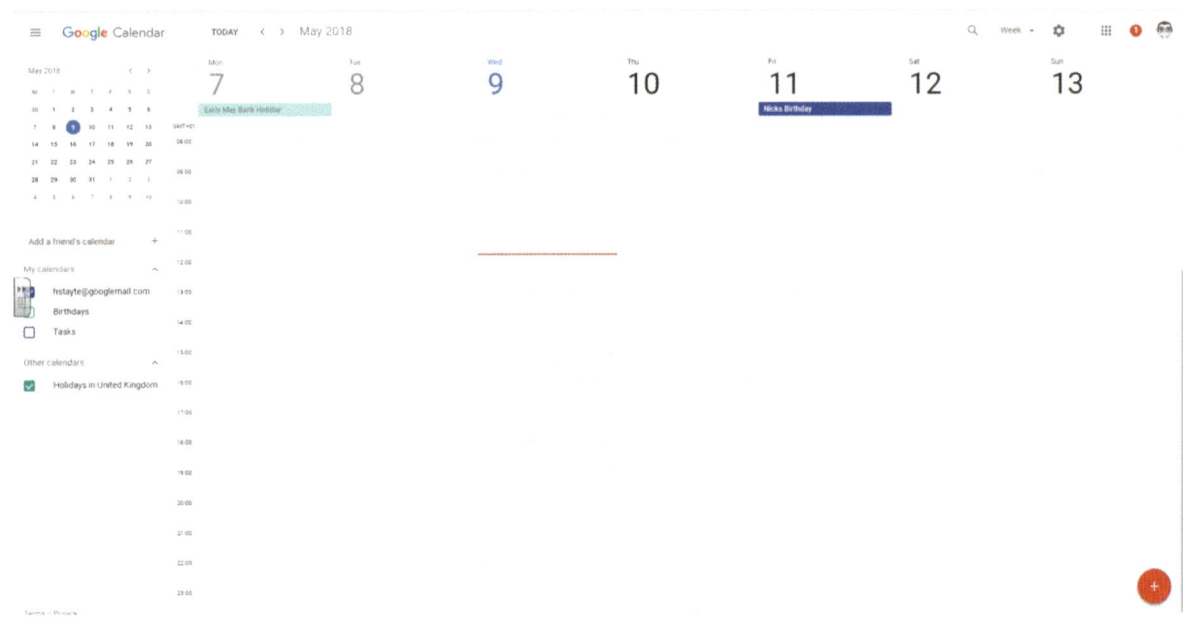

 The big red button! As with a lot of G Suite apps the use of a button in the bottom right hand side of the screen is common and in Google Calendar you can use this to add a new Event to your calendar. If you are using the tablet app you can also use this button to add a Reminder or Goal.

Events

Events are the main thing you will create using your Google Calendar and you can use the red button in order to create a new event. You can also click into the calendar at an appropriate place to create an event at the right date and time. If you click and drag you can also determine the length of the event very quickly.

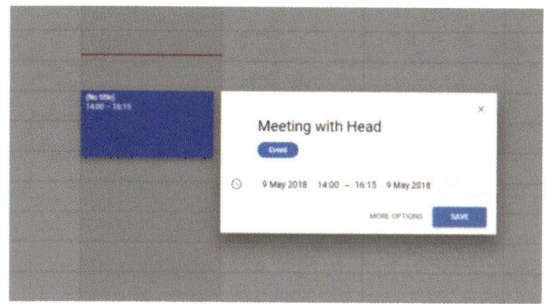

This also allows you to quickly add a title for the event and add it to your calendar in a couple of clicks.

From here you can also click 'More Options' to edit the event in more detail.

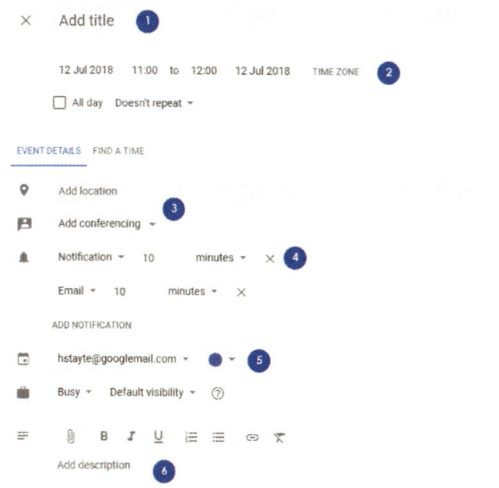

To load this screen menu, you can also just click on the red button to create a new event.

As you can see there are many new options available to you when you create a calendar event and they are all explained below.

1. Here you can add a title to your event
2. Here you can add all the time details for the event. If the event is an All Day event simply click the checkbox. You can also choose if this event will repeat which is incredibly useful for recurring meetings or even lessons if you would like to add your school timetable to your calendar
3. This is the Event Details section and allows you to add a location and conferencing options such as Google Hangouts
4. This is the notifications section which are some of the most powerful parts of Google Calendar as you can setup up emails and pop ups to remind you about any Google Calendar event you have created
5. This allows you to control which calendar you are adding the event to and all the calendars that you have access to will be listed here including all your Google Classroom calendars. You can also control how your availability is displayed
6. Here you can add a description about the event and some more details

Get more out of Google Calendar

Goal

Reminder

Event

<u>Reminders</u>

If you are using the Google Calendar App then you have the extra functionality to add Reminders using Google Calendar. These allow you to keep giving yourself prompts to complete tasks and the options to dismiss or remind you later about the task. These can be very useful to you if you need continuous reminding about certain tasks or events.

<u>Goals</u>

Goals are another option only available to you through the Google Calendar App and these allow you to set future Goals that you would like to achieve and Google Calendar will help you to schedule when you are going to do it.

You can easily choose from some of the predetermined options available or you can customize what you would like to do. Next you answer a few questions about how often and approximate times in the day and Google Calendar will do the rest.

Once scheduled you then have the ability to adjust the times and Google Calendar will start to learn your preferences and help you to find the time to achieve the Goal.

<u>Never Forget</u>

Using Google Calendar can turn you into the most organised person that people know and it is all done by machine with you doing as you are told. You will never again forget a meeting and will always know if a student doesn't turn up for a detention because your Google Calendar will tell you. The only thing you have to do is get yourself into a routine of adding all events of any kind to your own calendar with email reminders at appropriate times.

Daily Agendas

Daily agendas are a built-in function of Google Calendar that can be setup to send you an email in the morning of all the events in your Google Calendar for that day. I have mine setup to email me at 5am every morning and it is very handy to give yourself a reminder in the morning of everything you have got to do that day. More times than I can count it has saved me from forgetting an important early morning meeting or job to do.

To turn on your daily agenda you need to go to your calendar settings by clicking on the cog in the top right-hand side of the screen as shown here:

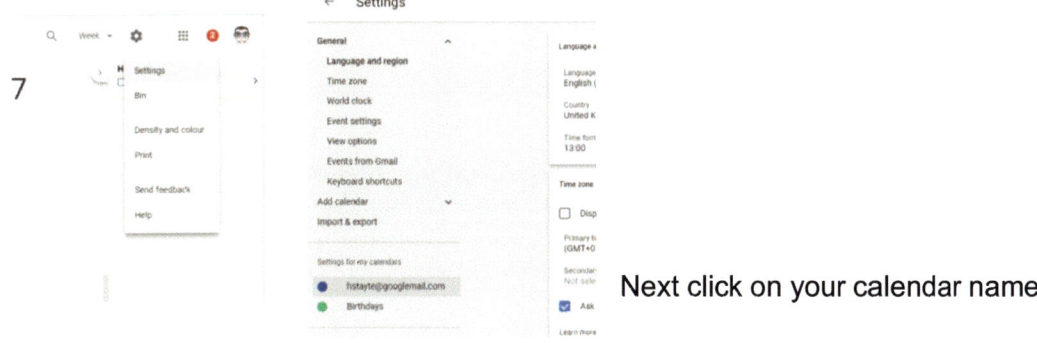

Next click on your calendar name

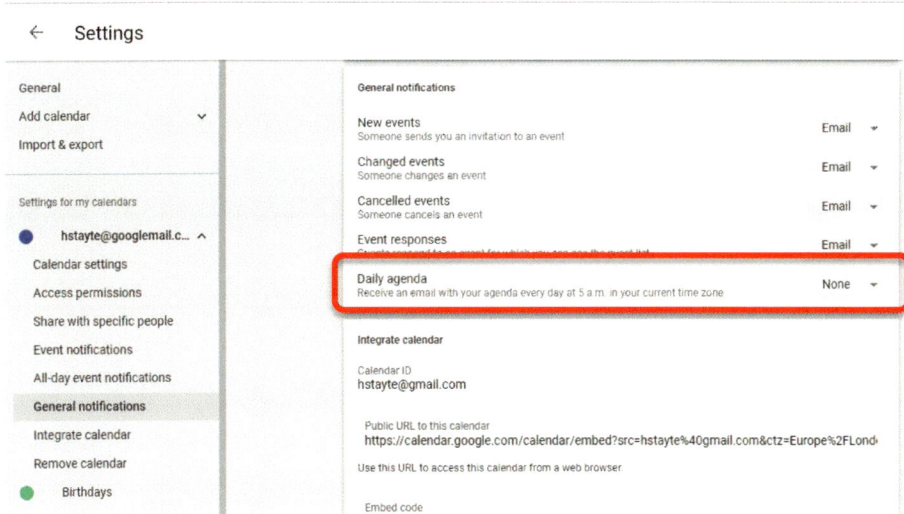

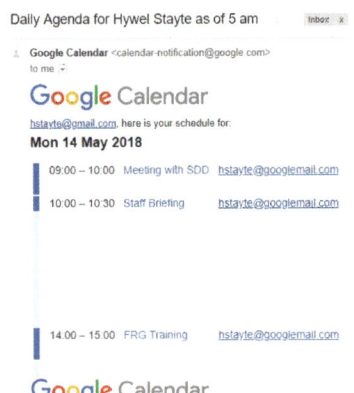

You can either scroll down through all of the calendar settings options here or click on the shortcut link on the left for 'General Notifications'. As you can see in the screenshot on the previous page you can select to receive a Daily Agenda by email by changing the settings and an example of what this could look like is shown here.

Adding & Sharing

You can also add colleagues or whole school calendars to your own calendar which can be set to a different colour and overlap against yours. This is very useful if your school calendar plan is available on a Google Calendar as you can easily see what events are on and select to copy any of the events to your own calendar and add your own reminders. You can also share your calendar with others also, allowing you to know each other's availability and plan things together.

Resource Booking / Appointment Slots

This is a very handy tool that can be setup through the Google Admin console for whole school bookings however individual users can also make their own appointment slots. The way this works is you can set up appointment slots for a resource such as a computer suite and then allow members of staff to be able to book the room using their Google Calendar. The advantages of creating resources across the school in this way is that you do not need to purchase any additional room booking software and can manage all of it through your G Suite domain. If a member of staff needs to cancel a booking, then they can simply delete the calendar entry created for them in their calendar and the resource's appointment slot will become available again for anyone else to book.

Using this same method an individual can create appointment slots on their own calendar for other members of staff to book meetings with them. This could be used for a variety of different reasons from booking to meet with SMT or booking a training session with a Google Trainer for example.

Invite to meeting

This allows you to invite participants to a meeting or event which you are organising and they will be notified and be able to add the event to their Google Calendar easily without having to manually add the event themselves. This is useful for when you are scheduling meetings with other people and you want to check if they can attend.

Find a time

This function built into calendar allows you to find a time suitable for all of the members you have invited to your event within Google Calendar. Provided all of the members you have invited have kept their calendar accurate you can use this feature to find an appropriate time when you are all free and available to meet. This can save lots of time and stop the countless emails trying to organise a suitable time for you all to meet.

Integration with Classroom

The use of Google Calendar is built into Google Classroom and every time you create an Assignment with a due date the Assignment will automatically populate into Google Calendar for the date which it is due in. This will also be added automatically to any students Google Calendar as well making it easier for everyone to manage their workload.

Integration with Tasks

If you use Tasks within Gmail you can also add due dates to your tasks which are then displayed as another calendar within your Google Calendar. You can also display your task list on the right hand side of calendar as shown below.

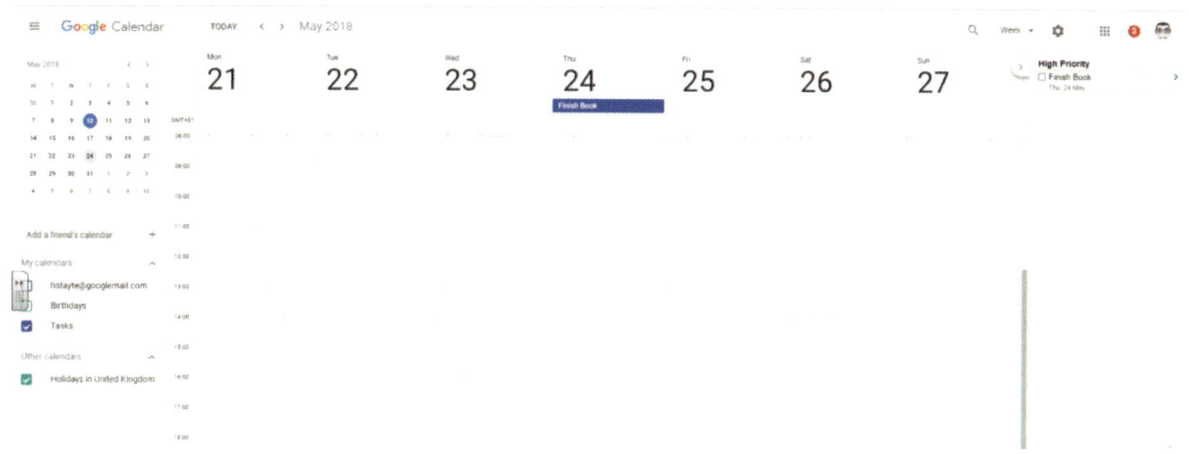

Google Keep

I feel like I was late to the party with Google Keep and I had been very happy using tasks within Gmail however I have now fully converted over to using Google Keep instead. Google Keep is very simply a post-it note board that you can use to keep to do lists however it is also so much more than that.

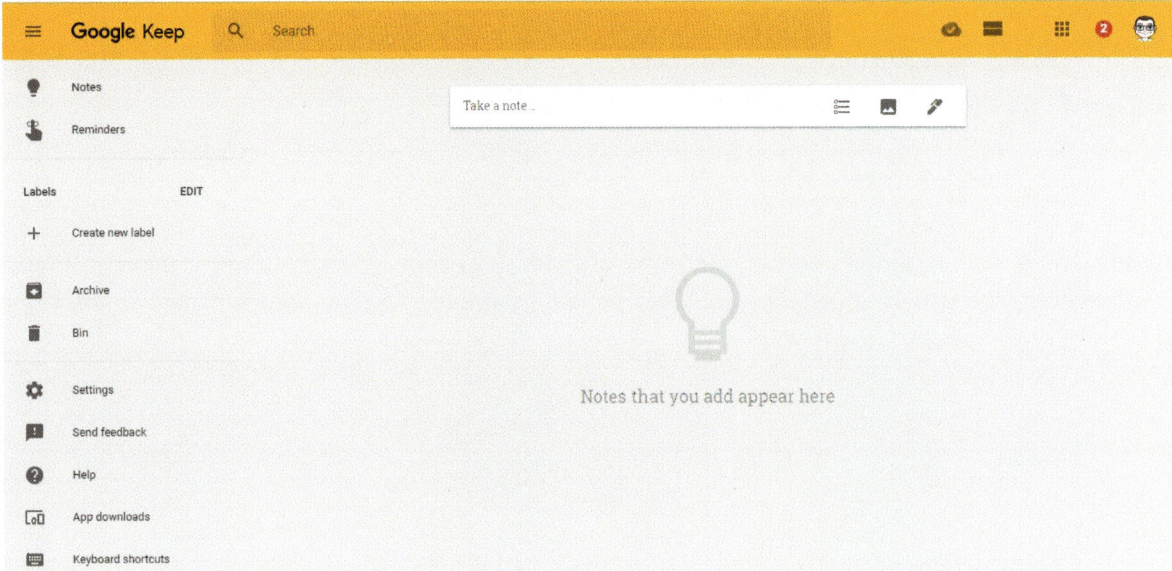

Notes

The first thing you can do is create a very simple reminder note by clicking in the 'Take a note...' box at the top of Google Keep.

You do not need to add a title to create your first note and you also do not need to do anything else using the options along the bottom of your note however I will go through what each one of these does.

1. Reminder Me.

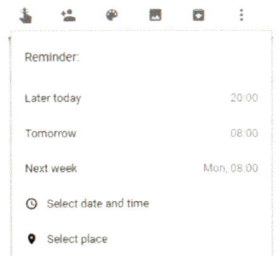

This function means that you can easily add automated reminders for any of your notes on Google Keep.

2. Add Collaborators - This is one of those huge advantages that Keep has over simple tasks list with Gmail as all of your notes can be shared just like a Google Drive file and you can allow other users to be viewers of your Google Keep list or indeed editors allowing you to have group to do lists for projects.

3. Colour Palette allows you to change the colour of your selected notes

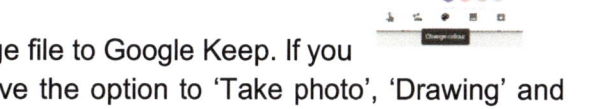

4. Add Image means you can upload any image file to Google Keep. If you are using a mobile device you will also have the option to 'Take photo', 'Drawing' and 'Recording' using your device's microphone.

5. Archive - Just like using Gmail this function allows you to remove your notes from the main display without deleting them meaning you can always get them back if you need to.

6. More options

Delete note	**a**	a) This allows you to delete the note
Add label	**b**	b) This allows you to create labels for your notes so that you can organise them within your Google Keep
Add drawing	**c**	c) This allows you to add a drawing to your note which will work on a desktop and will open a separate editor
Make a copy	**d**	d) Make a copy is a common feature amongst G Suite Apps and this lets you make a copy of your note
Hide checkboxes	**e**	e) Show tick boxes means that you can convert your note into a list of items with can be ticked off when completed
Copy to Google Docs	**f**	f) Copy to Google Docs will automatically create a Google Doc with you note copied to it

7. Undo - This will undo your last action
8. Redo - This will re-do your undo
9. Close - This will close and save the note

Sharing

As mentioned earlier you can 'Add Collaborators' to your Google Keep notes and this works in the same way as any Google Drive file loading up the following screen.

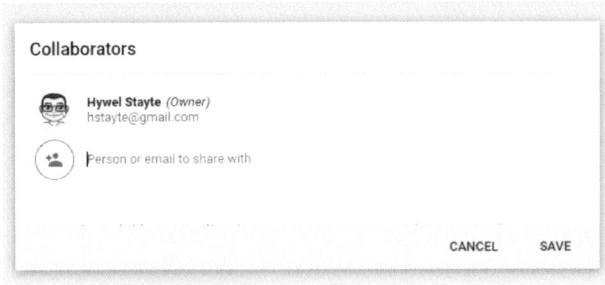

Simply add an email address in the box and the recipient will receive an email letting them know the note has been shared with them.

Get more out of Google Keep

<u>Grab Image Text</u>

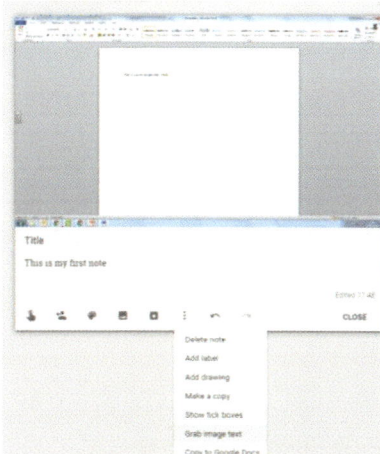

If you have an image that you have uploaded to Google Keep, then you can use the 3 dots (More options) to select a new item that will appear in the menu called 'Grab Image Text'.

This is built into Google Keep and will analyse the image and pull out any text that it can read and convert it into editable text in your Google Keep.

<u>Copy to Google Docs</u>

I identified this option earlier as one of the menu items from the More Options button on Google Keep and this will automatically turn your Google Keep note into a brand new Google Doc within your Google Drive. All of the content of your Keep note will be copied across but it will not delete your original note.

<u>Integration with Docs and Slides</u>

Similar to copying across to Google Docs you can also access your Google Keep notepad from within Google Docs and also Google Slides as mentioned earlier when looking at Gmail. In both applications you can find the Google Keep notepad on the right-hand side.

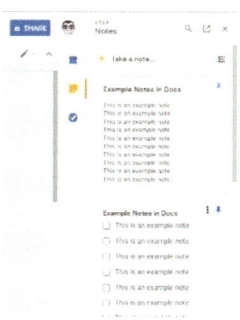

You can then drag and drop your notes from Google Keep directly into Google Docs or Google Slides.

If you have been using Keep to take notes and then wish to create a document or presentation from them then this feature is very handy.

Mobile Device App - Take photo, Drawing & Recording

These are some of the extra functionality that you have when you are using a mobile device such as a tablet or smartphone. When using the Google Keep App you are given extra options when you are creating your notes.

These extra options are fairly self-explanatory and allow you to use the built in functionality of your mobile device to add extra media notes to Google Keep.

Google Sites

Google Sites has had an overhaul recently and this has led to vast improvements in the way that Google Sites looks and also the ease in which you can create professional looking websites. Unfortunately, at the moment not all of the capabilities of the old Google Sites has been built into the new Google Sites however it is something Google are working on and I am sure it will be develop further as increased functionality is being added all of the time.

If you have never explored what Google Sites is then it is a way that you can create a website without any technical knowledge whatsoever. This is extremely useful for students especially when they have limited ability to use HTML code and they can just create a good looking website within minutes. Google Sites is ideal for any kind of school competition where a website is required but the actual technical ability of a website is not required.

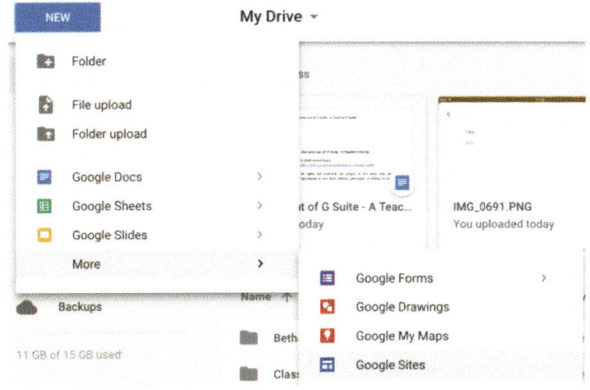

The new Google Sites now sits within Google Drive like many of the other G Suite applications and this allows much more integration with the other products and also ease by opening through Drive.

To create a new Google Site simply use the 'New' button within Drive and go to 'More' where you can select Google Sites.

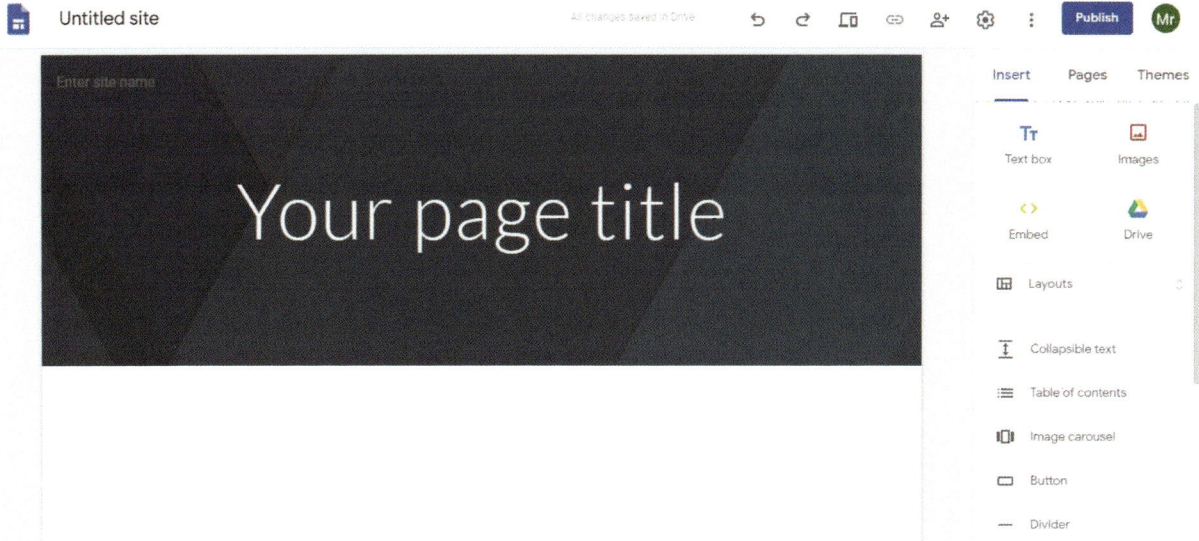

Now that your new site has been created you just need to give the site a name. Once you have entered a site name the file on Google Drive will also be renamed to be that name if you click at the top where it says Untitled Site. You can also now change the heading at the top of your first page to anything you would like. Within Google Sites you have many of the same components that you will be used to such as adding collaborators but there are also specific options relating to sites that you may not have seen before.

You have the familiar undo and redo controls here to help you with your design and creation of your site. The next button along is the button to preview your site. A great feature of the preview function is it allows you to choose the type of device that will be viewing the site and see what your site will look like.

The next control button is the copy website link and will only become available once you have published your Google Site. This will allow you to easily copy the link to your website which you can share with others.

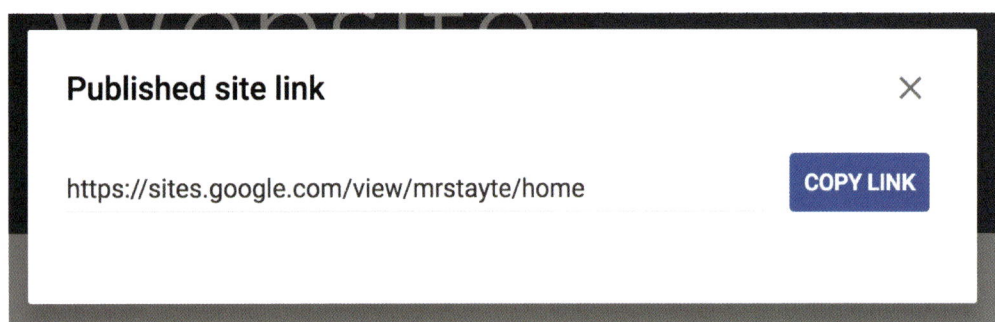

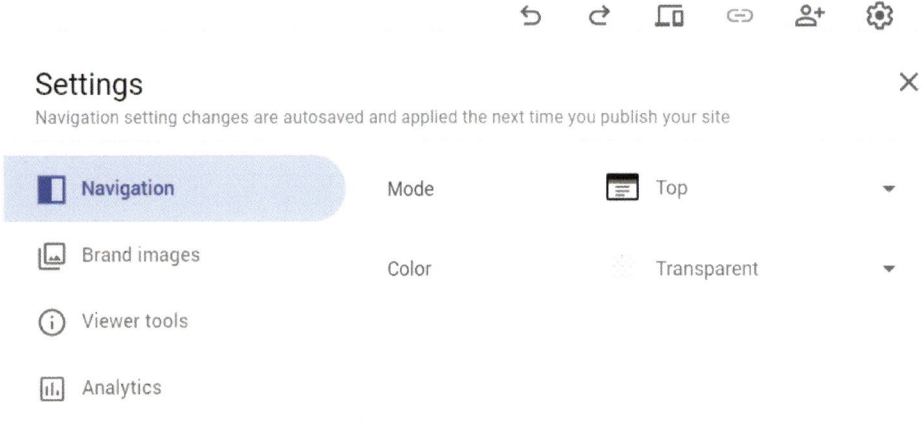

The cog like in most Google Apps is the Settings section of your Google Site. Click on this button will open this Setting dialogue box and allow you to adjust various aspects of your site.

- Navigation – Allows you to determine some settings for your navigation bar of your site
- Brand images – You can add a logo and favicon meaning that you can customize the icon displayed in a web browser when people are visiting your site.
- Viewer tools – Here you can turn on and off some additional viewer options such as when the site was last updated
- Analytics - In this section you will find site analytics which allows you to setup Google Analytics to monitor the traffic coming to your site.
- Announcement banner – This gives you the ability to add an announcement banner to your homepage or every page in your site. You can also have a button and link as part of this banner.

The 3 dots or more options button will give you these options for your Google Site.

Version history

Duplicate site

Report a problem

Help

Take a tour!

- Version history is where you can see all previous edits and changes and revert if needed
- Duplicate site creates an exact copy of your current site which is helpful when creating multiple sites with the same look
- Send feedback allows you to send suggestions and ideas to Google for improvement
- Help will open the Google support pages for sites
- Take a tour will give you an overview of the features of sites

PUBLISH

Publishing your site

Once you are ready to share your masterpiece with the world you can publish your Google Site. By pressing 'Publish' you are given the following option box where you can customize the name of your Google Site and the default web address that will be created.

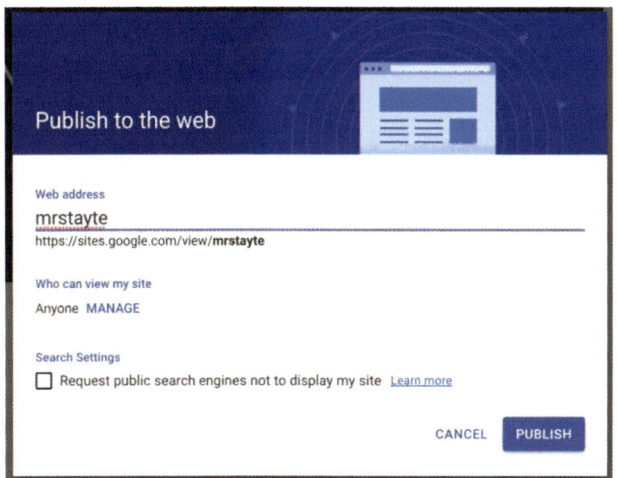

You can also click MANAGE here to customize further who will be able to view your site.

This will load the sharing box you will be very used to using G Suite however there are two options available in terms of sharing.

You first have the ability to choose who can edit and view the editing version of the Google Site meaning that you can add collaborators to your Google Site. You can access these options through the 'Add Collaborators' button but they will also appear here when you are publishing your site.

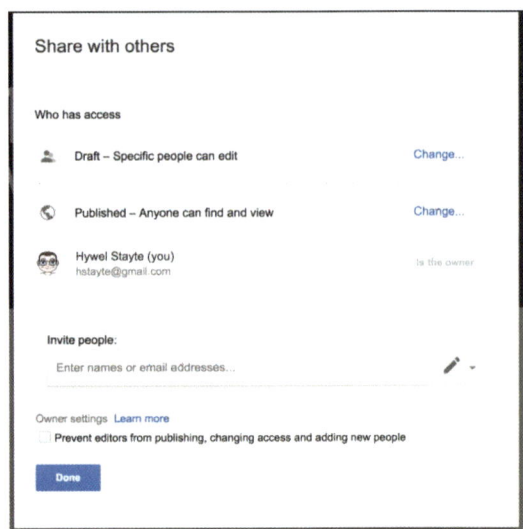

The second option is to do with who you are publishing to and if you want your site to be public on the web or if you want to only publish it to specific people. You can also publish to just your specific organisation and if your organisation has turned off Google Drive sharing with anyone outside of the organisation you will not be able to publish your site publically.

Editing Pages

When you are editing your pages using Google Sites you always have the menu sidebar on the right. This allows you to manage the design of your site and the specific page you are on. As you can see here you are able to insert text boxes, images, embed and upload and these can be easily dragged onto the pages.

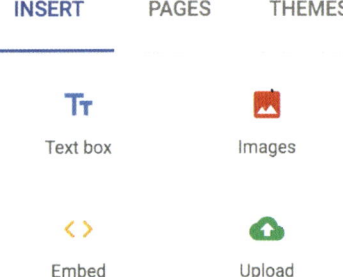

As you can see in the image above you can add text boxes easily to your Google Site and then fill the content with whatever you would like to. Once you have dropped objects like this into your site you can also drag and reorder the content as well as add hyperlinks. On the left hand side of all objects you have the options to change the background, duplicate or delete. You can also manually resize any object and Google Sites will snap to a set size as shown here.

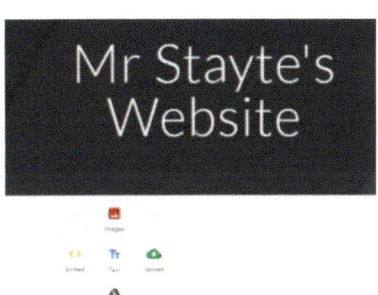

You can also just double click anywhere on your page in order to get these insert options.

Images allows you to select images from the internet to use on your website from a Google search and also from your Google Drive files. Upload allows you to upload an image that you already have saved on your computer.

Embed allows you to embed another website page into your Google Site either through a URL or Embed Code that you can get from some websites.

INSERT   PAGES   THEMES

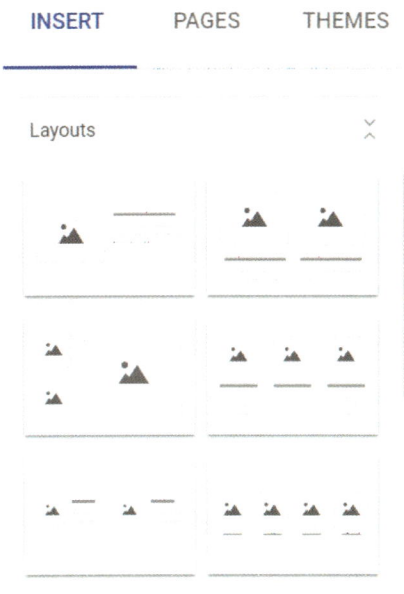

A recent update to the new Google Sites has seen the introduction of the ability to insert layout templates into your website.

These pre-made layouts allow the user to quickly pick a suitable layout for part of their site and build it up very quickly.

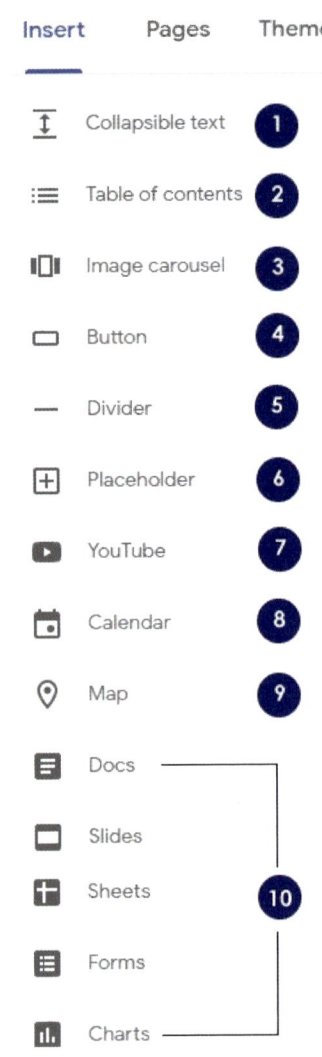

1. This allows you to add a section of text that can expand and collapse through the user's interaction

2. Add a table of contents to your page to allow links to section of the page to be easily clickable from the top of the page

3. You can add an image carousel here by uploading or selecting images saved on your Google Drive

4. This allows you to create a button on your site to link to a page of your choice

5. Here you can drag in the 'Divider' component to section out your site

6. Add a placeholder to your site ready for some media

7. Add YouTube videos either through search or copying the URL

8. Add a Google Calendar to your site - great for school calendars or Room bookings for example

9. Add Maps from Google Maps or indeed your own MyMaps to your site

10. These options will enable you to select the specific Google Drive file that you would like to embed into your Google Site

Adding Pages

The pages section will enable you to manage the different pages to your Google Site and these pages will automatically be included in the Navigation Bar of your site. You can adjust and manage this so that only the page you want to be listed in navigation are but more on this later.

In order to add a new page to your site you need to hover over this plus button at the bottom right of the site and you will then have these two options appear for you to select.

You can add your own URL links to your website and these will also be linked in your navigation or you can use the 'New Page' button to create a new page to your website.

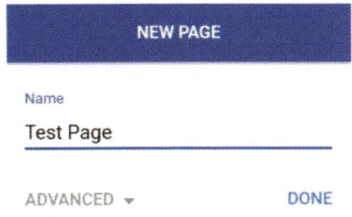

Once clicked on 'New Page' you can give your new page a name of your choice. This will generate the new page and it will be listed in the navigation across the top of your site and in the pages list as shown below.

Now that you have added additional pages to your site you are given extra options and settings for your pages.

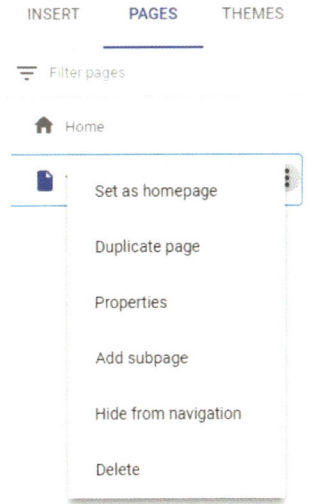

Set as homepage - any of your new pages could become your homepage through clicking this option

Duplicate page - make copies easily of existing pages

Properties - change the name of your page and advanced settings of customizing the website path

Add subpage - creates a new page underneath the current page selected

Hide from navigation - removes the selected page from appearing in the navigation bar

Delete - deletes the selected page

Themes

Google Sites also gives you a small sample of themes that you can choose from in the menu.

These themes have been carefully selected by Google and that is why there is such a limited number of them to ensure good quality sites are created using them.

Select the theme you would like, and it will be applied to your whole site. You are given some flexibility with the themes as once you have selected the one you like you can then choose the colour of your choice and the font style of your choice to be worked in with the theme.

Get more out of Google Sites

Using Google Sites for a class project

Instead of asking students to produce a poster or fact sheet about a certain topic why not mix it up a little and get the students to produce a Google Site about it. This can allow for real flexibility in presentation and also allow the students to easily embed videos and anything from their Google Drive. The sites can be easily shared with you as the teacher if students are creating individually but if you want to setup sites in advance for different groups of students then you can use Google Classroom assignments to give access to your students.

The new Google Sites is now a Google Drive file and therefore can be added to assignments but at the moment the only options you have are to allow the students to view or edit and not yet make a copy. This can still work well as you could only assign a site to a limited group of students and make another assignment for another group.

Using Google Sites for a Digital Portfolio

This is by far my favourite use of Google Sites and originally I have been using the old Google Sites to accomplish this however the vast majority of uses I have for it can be re-created in the new sites. Essentially I get all students to create their old Google Site which will be called 'Student Name Digital Portfolio' and this site is then shared with me as an editor.

Students are then required to make and manage pages of all of the topics we will cover in the year and are required to upload their completed work to the site. In the old sites you had the option of something called a 'File Cabinet' where students could simply upload completed work whereas now with the new sites if you get your students to become proficient with using Google Drive you can simply insert Google Drive folders into their pages displaying their completed work.

Part of the creation of the Digital Portfolio tasks can be to create all of the pages for your subject so that they have areas to store their work in advance of completing it and also you can allow them to experiment with some of the other features of Sites in their 'About Me' section that you can instruct them to create.

Marking & Feedback

Another reason why I am so keen on students creating their own Digital Portfolio is it means that I can conduct marking and feedback online through their portfolios. In the past we have used something called an 'Announcement' page in the old Sites however this is not a feature of the new Sites and therefore we need to be a little creative in how we do this.

The first thing I would get the students to do is create a new page called 'Teacher Feedback' which is where all the marking and comments will be posted. The way I am going to get around the lack of a blog page is that I will train my students on how they can insert Google Docs onto the page (which will contain a marking assessment usually generated using autoCrat) and then add text boxes with the date posted. Within the assessment sheets created there will be boxes for student comments or responses and these will be viewable from the Google Site. This is not ideal and the 'Announcement' pages from the old Google Sites were great for managing this however we cannot assume this functionality will be built into the new Sites.

Digital Badges

Thankfully this idea and feature works great in the new Google Sites just like in the old Sites and you can read more about the add-on Digital Badges later in the book but essentially what this means is that within Sites you will insert a Google Drive folder for viewing. The Digital Badges add-on creates a Google Drive folder for each student stored on the teachers account which they can insert directly into a page on their Google Site. The best setting to choose is the 'Grid' view as this will display all the badges awarded to the student really nicely and show at a glance what they have been awarded for.

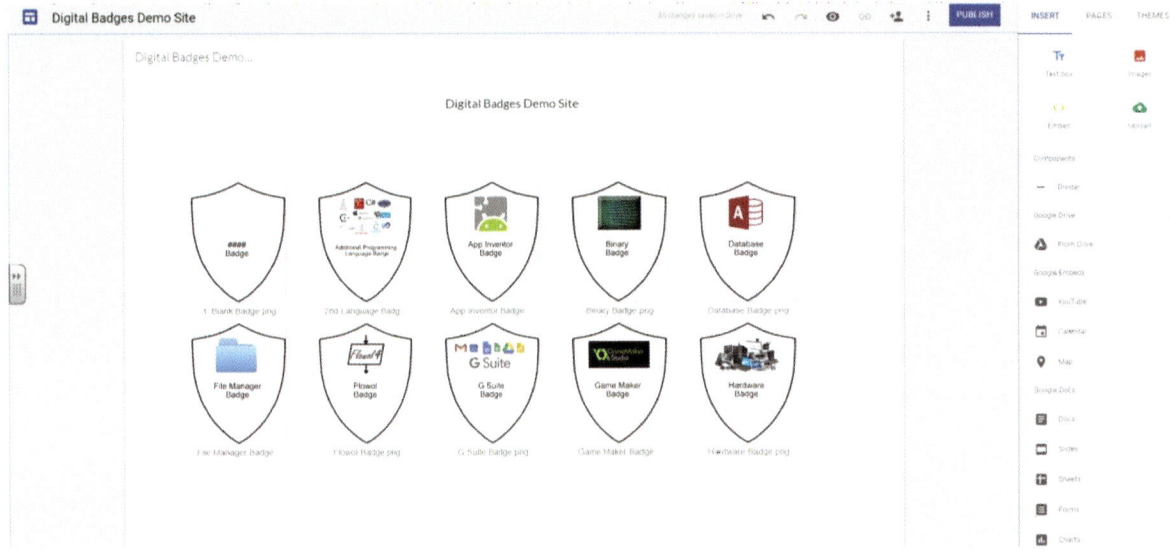

Google Chrome

I am sure many of you very familiar with Google Chrome and have used it extensively in your day-to-day jobs but it is important that you get the most out of what Google Chrome has to offer. As I am sure you are aware Google Chrome is a web browser developed by Google and I am of the opinion that it is the best web browser available to you and by far the most appropriate one to use if you are using G Suite within your organisation.

Although G Suite is designed to work in any web browser I often find that you avoid problems or issues by using Google Chrome when using the G Suite applications. The development of Google Chrome and its related operating system Chrome OS have allowed for some really exciting features and developments that can be used in Google Chrome and the next section will go through these with you.

Get more out of Google Chrome

Signing into Chrome

The first thing you need to make sure you do when using Google Chrome is that you sign in and not just into your G Suite account. By signing into Chrome you can have multiple Chrome users which means you only ever have one email address that is signed in on that Chrome user which means managing bookmarks and managing logins is much easier. Many of you would have used the 'Add Account' option that allows you to sign in to multiple accounts however sometimes switching between them can be difficult and you have to sign out of all and log back into one in order to load a particular Google Doc.

In order to combat this, you can create multiple profiles on Google Chrome and have a different one for every Google login account you have and use. This means that you can switch the entire Chrome browser to another login without getting the logins confused. This means that you can have different bookmarks and extensions depending on the account you are using.

Bookmarks

One of the major advantages to signing into Chrome is the fact that you can have shared bookmarks across the devices that you use. If you add a bookmark in Chrome and you are signed in on one device this will be available to you across all of your devices. By making use of this you are able to say goodbye to the days of adding a bookmark/favourite at home and not having access to it the next day in school.

Extensions

I will be exploring the use of Google Chrome Extensions in the next section of the book however this does go down as a big advantages of Google Chrome because you can easily add useful applications that run through your Chrome browser to help with your day to day work.

Extensions installed across domain

The vast majority of you reading this will have Google for Education domains in your organisations and one of the advantages of having this setup is the fact that your domain administrators can force install extensions for all of the users or a selection of users in the domain. Administrators could add extensions for just teachers to have and also extensions that you want students to have access to automatically as well.

Google Meet

Who would have thought how important this application would have become. With the Covid-19 virus in 2020 Google Meet has jumped to the forefront of important aspects of G Suite and it was one we all had to get up to speed with relatively fast. Fortunately Google Meet was already very easy to use and within the first few weeks of Covid-19 was undergoing huge upgrades to make it much more useful for a virtual classroom experience. Google has vastly improved the Google Meet experience and have added in many new features to aid classroom teachers through the integration with Google Classroom and Gmail and the already existing integration with Google Calendar.

So just like with the other sections of this book we will first go through the basic components of Google Meet and then consider the various ways that it can be used remotely to lead to the most effective learning experience for your students. First of all once you have loaded Google Meet you should find a screen similar to the one shown below which will allow you to join or set up a Meet. If you have been invited via Google Calendar to any Meets then they will be listed below the 'Join or start meeting' button and you can select the one you want to join. Nothing is scheduled below so you click on the green button to join or start a Meet.

Creating a Meet

There are many ways in which you can create and join Google Meets and some are better than others especially for an educational setting. These are all the ways (That I know of!) that you can create Google Meets and pros and cons of each one.

Method	Pros	Cons
Nickname	Only people in your domain can join a Nickname Meet Easy to do	An extra step If you use the same one as someone else you will join their Meet
Google Classroom	Built into Google Classroom Easy to turn on and off Only people in your domain can join Easy to do	Sometimes delay in link appearing
Google Calendar	Specify Time Invite attendees Good for finding appropriate time	Anyone with the link can join More steps than through Meet
No Nickname - Randomly Generated by Meet	Very quick to set up Easy to do	Anyone with the link can join
Gmail	Built into Gmail Easy to use	Anyone with the link can join
Invitation from Meet	Quick to directly email individual	Slow for larger Meets
Sharing Link	Quick way to share	Anyone with the link can join

I have highlighted the top two methods for creating Google Meets as the best practice for a school educational setting. There are two main reasons why these are better methods and that is because firstly they restrict the Meets to only users from within the school domain who can join them. Secondly they are not permanent links and therefore cannot be used again providing the teacher is the last one to leave. Throughout this chapter I will go through each of the methods above and how to use them.

Nickname / No Nickname / Link

When you click on the button to join or start a meeting you will be presented with this pop up screen. As explained in the box you can just press continue to create a randomly generated new Google Meet or you can type in an existing Nickname to join a Meet or a new Nickname to create a new Meet.

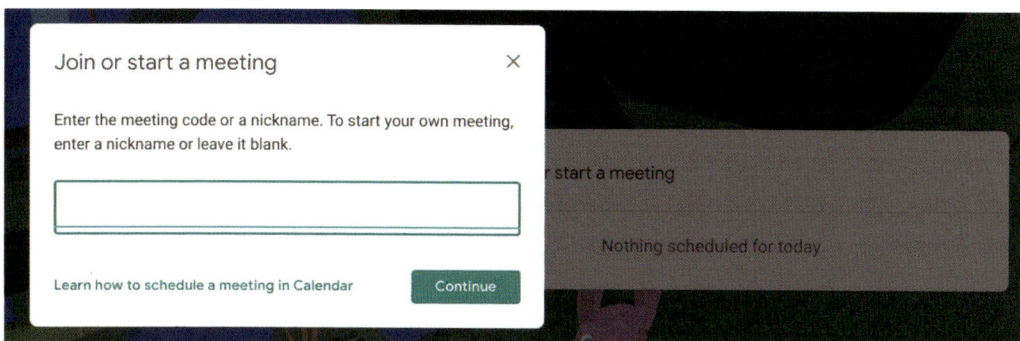

getmoreoutofgsuite

No one else is here

If you use a Nickname of your choice then you will be greeted by a screen similar to this one. You will notice that there is no link for this meeting and, as explained in the table before, only users from within your domain will be able to join this Google Meet.

Meeting ready

meet.google.com/xgp-fkut-eaf

Dial-in: (US) +1 574-218-0162 PIN: 233 538 783#

If however you use no Nickname then Google Meet will create you a random Meet link and on the next screen you will be presented with something similar to this.

Google Classroom

The Google Classroom integration with Google Meet allows you to have all of the benefits of the personally created Nickname Meet setup but done automatically for you within your already existing Google Classrooms. This means that any Meets created will only work for users within your domain and can also be ended forever if the Meet organiser is the last one to leave. In order to set this up within your Google Classroom you need to go to the 'Settings' cog at the top right as show in the image below.

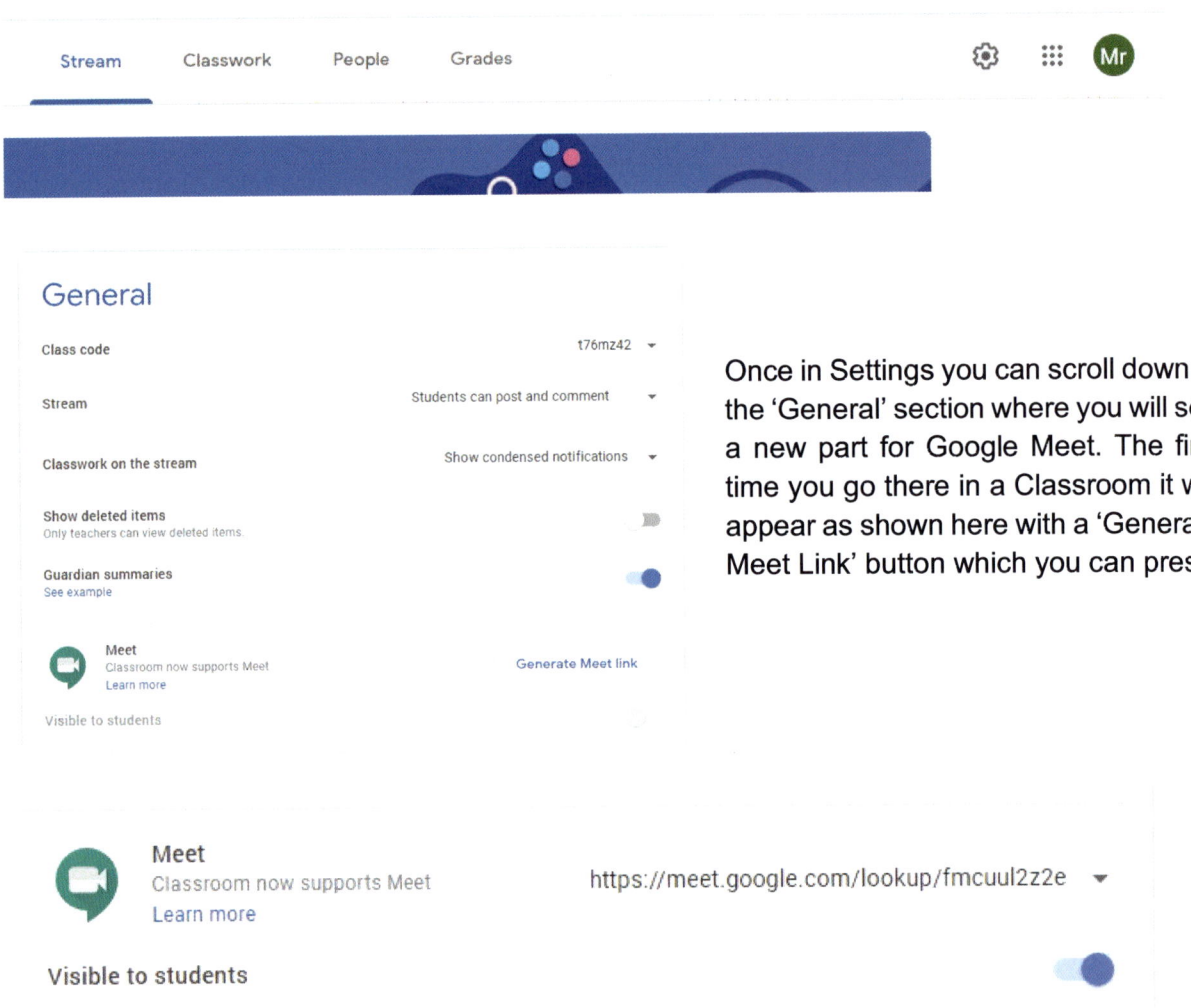

Once in Settings you can scroll down to the 'General' section where you will see a new part for Google Meet. The first time you go there in a Classroom it will appear as shown here with a 'Generate Meet Link' button which you can press.

You will notice that once you have clicked to generate the Meet link that a URL appears similar to the one shown above. You will notice that this URL is different to a Meet URL which would be created randomly from Calendar or no Nickname Meets. This URL has 'lookup' within it which indicates that this is a Nickname Meet and therefore the benefits of Nicknamed Meets apply.

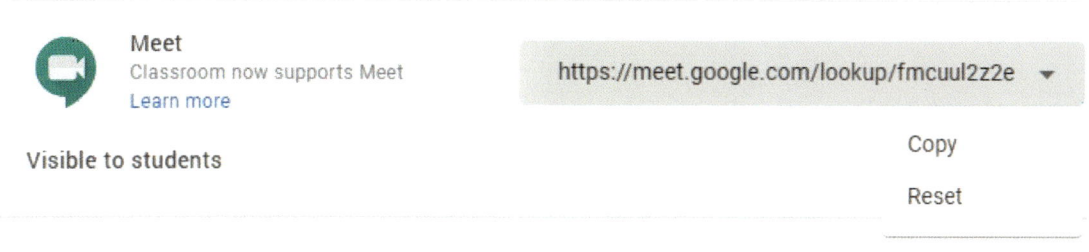

Because this is working like a Nickname Meet you can 'Copy' this URL and paste it for your students to use. You can paste this onto your Classroom Stream or within an Assignment in your Classwork section for example. At any time you can also use the drop down here to reset the link and therefore remove that Nicknamed Meet entirely.

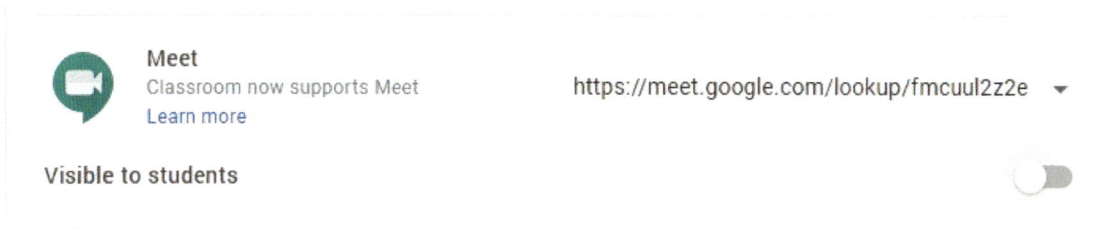

The only other settings you have here is whether or not you want this link to be visible to the students. This just means that you want it to appear on the Google Classroom page for this class. This button does not have to be on for the Google Meet link to work and is just a nice way to display the Google Meet link as shown in the image below.

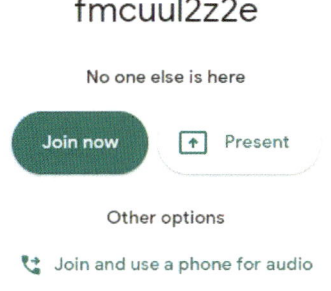

You can see here that if you click this Google Meet link then you are taken to the Google Meet login which automatically converts the 'lookup' to a Google Meet Nickname.

Google Calendar

Google Calendar integration is very handy for organising Google Meets as of course the date and time are created within the event and you can invite guests to the event so that it appears in their Google Calendar. The downside that all educators must be aware of here is that these Google Meets are created using links and not Nicknames and therefore none of the Meet updates, for example only allowing users from your domain, apply. Despite this it is still a very useful method especially when you are organising meetings with staff as depending on your Google Calendar use and setup you can use the find a time feature when looking to organise a Meet.

Firstly open Google Calendar and click anywhere to create an event. If you click and drag you can decide the length of time for your event. Once you have done this the box shown below will appear for you to use.

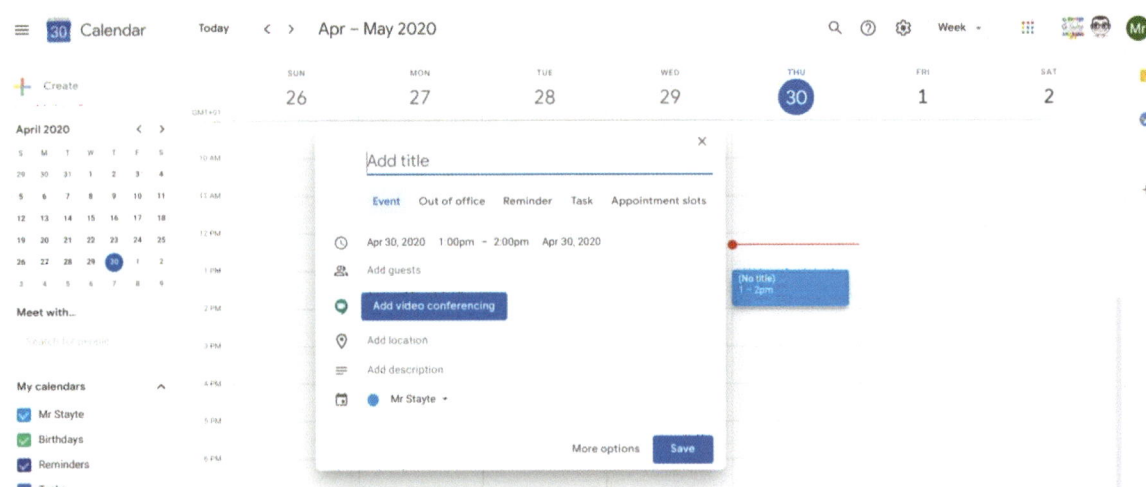

You will hopefully already be quite familiar with Google Calendar and I will not go through again all of the features here but focus just on the Google Meet aspect. As you can see there is a button to 'Add video conferencing'.

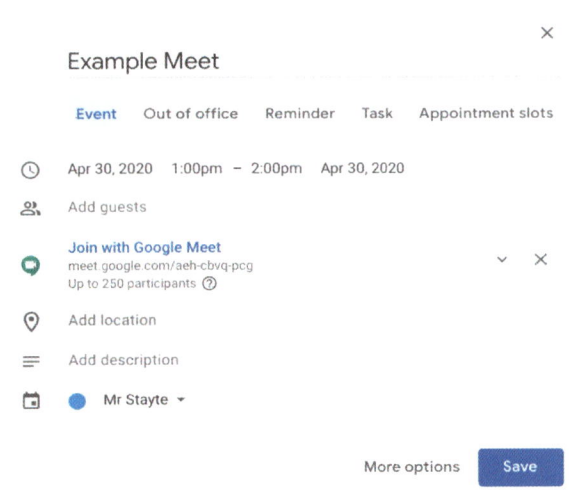

Once you have pressed the button you will see the Google Meet created with a direct link to the Meet.

You can use the little drop down to see more details and you can also click on 'More options' at the bottom in order to invite guests.

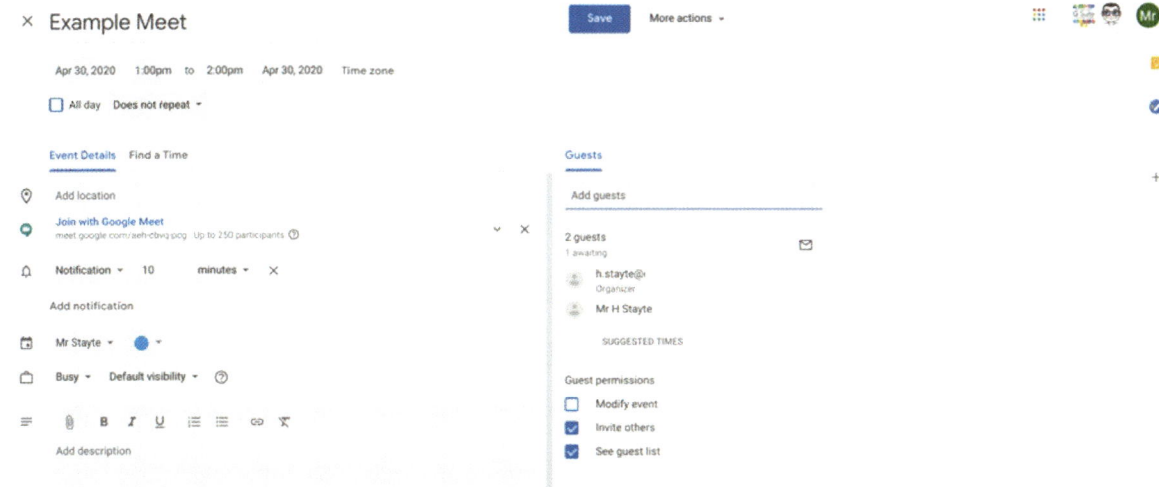

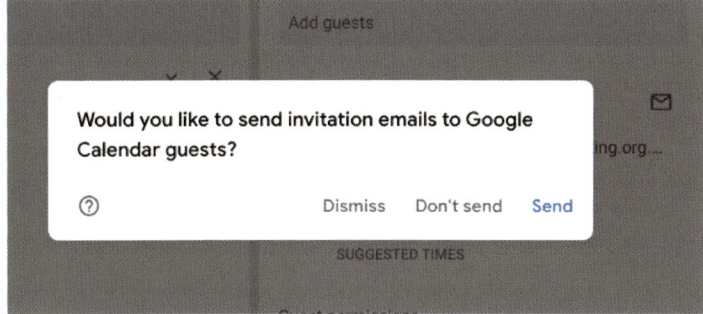

I have added a guest in the box above and when I press 'Save' it will ask me if I would like to send this guest an invitation.

The guests will then receive an email similar to the one shown below. How this is displayed will very much depend on what email system the invited guest is using.

Gmail

Outlook

From within both of these systems the user can easily indicate whether or not they can attend the event and also click on the links to join the Google Meets.

If you are outside of the domain then you will get a slightly different joining screen and have to ask to join the Meet.

Gmail

Gmail integration is relatively new for Meet although hangouts has been part of Gmail for a while. This method for creating a Meet is very similar to Calendar in that the Meet that it creates is a link Meet and therefore could be joined by users outside of your domain. It is handy as it is started from within your Gmail and you will see the new options on the left in the image shown below.

You are given two options within Gmail to 'Start a meeting' or 'Join a meeting' and both of which will open another window.

Start a meeting

Join a meeting

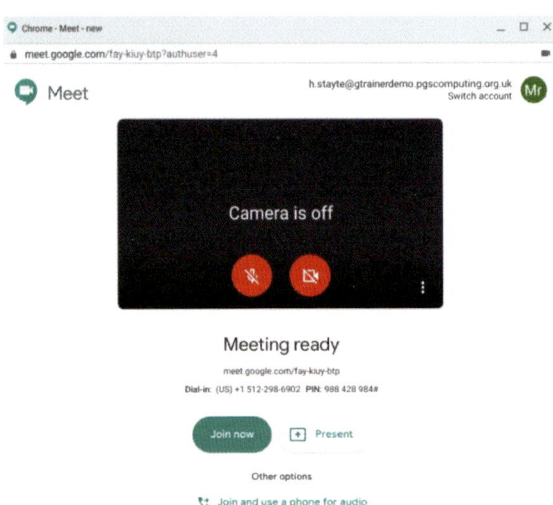

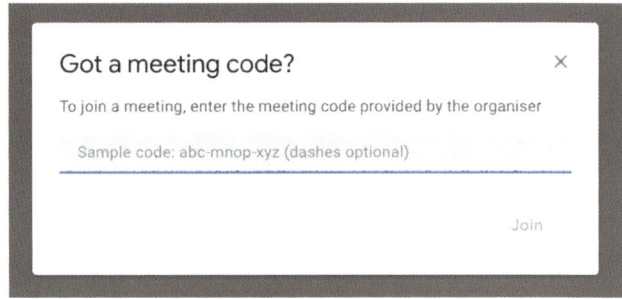

Invitation / Sharing Link

Once you are into a Google Meet you also have the option to invite users directly, similar to sharing a document, and the users will get a direct email with the details of the Meet which they can click. Alternatively, if you have the URL link from setting up a Meet you can of course copy and paste this link directly into an email or message as a very fast way to get users onto the Meet.

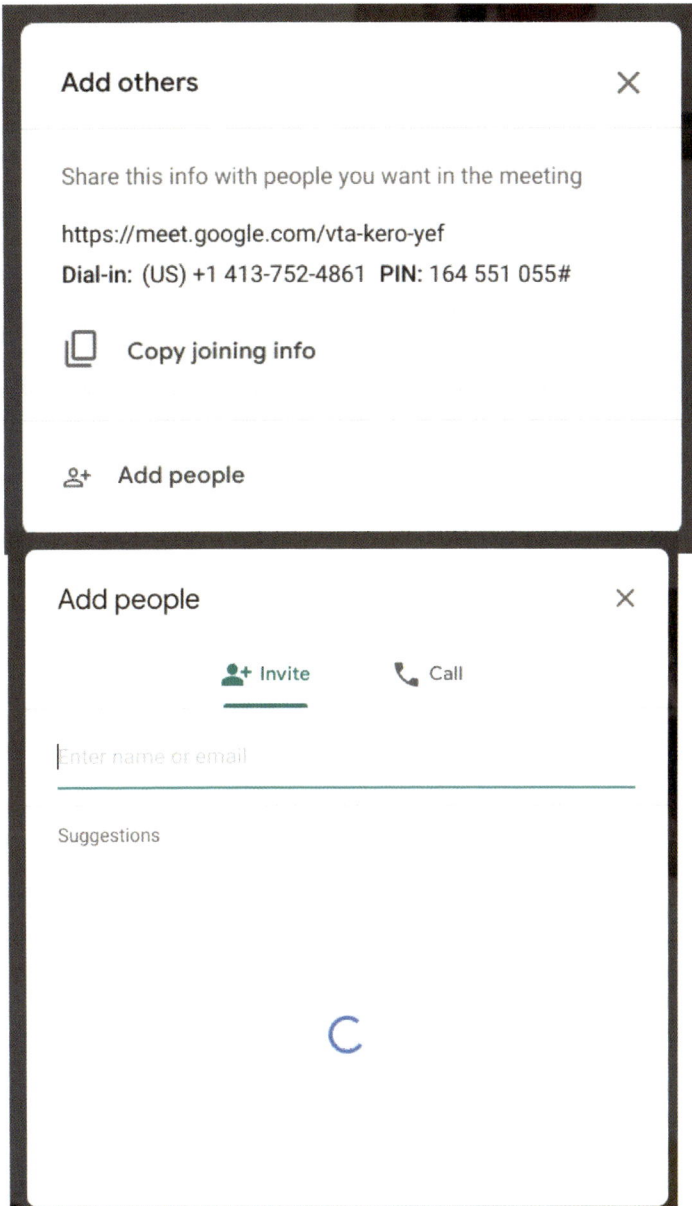

Here is the box that will appear once you have created your Google Meet (More on that later) which allows you to copy the joining info to your clipboard or to invite users directly.

You can also click this button to 'Add people' directly to your Google Meets.

Once clicked this box will appear and allow you to search your domain directory for anyone you would like to invite to the Google Meet.

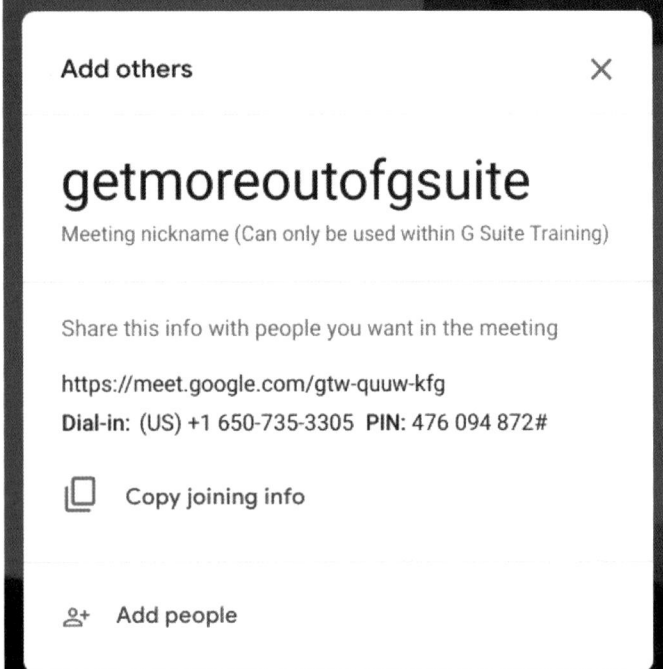

You get a slightly altered box if you have used a Nickname to create the Meet.

Please note that even if you have used a Nickname if you send anyone this link it will work and allow anyone to join the Meet. In a school setting always send them the code and not the link.

Joining the Google Meet

Before you join a Google Meet, whether you are the organiser or not, you will be presented with this screen shown below where you can check your camera, microphone and settings.

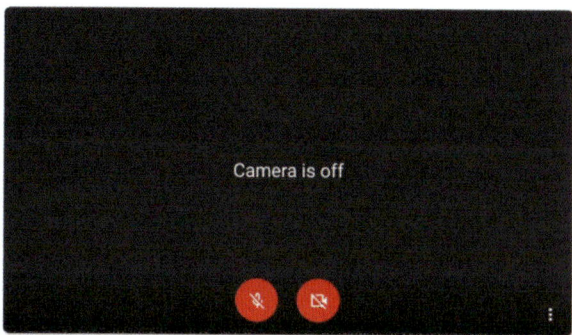

This landing screen will allow you to test out your webcam before you enter the meeting and in the image above both the camera and the microphone are currently off. You can press these buttons in order to turn them back on.

You also have two options here about how you join this Google Meet. You can click the button here to 'Join now' which will enter you directly into the Meet or you can click on the 'Present' button which will allow you to present directly to the Meet but you will not actually have joined the Meet in a video conferencing format but rather just send directly to the Meet.

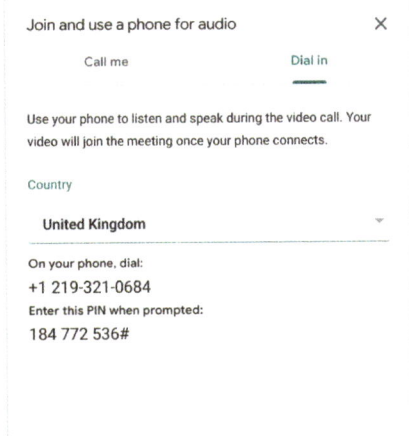

The 'Join and use a phone for audio' button will bring up this box which will provide you with the details on how to use your phone to call into the Meet which is useful if you have no internet or a poor connection.

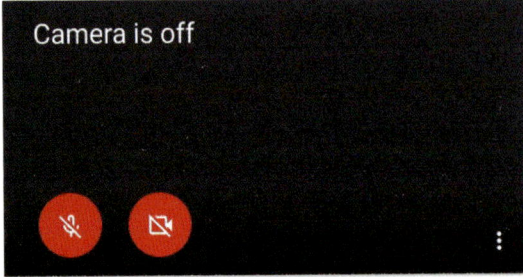

You will also notice that there are 3 dots at the bottom right of the video screen before you join the Meet. These give you extra options.

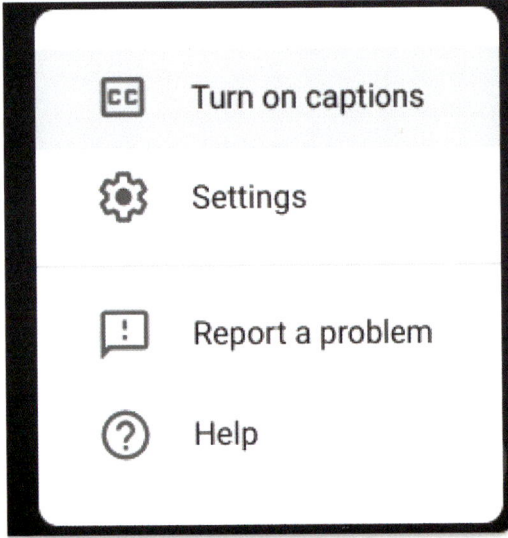

You can choose to 'Turn on captions' before you even join the meeting which will automatically convert anything someone is saying into text/subtitles for you to read.

You can also 'Report a problem' or submit a feature request here as well as get extra help for how to use Google Meet.

The 'Settings' option allows you to determine your camera and microphone settings before you join the Meet.

Settings

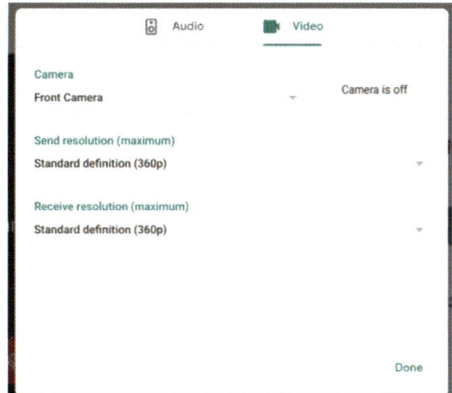

The settings box that will appear allows you to control the settings for both Audio and Video by clicking the tabs at the top of the box. The audio options are simply a selection of your microphone and your speakers or headphones. You may have multiple audio devices on your computer and this allows you to select which you would like to use.

The video is much the same and allows you to select which camera you would like to use (if you have multiple) and also gives extra settings on the quality of your upload and download.

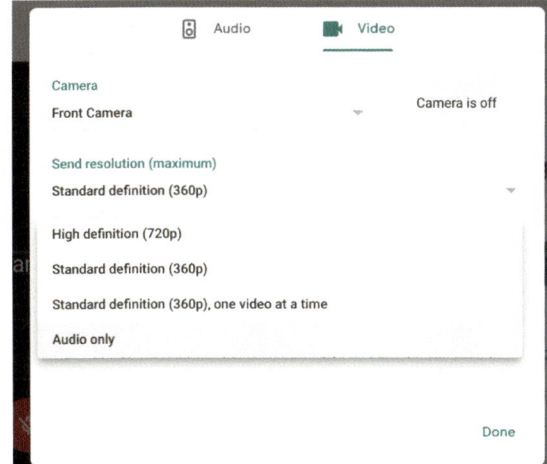

Your send resolution allows you to send either standard quality or high quality resolution to others in your Meet.

Your receive however gives you a few extra options as shown here. If you have a slower internet connection you can adjust your settings here to only send Audio which can improve your overall experience.

With all of these settings for Audio and Video there is some personal preference about whether or not you are going to engage in a full video conference or you would like to have just the audio aspect. You also need to consider the speed of your internet connection and how many others in your household are also using the connection. There will be an element of trial and error to find the best settings for you. Even though you may have a fast internet connection, keeping to a standard definition may be best all round as others in the Meet may not have as good a connection and sending high definition video may cause them to not be able to receive video at all.

External Joiners

If you want to join a Meet that has been organised by someone outside of your domain then you have to request to join that Google Meet.

You will get a slightly different screen than usual and be presented with these options. You can click 'Ask to join' and all members of the meeting will be shown a pop up box.

Providing someone in the Meet presses 'Admit' you will be entered directly into the Google Meet. If 'Deny entry' is pressed you will receive the following message.

Someone wants to join this meeting

M   Mr H Stayte (outside G Suite Training)

Deny entry   Admit

You can't join this call

Someone in the call denied your request to join

Controls in a Meet

This next section will go through the controls which you have once you are in a Google Meet video call. The image below shows what Google Meet looks like if you are the only person on the call with your microphone and camera turned off and in this particular image you will also see extra icons that are added through two Google Chrome extensions Nod and Grid View.

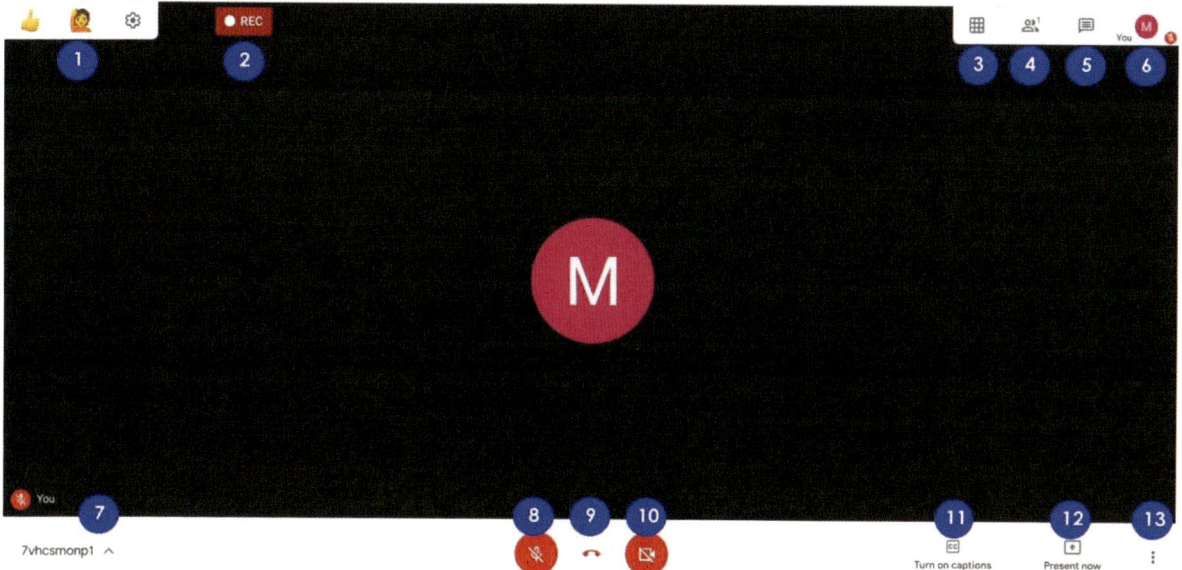

1. Nod icons extension
2. Recording is indicated here (Live streaming is similar)
3. Grid View extension
4. People Tab
5. Chat Tab
6. Participants (You) - more show if you have sidebar view
7. Room Information and meeting attachments
8. Microphone on or off
9. Leave call / Meet
10. Camera on or off
11. Turn Captions on or off
12. Present to the Meet
13. Options

Most of the controls indicated above are fairly self explanatory however I will go through a few of them in more detail and the extensions are covered further on in this chapter.

4 - People tab offers some quick and easy controls for you during the Meet as both the Meet organiser and a Meet participant.

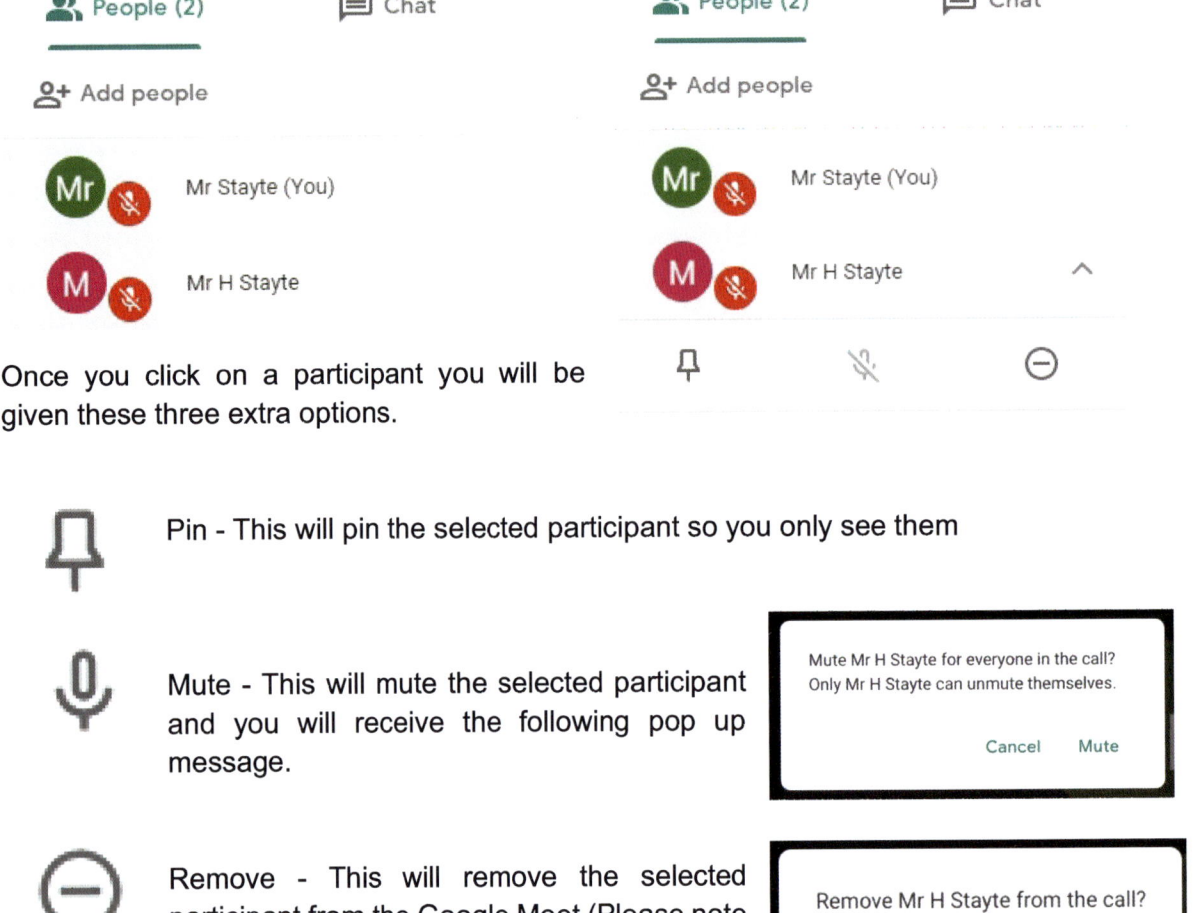

Once you click on a participant you will be given these three extra options.

Pin - This will pin the selected participant so you only see them

Mute - This will mute the selected participant and you will receive the following pop up message.

Remove - This will remove the selected participant from the Google Meet (Please note that it will not stop them joining again)

Hide - This will hide the participant from your view. (Added when using Google Meet Grid View extension)

5 - Chat function is quite useful here and good if you have some students who do not have working microphones or do not want to speak out loud as they can simply type their questions and you can answer in real time. To use, click on the icon and start typing.

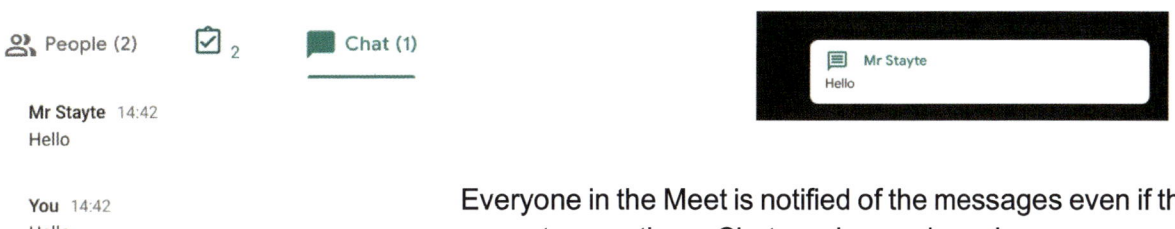

Everyone in the Meet is notified of the messages even if they are not currently on Chat as shown above here.

7 - Room information and meeting attachments is a useful section if you need to share the meeting information with someone else as the box it opens contains all of the joining information that appears when you first create a Google Meet.

You will also notice there is an 'Attachments' tab across the top which will contain any attachments that have been added to the Meet via Google Calendar.

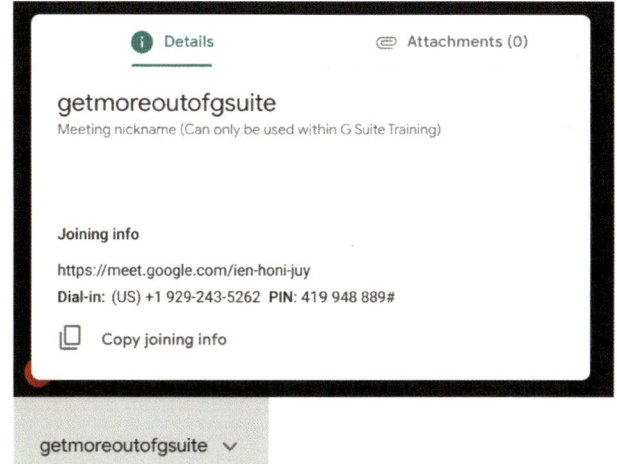

This example of a Meet has been created with a Nickname and therefore there are no attachments.

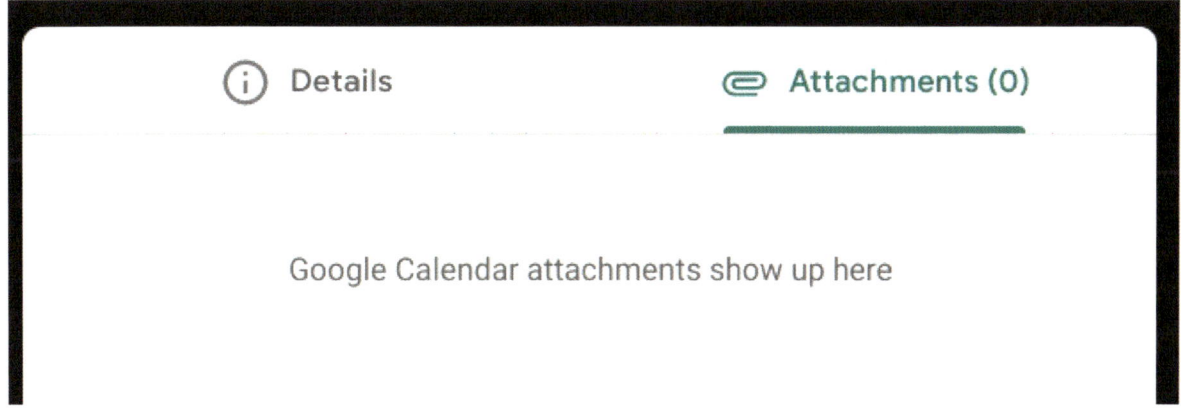

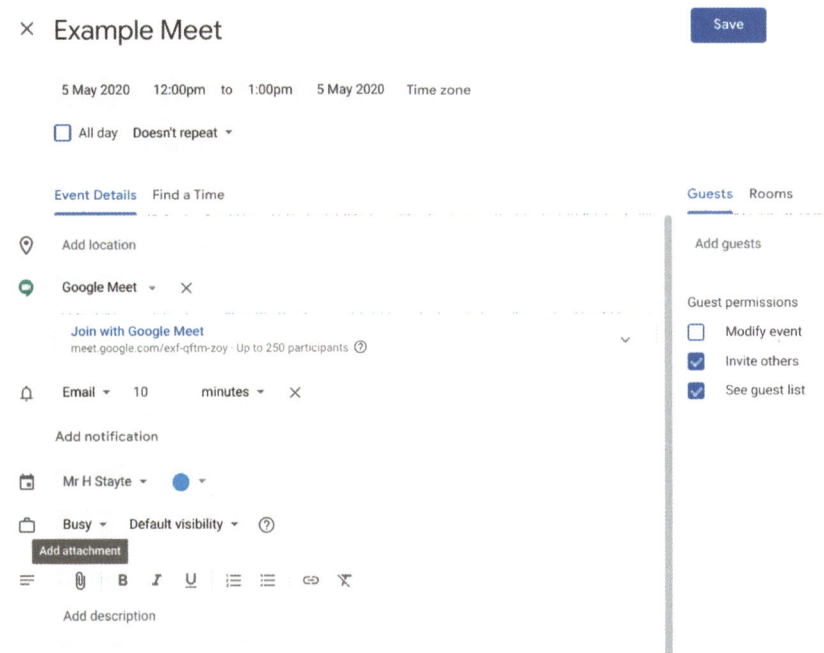

When you use Google Calendar to create and set up your Google Meet you can add attachments from Google Drive or even upload files. Shown here is where you attach the files in Google Calendar.

Once files have been added to the Calendar entry they will appear in the Google Meet. This is a live link so if you go back and edit the Calendar entry with additional files they will automatically appear in the Google Meet attachments section as in the example shown below.

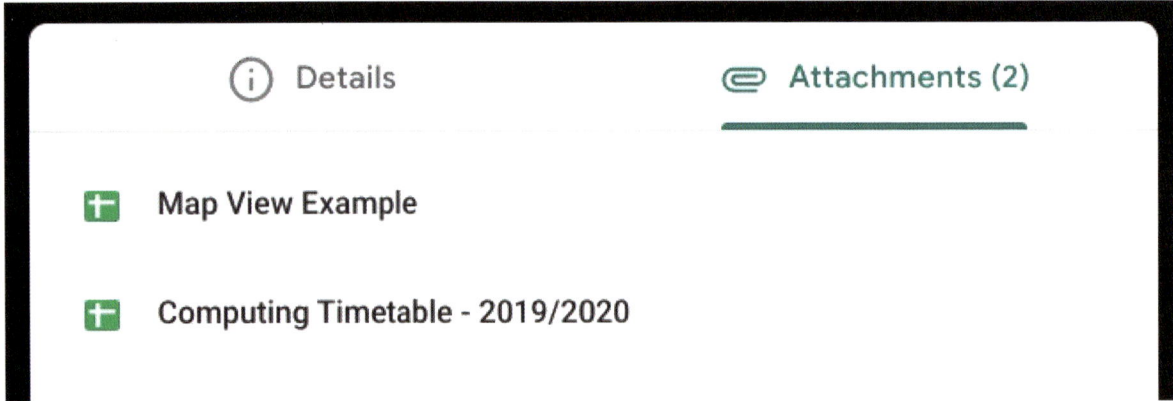

12 - Present to the Meet gives you several options of how you would like to present to the participants of the Meet. This is a tool that allows you to show everyone else in the meeting your screen and Google Meet currently has three options available for you to choose from.

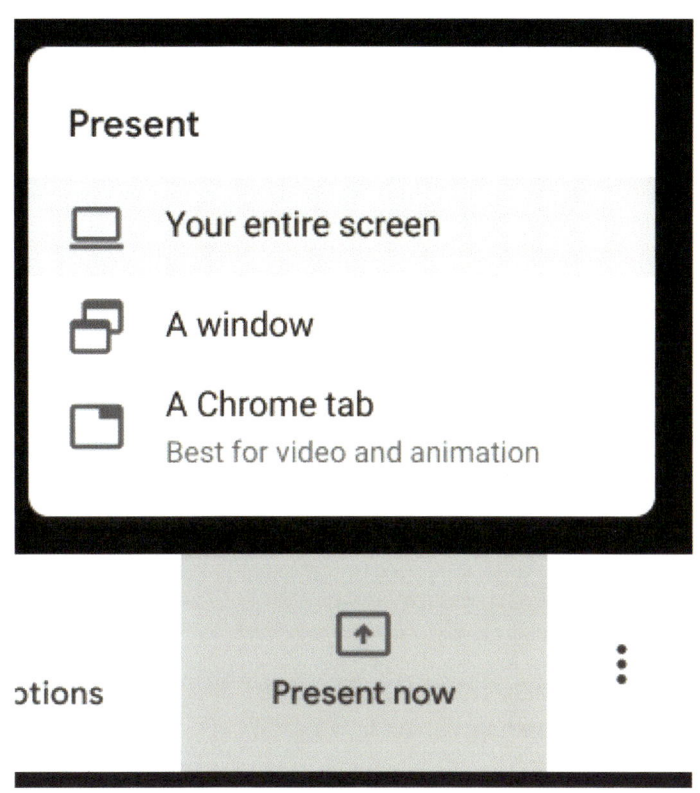

Your entire screen - useful if you would like to switch between programs and lots of different things you would like to present to the students.

A window - A certain window you have open on your computer (not just browser)

A Chrome tab - A particular tab that you have open in the same Window as your Meet.

Depending on your choice depends which of the following boxes will appear for you to use.

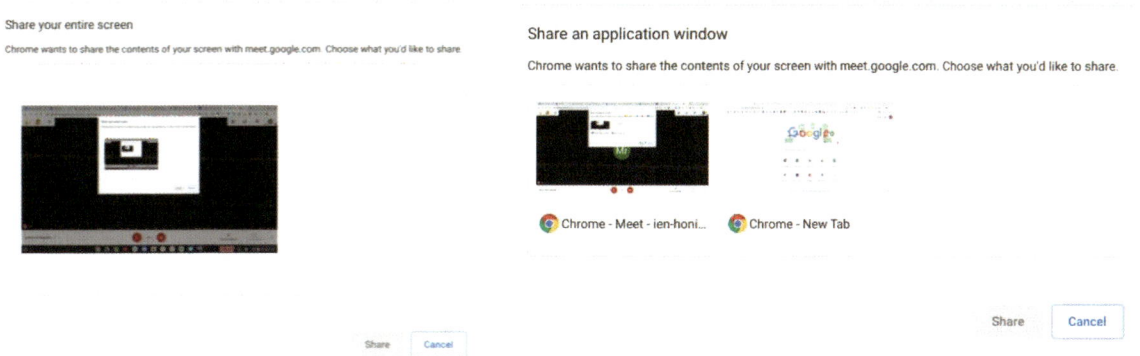

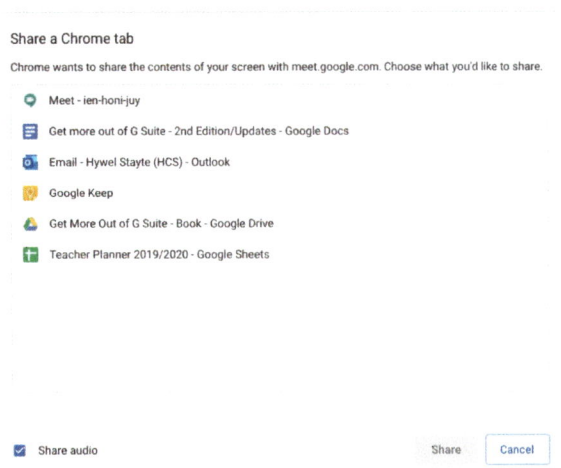

If you want to share a video or animation with your students through Meet then the best choice is the present tab option as shown here. You will notice that at the bottom of the pop up box is an option to share audio which is something that does not work with the other methods.

13 - Options provide you with some extra Meet functionality some of which I have already explained. The menu is shown below.

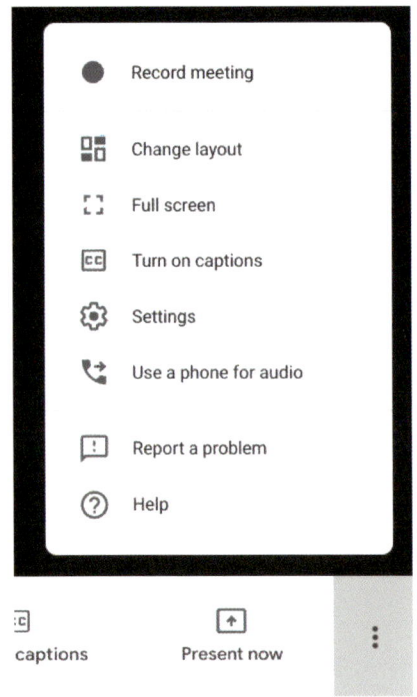

Record meeting - This allows you to record the Google Meet and the file is automatically saved to your Google Drive. (Admin can turn this on and off so check with them if you do not have this option).

Full screen - makes the Google Meet window go full screen so you can avoid distractions.

Turn on captions - converts what any speaker is saying into subtitles that you can read.

Settings, Use a phone for audio, Report a problem and Help - explained in the Join a Google Meet section.

Change layout

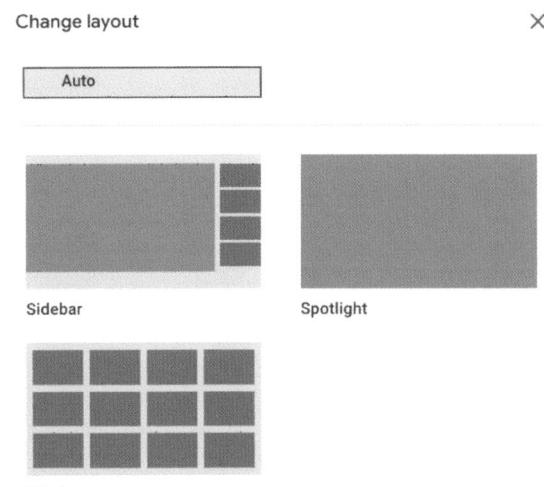

These controls allow you to choose how you would like to view the Google Meet. This has been another element that the Google team have been working on recently and the 'Tiled' option for layout is a very recent addition.

The light grey boxes indicate the current speaker and will change as different people in the Meet talk. The darker grey indicates a smaller thumbnail of each individual within the Meet.

I prefer the 'Tiled' option so that you can see as many people as possible (16) at once. The Chrome extension Google Meet Grid View allows for more than this and I will explain how that works further on in the chapter.

Google Meet Shortcuts - in a Google Meet video press 'Shift'+'?' and you will get the following window that shows all of the keyboard shortcuts for Google Meet.

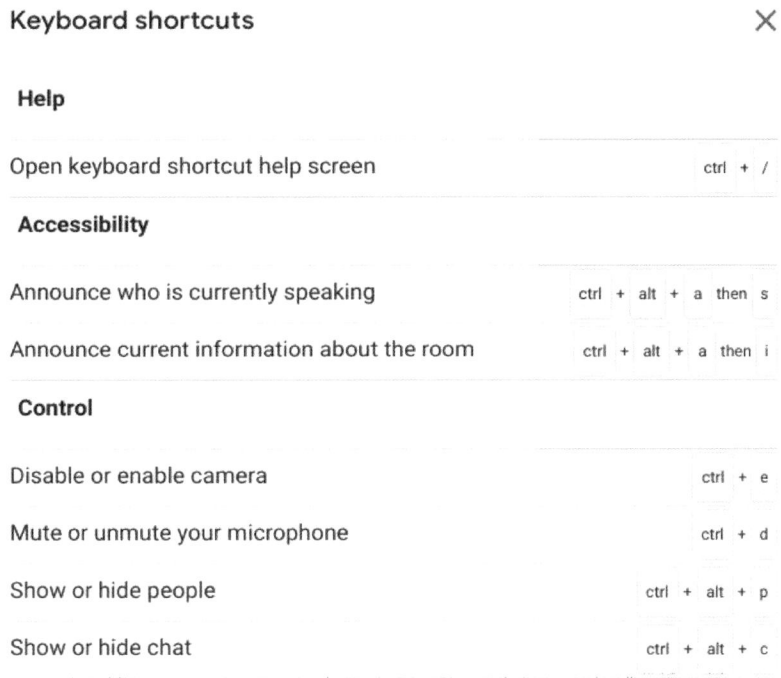

Get more out of Google Meet

Extensions

In order to maximise Google Meet for the virtual classroom installing certain Google Chrome extensions are a must. So far there are two that I would strongly recommend that you install and even push out via admin controls to all staff and students. The first one is Google Meet Grid View which allows for you to see everybody in the Google Meet at once in a tiled display. Google has recently updated Google Meet to have it's own built in tiled view however Grid View still offers a larger number of participants on view than the tiled view does so it is still a very useful extension to have. The second extension I would suggest all need to have is Nod - Reactions for Google Meet as this extension enables students to send emojis to the Meet and most importantly raise their hand to get your attention.

Google Meet Grid View

Shown below is an example of what a Google Meet will look like with Grid View turned on.

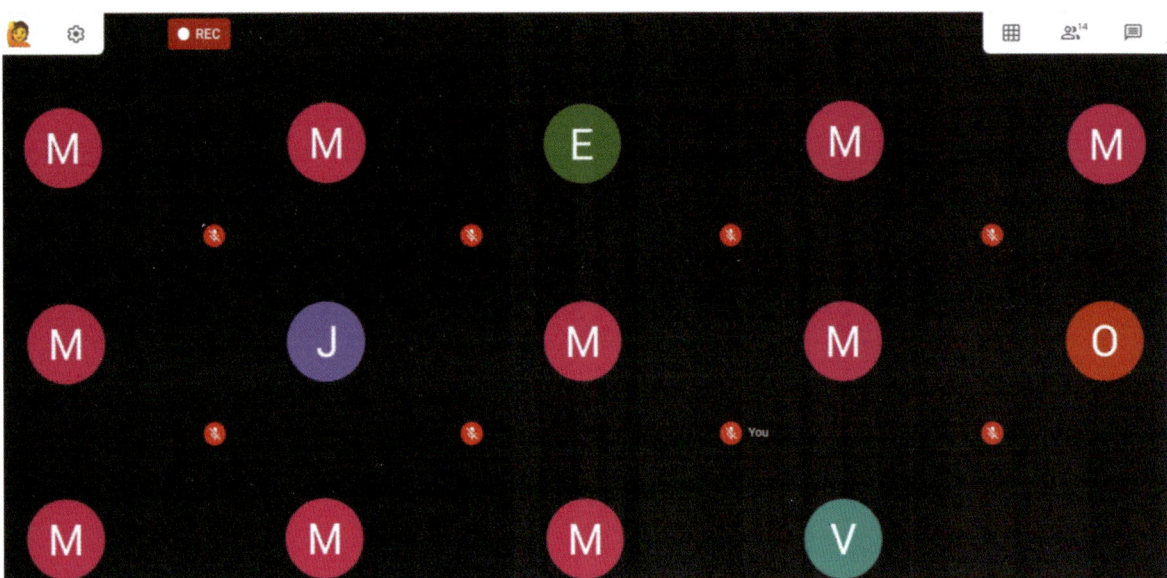

Please note - names/image icons have been covered

You will also see at the top right of the Meet you have the Grid View icon that looks like this. This indicates that the extension is turned on and if you see a diagonal line running through it that means that Grid View is turned off.

If you hover over the icon whilst in a Google Meet the following options will appear for you to use.

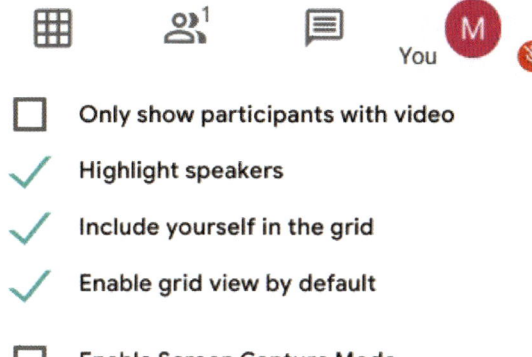

These drop down will give you some very straight forward options and settings for you to change. Shown here is the way I like to have it set up but obviously you will be able to find your own personal preferences here.

☐ Only show participants with video

✓ Highlight speakers

✓ Include yourself in the grid

✓ Enable grid view by default

☐ Enable Screen Capture Mode

Forces 16:9, Disables names, Locks videos in place

Nod - Reactions for Google Meet

You would have noticed earlier in my screenshots of Google Meet that in the top left corner I always had these three icons available. This is a Chrome extension called Nod that is fantastic to use with Google Meet.

The main function is to allow for simple unobtrusive interactions between you and the students by allowing them to send emojis everyone can see and also to get your attention by raising a hand.

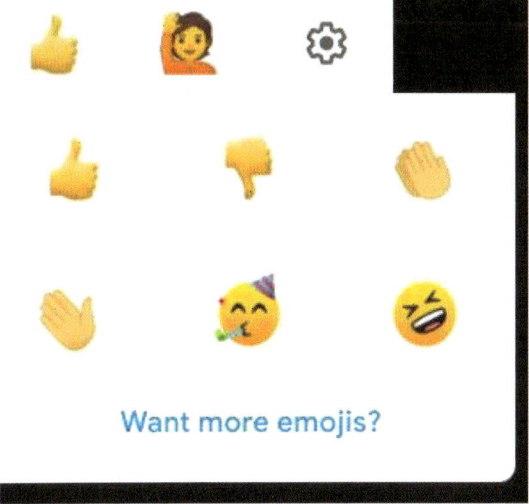

The first icon is the emoji tab which when hovered over will load all of the current emojis as shown below.

All you now have to do is click on one of them and they will appear at the bottom left of everyone in the Meets screen for a couple of seconds before disappearing again.

177

The next icon is the raise your hand feature which allows the students in the Meet to get your attention without rudely interrupting you. This is ideal if you are in the middle of talking. The following is an example of what will appear and it will not disappear until you cross it off.

Finally you have the settings that you can adjust within the extension. They are all easy to understand with the top part of this box being the most important. You can adjust your skin colour, choose to fully display your name and finally enable notifications.

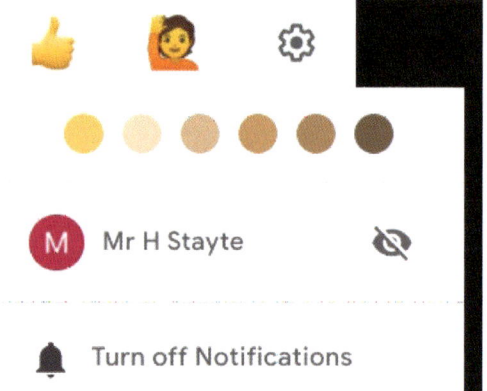

Meet Attendance

 There are several attendance extensions available for Google Meet and at the time of writing this book there were three main ones that you can choose from. Each one has advantages and disadvantages over the others, but I personally like the one called 'Google Meet Attendance' and it has a green tick as an icon. The reason I liked this one is that you can feed it an existing class list and the extension will automatically tick off those students that are present. I have also found it is much more reliable than the other most popular attendance taking extension. The only aspect that this extension does not have is the ability to save to Drive however personally I have found that the ability to download as a csv file is perfectly adequate for my needs.

Interactive Whiteboard (Jamboard & Canvas)

Many teachers like the ability to have some form of interactive whiteboard that they can use to show students calculations or drawings for example. Some people like to have a document camera or visualiser that they can present into the Meet whereas others like to use an already integrated application. Google provides two very neat solutions to this problem in the form of Google Jamboard and Chrome Canvas. Simply use the Meet controls to present your screen and then load up one of these applications and you have instantly got a whiteboard. The beauty of using Jamboard is the students can also be editors or viewers so they can contribute or watch from the Jamboard application rather than just through your Meet. You can checkout the chapter on Jamboard in this book and go to https://canvas.apps.chrome/ to get started with Canvas.

Breakout Rooms (Mute Tab Extension)

One of the great things about using Google Meet is the ease in which you can open a new Chrome tab and go to a Google Meet multiple times. You can enter your own Meet many times (just turn off the microphone and speakers else you will get a feedback loop) and this is useful for lots of reasons.

Because of this ability you can set up breakout rooms for your students which you can still monitor however you will need to install the 'Mute Tab' Chrome extension because otherwise you will receive too many sounds all at once. Mute Tab will allow you to turn the sound on and off of each Meet, as you require, meaning you can dip in and out of the conversations easily.

All you need to do is create multiple Meets using Nicknames and post to your Google Classroom the codes but you can be a little clever here and have a different post for each of your groups and set it to only show for those students meaning students can't join the wrong group unless one of the group intentionally shares the code with others.

Live Streaming

Sometimes it is just better to conduct a Live Stream instead of a video conference especially within an educational setting. Live Streams are ideal for assemblies and very large classes as it means that the interaction is generally only one way, allowing you to concentrate on what you are delivering without any distractions. If you record a Live Stream as well you can easily post it for anyone who misses it to re-watch at a later stage.

In order to set up your Live Stream you must use Google Calendar. Firstly just simply create a Google Calendar event and add video conferencing to it. Next you need to click on the drop down to view the conferencing details and once clicked you will see the extra option to 'Add live stream' at the bottom which you need to click on.

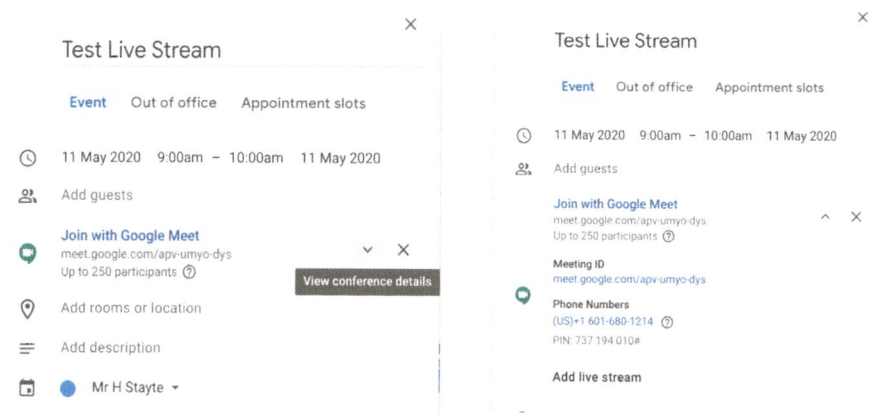

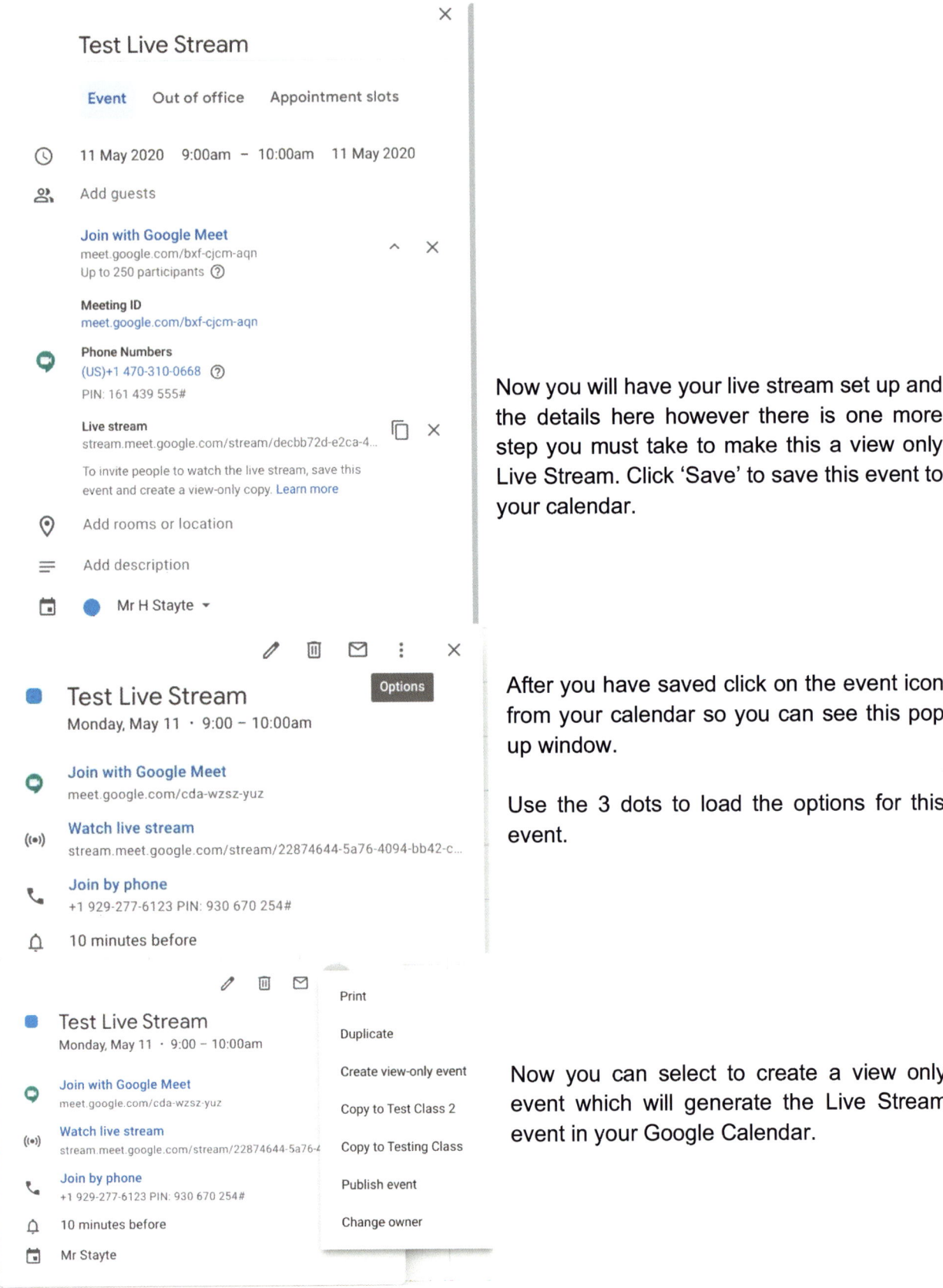

Now you will have your live stream set up and the details here however there is one more step you must take to make this a view only Live Stream. Click 'Save' to save this event to your calendar.

After you have saved click on the event icon from your calendar so you can see this pop up window.

Use the 3 dots to load the options for this event.

Now you can select to create a view only event which will generate the Live Stream event in your Google Calendar.

You can see the new event is created below and the use of [Live stream] is added to the title in your Google Calendar.

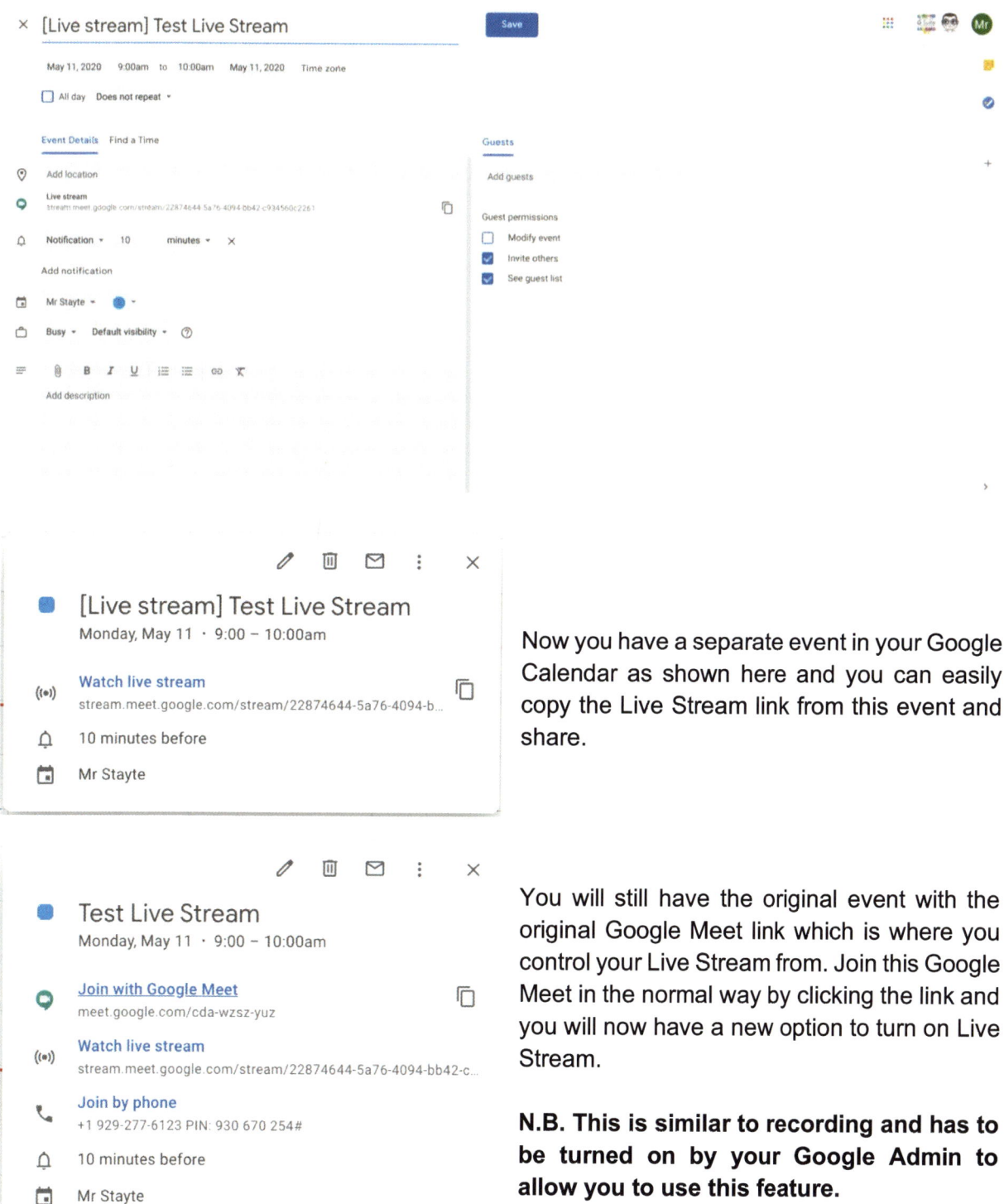

Now you have a separate event in your Google Calendar as shown here and you can easily copy the Live Stream link from this event and share.

You will still have the original event with the original Google Meet link which is where you control your Live Stream from. Join this Google Meet in the normal way by clicking the link and you will now have a new option to turn on Live Stream.

N.B. This is similar to recording and has to be turned on by your Google Admin to allow you to use this feature.

Slides Q&A

For more detail on how to use this feature please do refer to the Google Slides section of the book and in particular the use of the Q&A feature. This is a very nice way in which you can allow for student interaction with your lessons and more specifically when you are conducting a Live Stream. As part of your Live Stream if you are presenting your screen and a Google Slides presentation you can turn on Q&A mode in order to allow for the students to ask you questions whilst you are presenting.

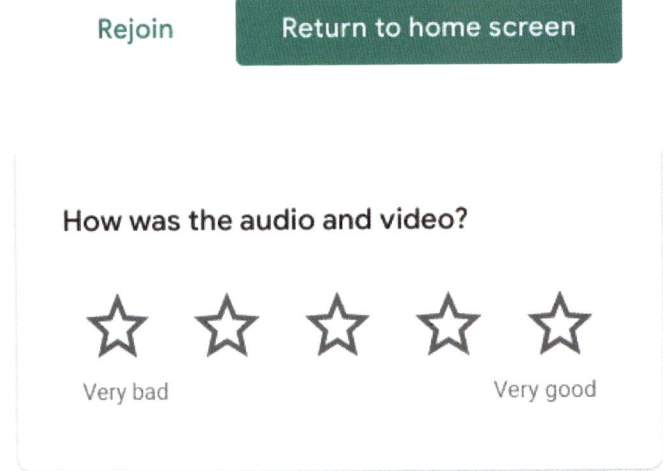

Extensions & Add-ons

Google have clearly worked very hard to allow for greater flexibility with their web browser and G Suite applications by allowing extensions and add-ons to be created by independent developers. Extensions are created to be added to Google Chrome and Google provide all of the necessary documentation to allow developers to do this. These extensions are installed to your browser and will also sync with your login providing you are signed into Google Chrome. This is very useful when you are changing computers as once you sign into Chrome not only do your bookmarks and settings sync but also all of your Google Chrome extensions.

Add-ons are created for use with G Suite applications such as Docs, Sheets, Slides and Forms. These add-ons use Google Apps Script to create extra functionality to your Google files and can be privately created for just your Google file or shared more publically as an add-on. If you have not already done so it really does pay to look through all of the extension and add-on stores for any program that can save you time as a teacher. This next section of the book will go through the extensions and add-ons that I use and I believe will save you time or make your work easier.

With all of the following extensions and add-ons I will give a very brief overview and explanation of how they work but I will not give full details because for each one there are videos and documentation provided through the add-on and extension stores. Most of the developers of these will have created user manuals and YouTube tutorials on how to use them effectively.

Google Chrome Extensions

App Launcher

App Launcher is definitely the extension that I use everyday both as a teacher and personal user of Chrome. This extension allows you to fully customize your Google App Squares

You can use App Launcher to select any of the G Suite applications to be easily displayed in your app square panel. This is especially useful as a teacher as many of your will get frustrated with Google Classroom not being listed in the default apps listed.

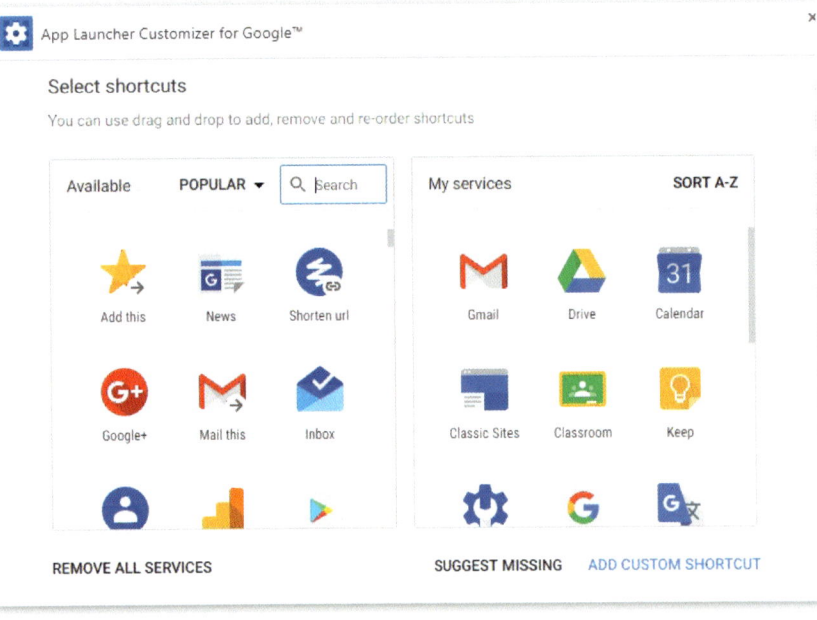

Shown here is the menu where you customize the apps you want displayed from a list of commonly used apps.

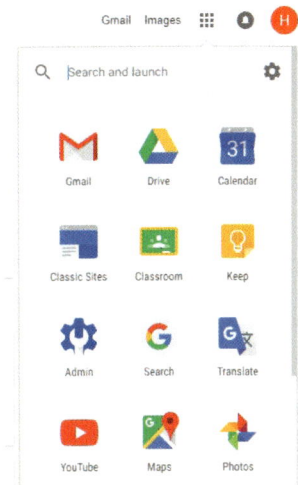

Here is an example of what App Launcher could turn your squares into and as you can see it is much more useful this way to what you need.

You can also use this extension to create your own custom links to any site you like as shown here with the Facebook, Hotmail and Yahoo links.

Share to Classroom

Share to Classroom is definitely going to be a must app for a large number of people and depending on your G Suite setup in your school could be one of the most useful extensions you have.

You can use this extension to quickly share links to websites you are on without the hassle of loading Classroom and copy and pasting links. Simply visit the page you are on and use the 'Share to Classroom' icon in Chrome to quickly create posts for your classes.

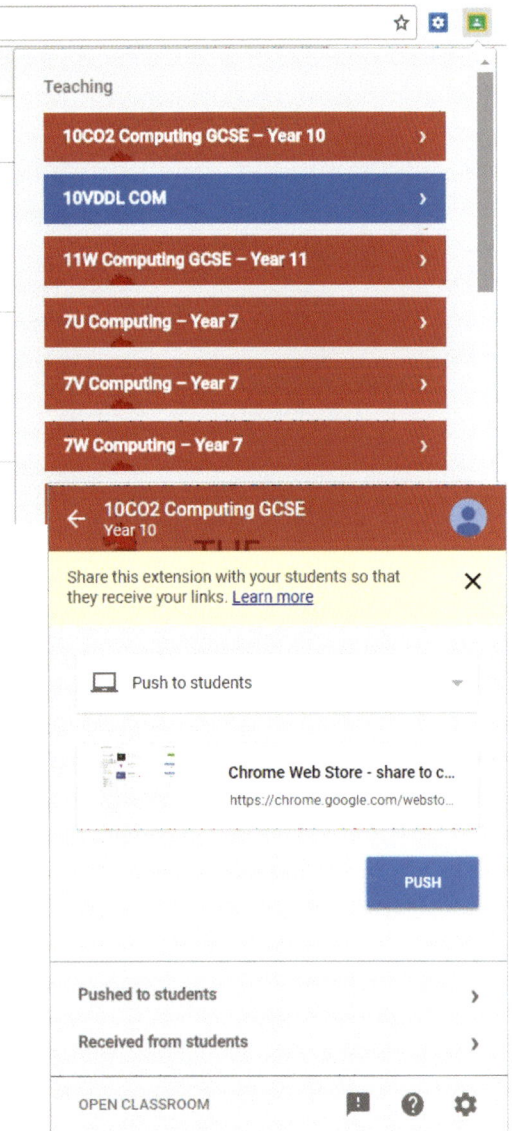

Once selected you can see all of the possible classes you have access to via Classroom as shown here in this image.

You can then choose which class you would like to send the link to and the next screen will give you the different options available for doing it.

The first option available to you is called 'Push to students' which will send the website page to all of the students in your Google Classroom. The website will magically appear in their Chrome browser.

This is where the setup of your school will matter as if your students in your Google Classroom are all using Chromebooks then they will be already signed into Chrome and this will work providing they also have the extension installed. (This can be done via the Google Admin console so easy to set up)

If you do not have Chromebooks this can still be used providing all of the student have signed into Chrome on their desktop/laptop and also have the extension installed.

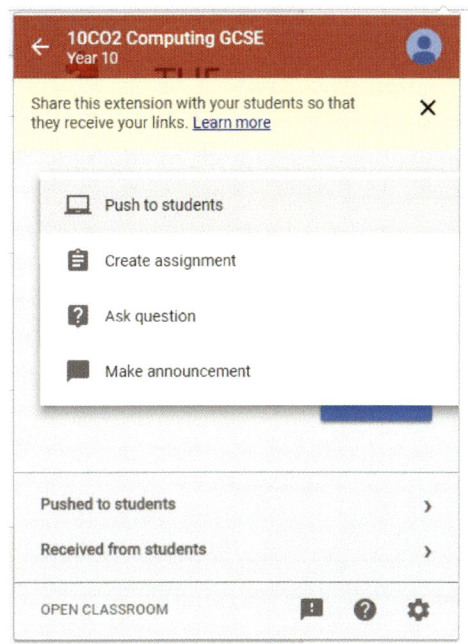

The other options available to you via the drop down menu are all of the Google Classroom posts you can normally create in Google Classroom.

If you use this drop down, you can choose the type of post you would like to create and Share to Classroom will include the link to the page you were looking at automatically.

Once you have this set up and working you will also notice that students can send you links as well via the extension and this is something you can manage as well.

Overall Share to Classroom is a fantastic time saver and also very useful for getting all students onto a particular website quickly if you have the setup right.

Screencastify

This extension has proved useful to me in so many ways from recording technical training for people on using specific ICT tools to providing students with feedback. Screencastify is essentially a screen capture piece of software however being a Chrome Extension its functionality is built into your browser. You can use Screencastify to record anything you would like to demonstrate and it will record and store in Google Drive all of the video files.

In my personal role I have run many Google training sessions and often people are very receptive but cannot always remember everything that you have shown them. By activating Screencastify at the beginning of my training session at the end I can share the video with all of the delegates by simply sharing the file from my Google Drive. You can also fully customize what Screencastify is recording and you can choose to turn off your microphone and make a silent movie. You can choose to record your entire desktop or a specific tab depending on your need and requirements.

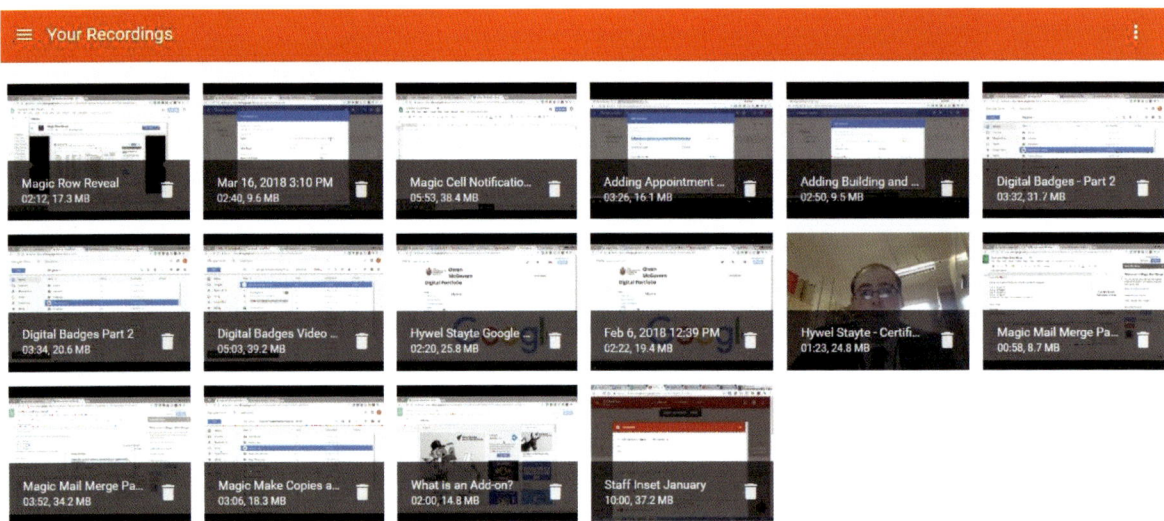

Screencastify can also be used to provide really quick visual feedback to students. You can record looking at a student's piece of work and quickly dictate what the problems and improvements required would be (just like in a lesson!) and then send the video to the student. You can also use some of the inbuilt tools to highlight areas or circle areas on screen in your videos as well. Screencastify can make use of your webcam and you can record yourself giving the instructions or explanation.

Mote

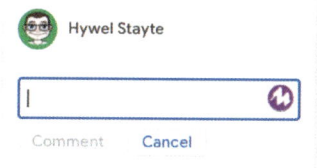

This is a relatively new Chrome extension however in my mind an extremely valuable and useful one. Mote allows you to leave voice comments on your Google Doc in a matter of seconds. It is designed to work perfectly with Google Doc comments and therefore is faster to use than some other options available such as Screencastify which could achieve a similar goal of leaving voice comments for your students.

Where Mote takes the lead here is the fact that it can also transcribe what you record into written text instantly and allow you to add the text to the Google Doc comment.

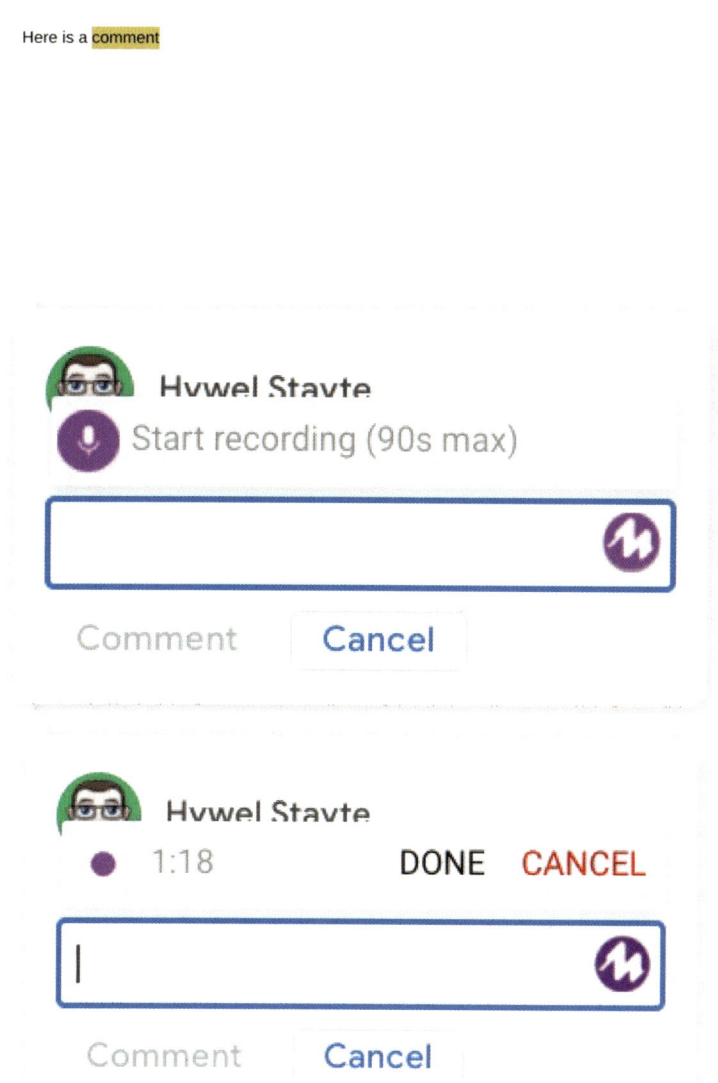

When you leave a comment on a Google Doc you now get the Mote icon in the right hand side of the comment box. Click on this button to record your voice comment.

Whilst recording you are given an on-screen timer so you know how much of the 90 seconds allowed you have left to go and you can press Done once you are finished.

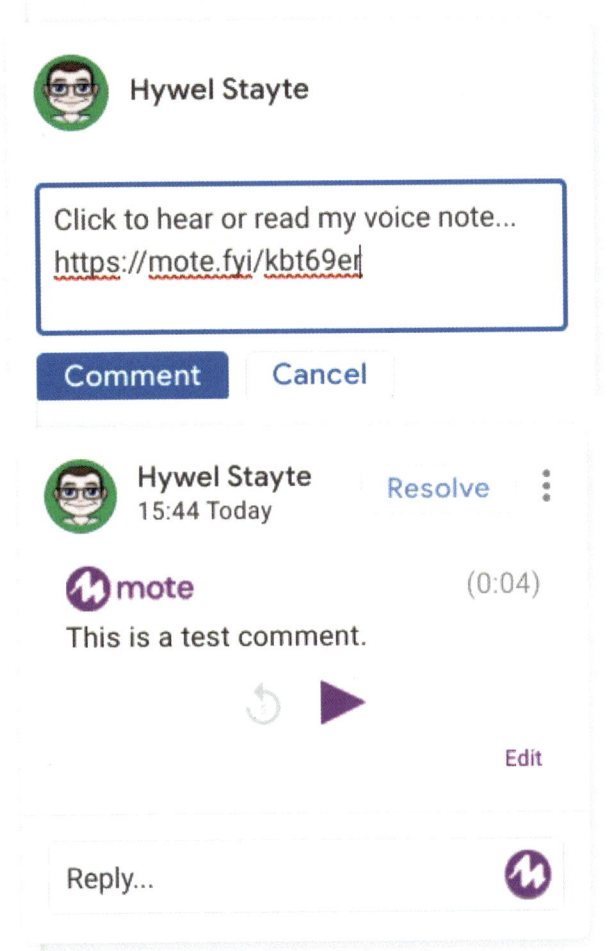

The default message is put in here which you can then post or use the link to listen to on the Mote website. After you press comment, Mote will transcribe the audio into text and post that with the comment as well as the audio.

Here you can see the transcribed comment and the button to play the audio. Sometimes the translation is not perfect but you have an easy edit button so you can adjust what is written as shown in the images below.

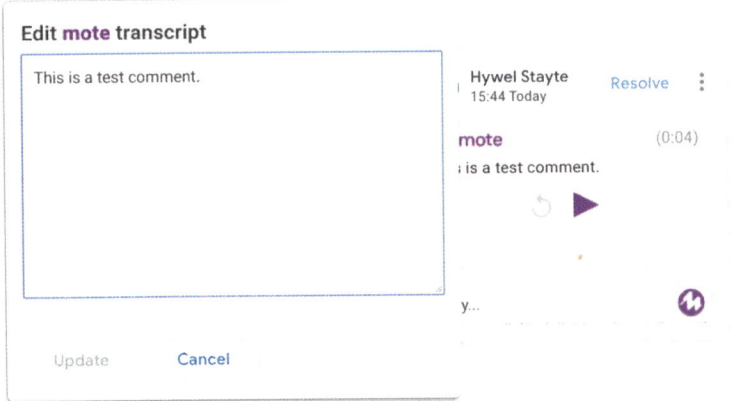

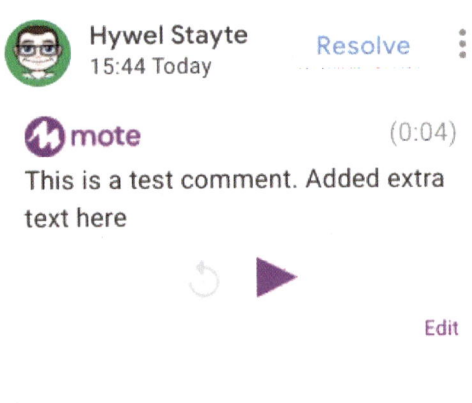

Draftback

This can be a very useful extension that will load and activate automatically whenever you are on a Google Doc. Draftback uses all of the revision history to produce a video of all of the edits and shows you a very cool progression.

This can be used to demonstrate progress and development for the student as well as allowing the teacher to show the influence they have had on a Google Doc through comments and suggestions.

Along with these benefits mentioned above it is also very cool to watch a documents creation with all the edits and revisions that go into it!

Cast for Education

This Chrome Extension definitely has great potential as a way of allowing a student to send their screen to the teacher's screen and demonstrate their work.

This is so useful for demonstrations and also incredibly helpful if students are bringing in their own Chromebook which you can still Cast to without additional software or setup.

Save to Keep

Quickly save a website link and/or highlighted text on the site you are on straight to Google Keep. Just hit the extension button, add a note and it will automatically populate to your Google Keep.

Save to Drive

 You can use this extension to save web content or screen capture directly to Google Drive. Simply click on the icon listed in the extension area and your default settings will be used to capture to your Google Drive.

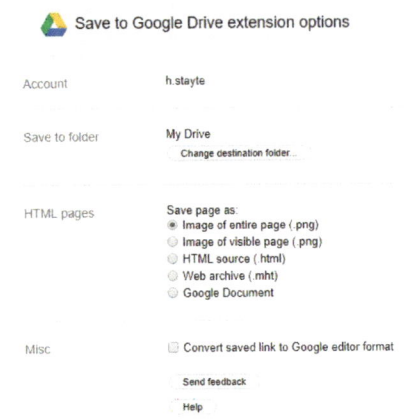

These options can be set up in advance to be your preferred settings when using Save to Drive so that you can use the extension quickly and efficiently.

Random Student Generator for Google Classroom

 This is a great little extension to have in the classroom and allows you to very quickly randomly select a student from your classroom. The way the extension works is it is integrated with your Google Classroom meaning that all the names of your students are already populated into the extension.

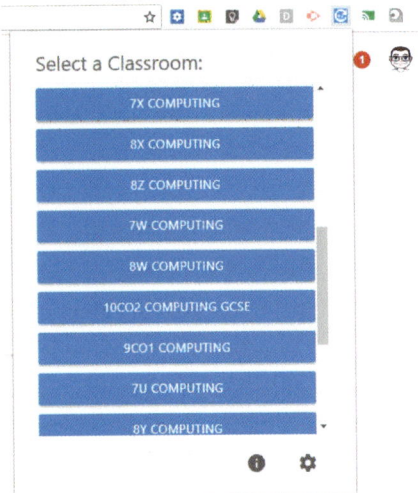

Once you select the extension from the menu you can choose from all your Google Classrooms available. Upon choosing the class automatically a random student will be selected and displayed in a pop out web page window.

Google Sheet Add-ons

Flubaroo

Flubaroo was the first add-on I ever used and I have not really looked back since. This add-on allows you to create an assessment or quiz in Google Forms and then Flubaroo will automatically mark it for you and provide email feedback to the students. Originally this only worked with multiple choice assessments but now there are extra features such as grade by hand allowing you to set free text answer questions which you can review and mark yourself before sending all of the assessment back to the students. You can also now share grades via Google Drive and assign stickers to the students who score particularly well as well as other options and features.

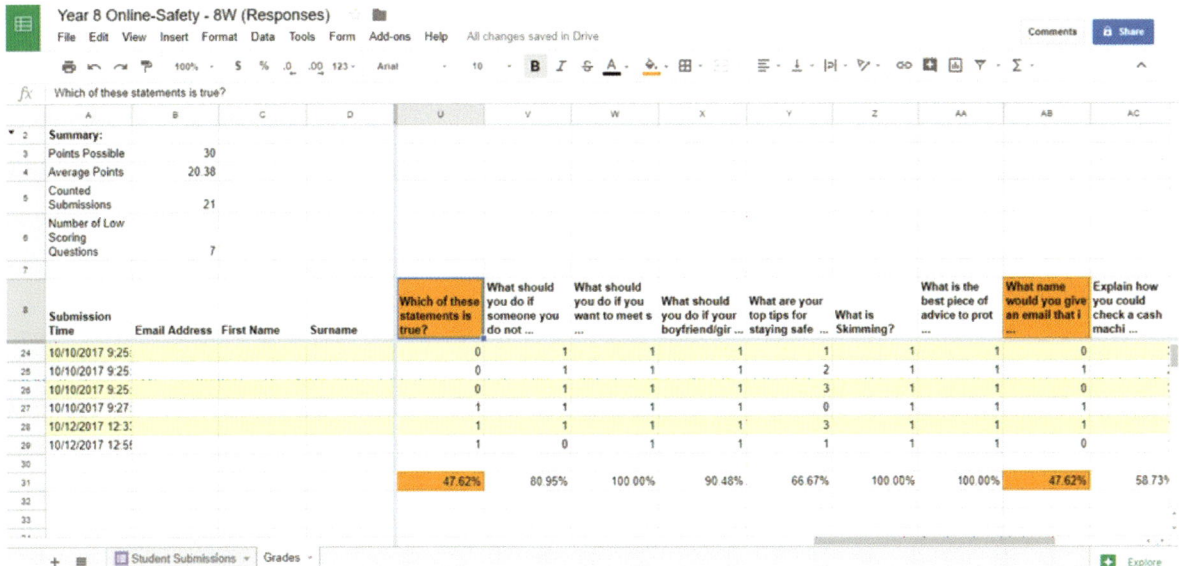

Google Forms has now been developed to work as quizzes and the main features of automatic marking can now simply be done using Forms and this data can also now be directly imported into Google Classroom from a post in the stream. Flubaroo still has many advantages over this however and the analysis conducted on the assessments is very helpful and it easily identifies the student or the whole class weak areas.

Doctopus & Goobric

Google Classroom, Doctopus and Goobric
The Ultimate Workflow!

This Google Sheet add-on and Chrome extension has enabled me to speed up the amount of time it takes to complete online marking through Google Classroom. As many of you will know marking through Google Classroom, before the recent update, can be quite time consuming to load all of the various files, read, mark and provide feedback through the comments section. Doctopus and Goobric allow you to setup reusable marking grids that can be specific to the assignment or more generic and allows you to progress through all off the students in the classes work very fast. The window opened and Chrome extension allow you to see the work and your marking grid all in the same place with the ability to add comments and automatically email students. Another powerful element to this is that your marking grid and comments are also automatically added to the Google Doc of the student's work which can also be done multiple times demonstrating improvements and progress made from the marking.

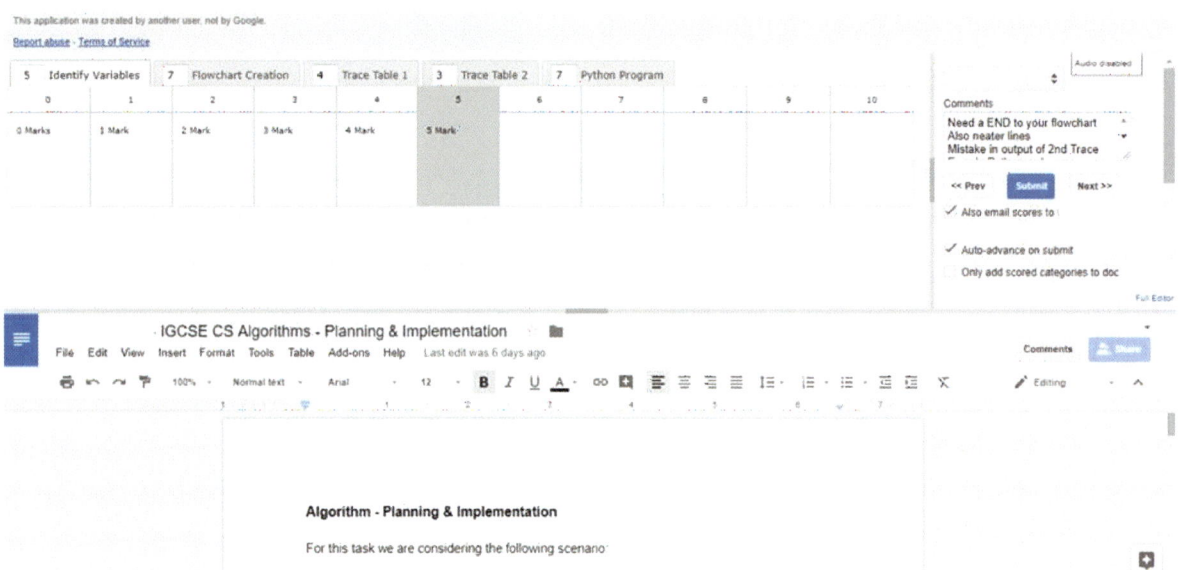

This is a truly powerful tool and it has allowed me to review students work at a much faster pace as well as giving better feedback on how to improve. The only downside is that for the average user the use of an add-on, Sheets Goobric and a Chrome extension together are an extra complication that can be off putting and too hard. If you follow the instruction and guidance in reality it is not that difficult and once confident in the setup process it will revolutionise the way you mark work on Google Classroom.

autoCrat

This was another recent discovery for me however has already saved me vast amounts of time and allowed me to remain completely cloud based even though I wanted to mail merge an assessment sheet into a document. autoCrat allows the user to produce a Google Document template that they can mail merge fields from a Google Sheet to it just like if you were using a local word processor and spreadsheet. autoCrat will make a completed Google Doc and then share it with the specific student automatically for you. Not only does this allow you to merge all of the data from your Google tracking sheets or even Flubaroo/Google Forms responses sheets but it also generates editable Google Docs which you can manually change again if you need to.

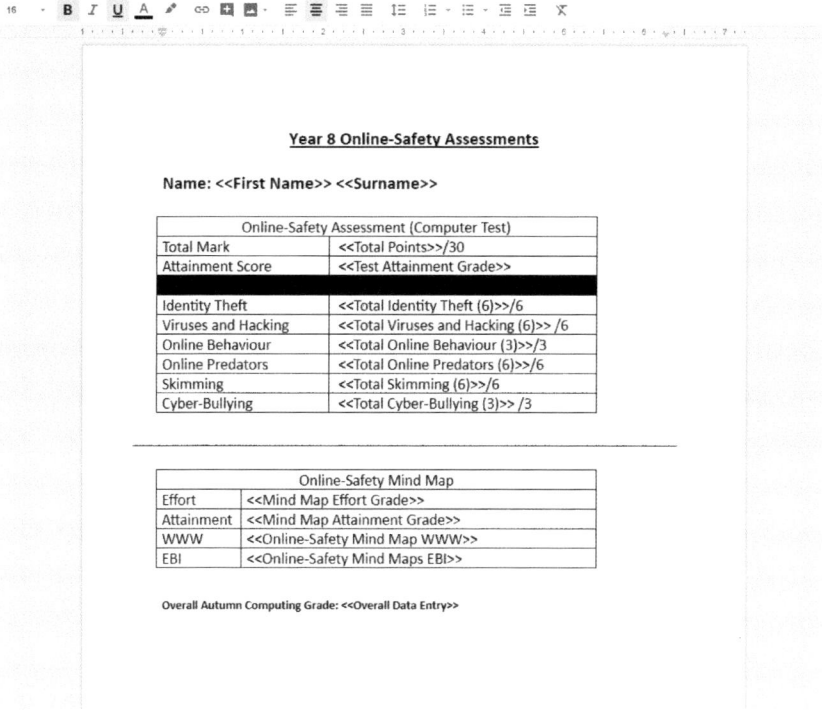

I have found autoCrat incredibly useful for a wide range of uses from sharing a Google Doc with a student's login details for an online competition to a full on detailed assessment sheet merged from a Google Form Flubaroo assessment including additional work marked and assessed on my main tracker. Once shared students can then complete a student response on the assessment sheet which the teacher owns and can see. These Google Docs can be easily embedded into a student's Digital Portfolio created using Google Sites and will demonstrate both marking, assessment and student responses all in one place.

Magic Mail Merge

Magic Mail Merge allows the user to email students grades and any data stored in a Google Sheets into mail merged emails. Before I created this add-on I used to use another add-on linked with Gmail however I created my own version for two main reasons. The first reason and the huge problem with lots of the add-ons available is that you have email quotas of 50 emails per day that you can send for free. This is fine if you only ever send 50 emails a day but for me this was not practical as one of the uses I have for MMM is that I want to email all students I teach (300-500 depending on number of classes and exam groups) their end of term grades. I want to be able to do this all at once and not have to keep using all of my quota and then continuing the next day where I left off.

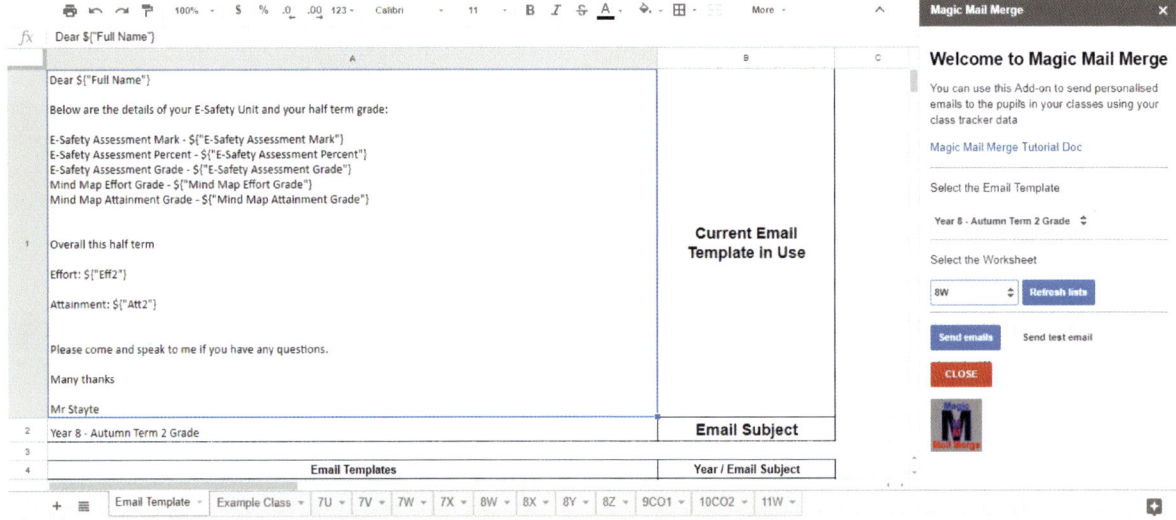

The second reason why I needed this add-on was because my organisation has G Suite except for Gmail and I suspect I am not alone here as getting any organisation to change from any email system does seem to be like parting the seas! Therefore, I cannot use an add-on that makes use of Gmail to run as I would have to use a personal Gmail account to email my students and it is not appropriate. So this add-on will run all from within Google Sheets and has no email limits other than the G Suite limits which are far more than most people would ever need especially if you are emailing inside your domain.

Magic Digital Badges

Magic Digital Badges add-on allows you as the teacher to assign badges that you have created (image files) to the students in your classes without having to manually copy the images to them all. This add-on is controlled through Google Sheets and you set it up with all of the names and email addresses of the students in your classes. You also upload all of your completed badges to a Google Drive folder and enter their IDs onto the Google Sheet.

Once setup Magic Digital Badges will generate a Google Drive folder on your own Drive area and share them automatically with the students. All you need to do is enter a Y in the correct cell to indicate a badge has been awarded to a student and this also indicates which badge. Once you have entered all of your Ys then you can run the add-on.

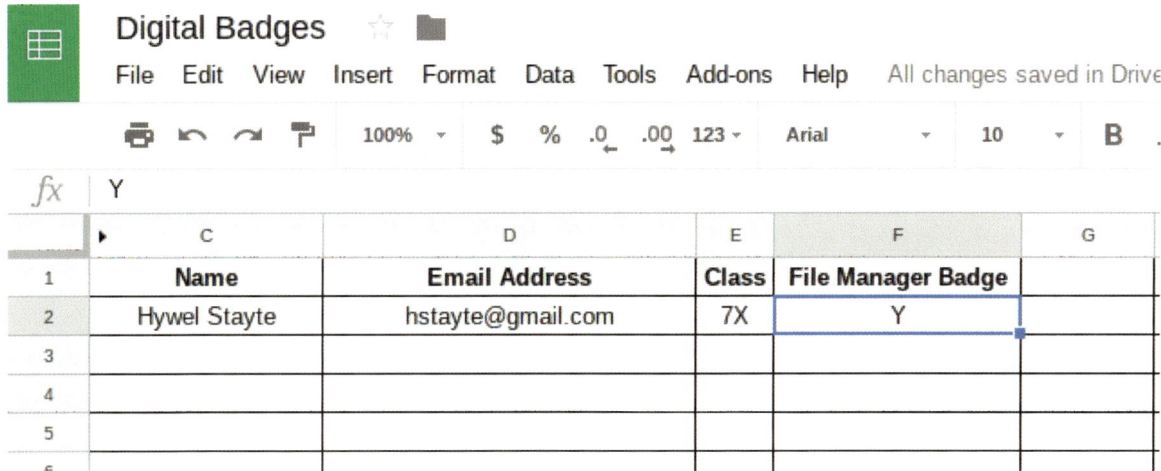

The add-on will replace all of the Y with the word 'Copied' once the specific badge has been copied across to the relevant student folder. The add-on will copy up to 100 badges at a time but can be run multiple times until all of the badges assigned have been copied. There is no limit on the numbers of students that can be added to the Google Sheet other than Google Sheets own limits in terms of number of rows as this is also the case for how many badges you need.

As shown earlier in the book this is great to include in a student's Digital Portfolio as the Google Drive folder shared with them can be embedded into a Google Site really easily and it displays them nicely for the students to see.

Magic Cell Notifications

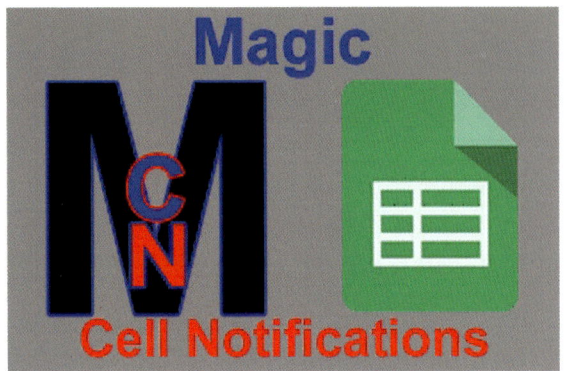

The popularity of this add-on has taken me a little by surprise and it was originally an idea that another teacher gave me however it is not something I have personally used myself however I can see some good uses for it in an education setting.

Magic Cell Notifications allows you to set up rules for when you want to be notified via email of changes made to your Google Sheet.

This could have many uses in a school environment and some examples of how it could be used are with tracking students where other staff would fill in certain sections of a Google Sheet and depending on the changes made another member of staff could be notified.

The add-on can also be used to notify when a Google Form is completed and certain values are filled in as the rules can be setup to read from the Form Responses worksheet.

I am sure there are many other uses of this add-on simply through how many people are using it and you may find that it provides you with a solution to something you need.

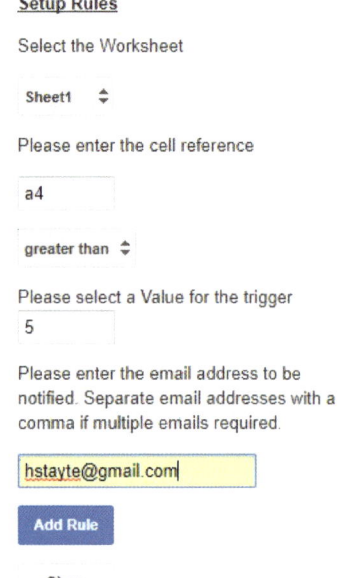

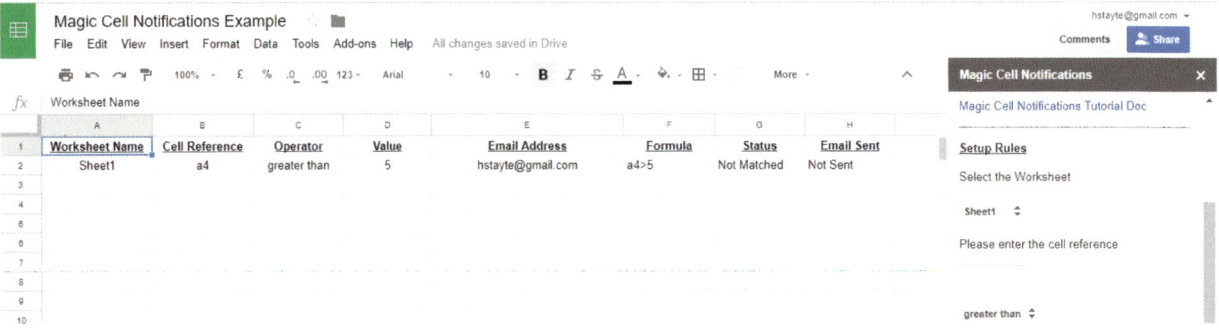

Magic Make Copies

This is one of the add-ons that I created to solve a time consuming problem I was having with Google Form assessments. Once I had created my master assessment on Google Forms I wanted to separate out forms for my different teaching classes and therefore I would often need to make multiple copies of the same file. Although 'make a copy' function is built into Google Drive it is quite time consuming to keep right clicking and making copies and that is where Magic Make Copies comes in handy. It was first built to work from within Google Sheets but now is also available from within Docs, Slides and Forms and it works in exactly the same way in all 4 products.

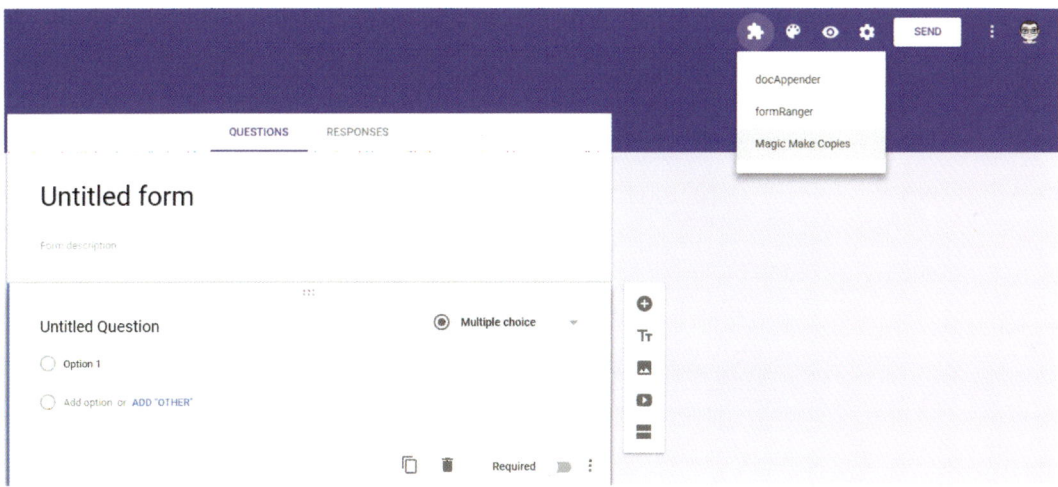

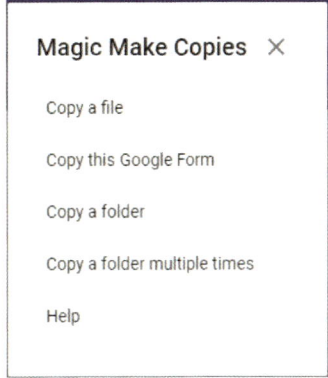

No matter which product you are using you can load the add-on menu for Magic Make Copies and you will be given the options to 'Copy a file' or 'Copy this Google Sheet/Slide/Doc/Form'. The first option allows you to copy any file from within your Google Drive and a new window will open allowing you to do this. Once selected you will be asked how many copies you would like to make and upon completion all of the copies will be added to the same Google Drive folder as the original file. When you copy the file you are working on it works in exactly the same way but of course you skip the step of having to select the file as the add-on already knows what file you would like to copy.

Copy folder will open a Google Drive selection window and allow you to choose a folder you would like to make a copy of. This option will copy the selected folder once which is not currently a feature of Google Drive. The Copy a folder multiple times does just that and will ask you to input how many copies of the folder you would like to make.

Currently the copy folder functions will only copy the files of a folder. It will copy the folders in the main selected folder and their file contents but will not copy any further folders. If you have lots of folders within folders then they will not all be copied.

Google Doc Add-ons

Easy Accents

Here is an add-on that I do not personally use however I can easily see the benefits to language teachers and for the students to use for their language work. Once you have installed the add-on you have the sidebar on the right hand side where you can select your language of choice.

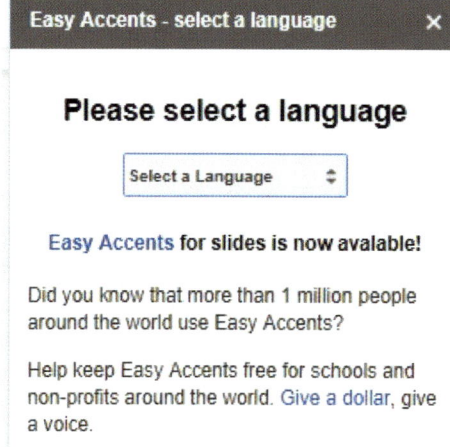

From here after your selection you are given all of the Accents you are likely to need and use when creating documents in that language.

Of course there are keyboard shortcuts for this kind of thing however I am sure there are many people who would find this incredible useful.

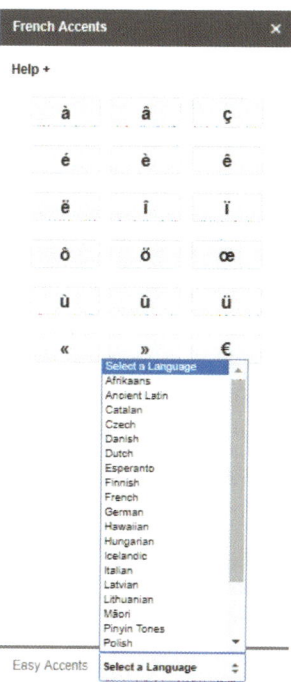

Magic Link

This is a relatively simple add-on for Docs/Slides that allows you to easily add hyperlinks to other Google files in your Google Drive without having to open and copy the URL into your doc. If you are building a worksheet for students or some kind of report for staff this could be incredibly useful to have and save yourself a little time.

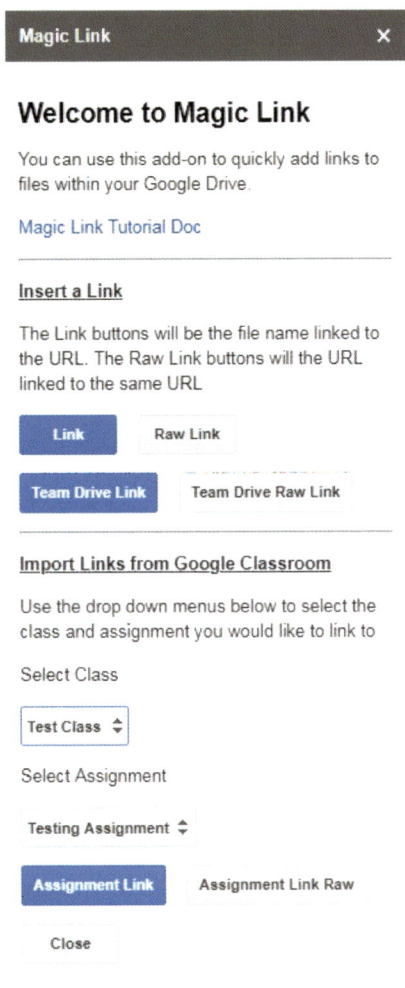

You can choose to insert the link as the filename with the URL to the file or even have the raw URL link inserted into your document. You can also select files from within Shared Drives using the extra buttons provided.

The new addition to this add-on is the ability to select any Google Classroom class you have and then choose any of your published assignments. Again you can choose to have the name of the assignment linked to Google Classroom or the raw assignment URL added to your document.

Magic Exercise Book (Docs & Slides)

This add-on was developed after a discussion on a Facebook group around being able to add additional pages to a Google Doc after it had already been assigned through Google Classroom. People wanted the ability to create a virtual exercise book that they could add to throughout the year without having to open each one and manually add to it therefore Magic Exercise Book was born for Docs as well as for Slides.

This add-on works in two main ways. Google Classroom and Google Drive. Using Google Classroom assignments allows the user to select a Google Classroom and then select the assignment you would like to add the text to. The best way to use this add-on is to first create a Google Classroom Assignment with a Google Doc set to 'Make a copy for each student'. Once this has been done you can then use Magic Exercise Book to add additional text or slides to each of the students' work. The second way is to use Magic Exercise Book with a Google Drive folder. (This can be a Google Classroom folder also) This will add the text to every Doc/Slides in the Google Drive folder.

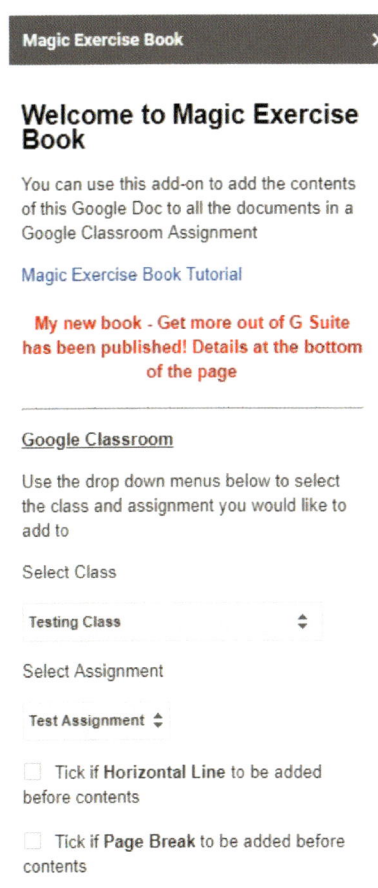

This sidebar menu allows you to control Magic Exercise Book and from here you have first got the controls for Classroom where you can select the class you want and then the assignment you would like to add to.

Additionally, now you can also Delete from a Classroom Assignment as well so if you make a mistake you can undo what you have done which can be very useful.

Not shown in this screenshot is the ability to add to all of the files in a Google Drive folder that can be useful too and is the way some other add-ons work. Magic Exercise Book gives you the best of both worlds and I personally think that the integration with Classroom is by far the advantage that it has over other add-ons.

Google Slides Add-ons

Pear Deck

If you have ever used interactive presentation software or apps then this may be worth looking at as an alternative if you already deeply use G Suite as this is a free version making use of Google Slides. Firstly, you can create your Google Slides presentation and then you can use Pear Deck to add questions and interactive elements to it whilst you are presenting. Students join your presentation by going to a website link and typing in the code you show them.

Once your students have joined you can control the progress of the presentation and add in extra interaction with your class and group as you go.

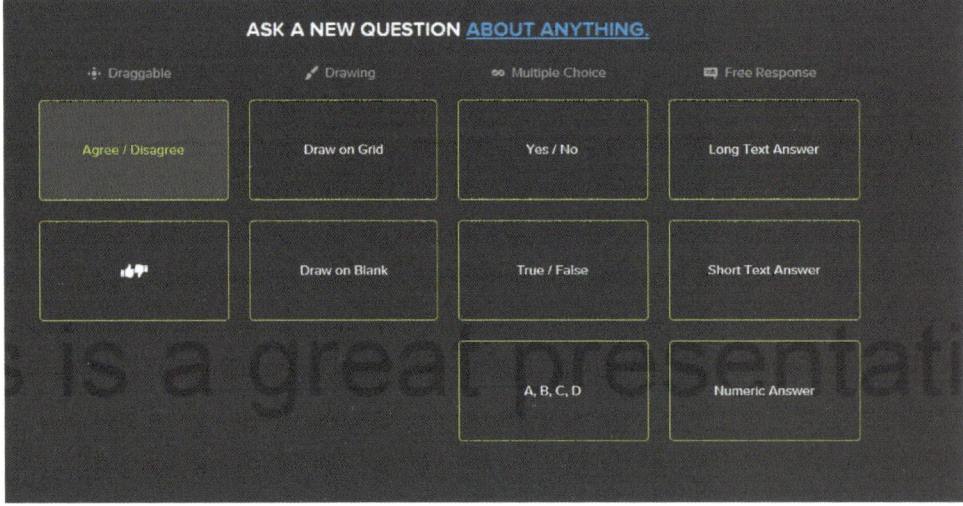

One downside here is that the free version of the add-on does not allow you to save the results of the questions you have asked and therefore there is a limitation if you wanted to use the results for any kind of assessment or logging. For me generally I think that you can still get good use out of it and good general assessment of your classes knowledge even though you cannot save the results. As you can see from these screenshots there are live interactions that you can manage and the screenshots below when live would show all of the students moving their blue dots or drawing their pictures for example.

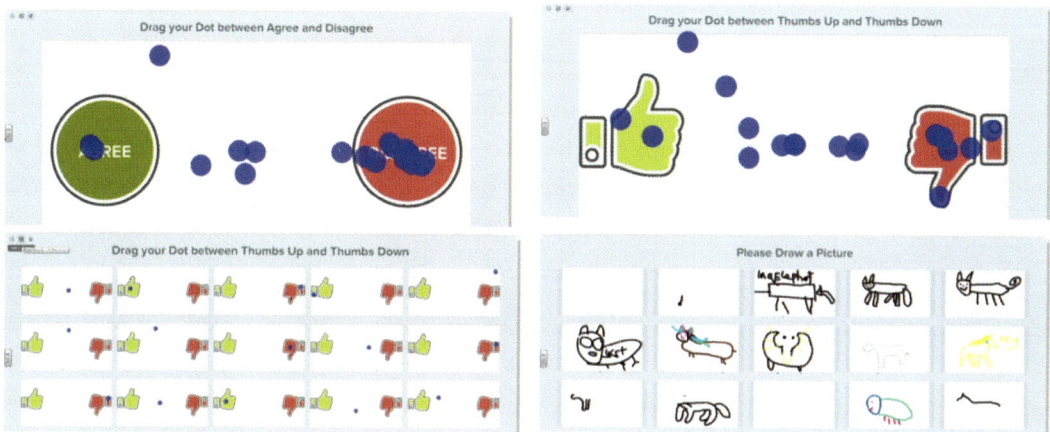

You could of course pay for the extra features and if you are a heavy user of the add-on then that would be an advisable thing to do however to the average user who does not have many presentations that would make the most out of Pear Deck then the free version should suffice.

Unsplash Photos

This is a great little add-on that you can add to Google Slides that will enable you and your students to create presentations which do not infringe on copyright. All of the images provided by the Unsplash Photos add-on are free to use and therefore can be used in the creation of all of your presentations even if they are being used publically and professionally.

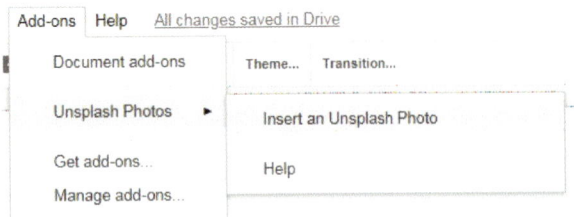

Once selected from the add-on menu the sidebar will load where you can browse, search and select the image of your choice. Upon selection the image is added to your presentation seamlessly. All images are also high resolution and are fantastic for creating quality presentations.

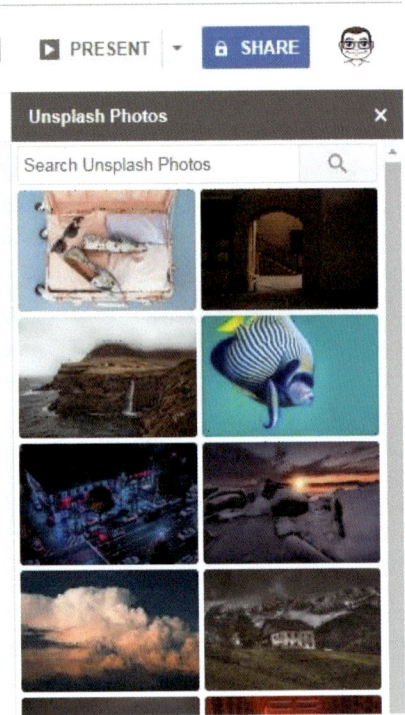

Google Form Add-ons

formRanger

This add-on is perfect for anyone who wants to create forms with lots of option choices without having to manually create every single one. A specific example for a school setting is when you want to include a list of teachers within your form and allow the student to select their teacher from a list. This would be very time consuming if you were to add all of the names manually to your form and that is where formRanger can help.

Simply create a Google Sheet which contains your list of teachers and this of course could be exported from your school system directly into a spreadsheet and uploaded to Drive. Once you have created this Google Sheet you are ready to use formRanger to insert the list of names into your form. Load up the add-on and select the question you would like to add the names to. You can then use the 'New range' button which is a little plus and select your Google Sheet.

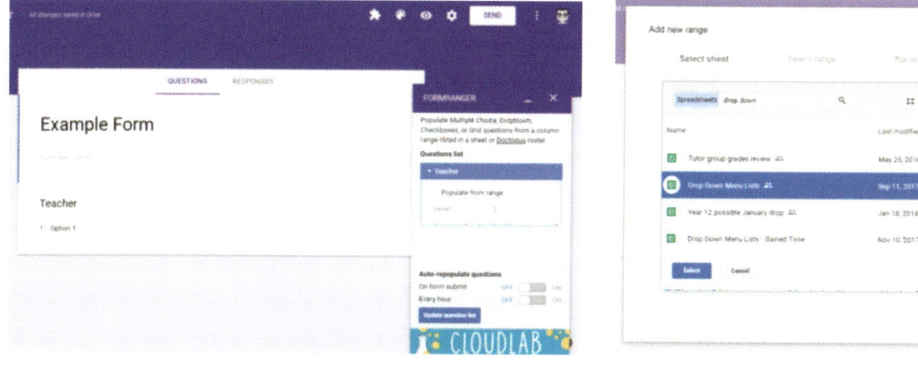

Once you have completed the steps formRanger will add all of the names to the option or drop down box for you. You can also use formRanger to automatically populate these questions regularly so that you can just update the Google Sheet and your form will also be updated. In some of my larger form projects having the ability to use a Google Sheet to populate questions has saved me hours of time than if I had to do each one manually and this is definitely an add-on that I personally use and would recommend to all.

docAppender

This add-on can be a fantastic way to complete peer assessment using Google Forms and Google Classroom assignments however can be a little complicated at first to get your head around but once you understand the process this could really revolutionise the way you use peer assessment electronically.

Firstly, you need to have used a Google Classroom assignment with a Google Document that you want the students to complete a peer review of. Next you need to setup your Google Form with all of the peer assessment questions you would like them to answer about the other student's work. You must include here a multiple choice question at the start that will be populated automatically with the names of the files being reviewed. You leave this blank at the beginning and call it something like 'Students work Reviewed'.

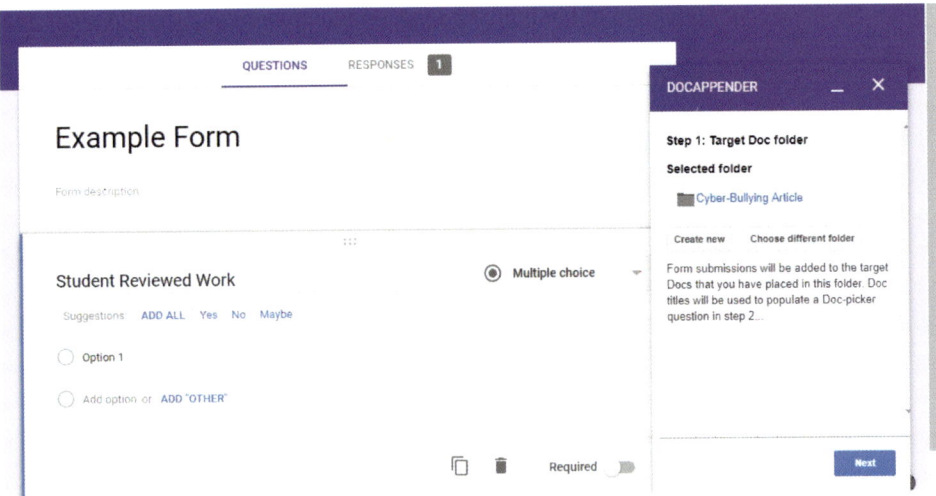

When you run docAppender you are first required to select the target folder of all of the documents to be reviewed and this is where Google Classroom Drive folders come in handy. Because you have created an assignment with documents attached you are able to find it within your Classroom Drive folder and select the assignment folder.

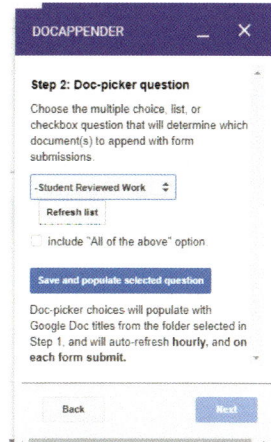

You can then tell docAppender which question needs to be populated with the list of students work to be reviewed and then all of the names of the files in the previous selected folder will be added as options to this question.

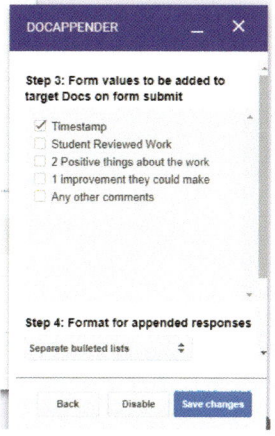

You can now select which of all of your other form questions you would like to include in your peer feedback. These are the responses from the form that will automatically added to the bottom of the Google Docs being reviewed.

You can select to include the form responses as a bulleted list, vertical table or a horizontal table and finally save changes. This will setup the form so that every time a form is submitted the responses are automatically added to the correct student document.

Using this add-on means that you can very quickly share a Google Form with your students and then give them access to the Google Classroom assignment folder and thus allowing them to peer review and assess other members of the classes work. Students can review multiple peers work using this method as the form can be setup to accept multiple responses and the responses will be added automatically to the bottom of the documents.

Once completed the students can go back to their document and review what has been said about their work by their peers and make the improvements directly onto their document. I think you will agree this has great potential as a quick and effective way to complete peer assessment using the Google tools.

Conclusion

In writing this book I have discovered many useful tools and I really hope that by reading this book you have found at least a few things that you would not considered using Google Apps and G Suite for. One interesting thing that I've noticed is every time I think I know how to do everything and I know how each of the apps works there is always an update that comes along or something new to improve it. Alongside this is also the fact that Google keep updating everything they do and this is so helpful in the world of education with new apps and improvements making life easier on a day to day basis.

The downside here for me is that on several occasions during the writing of this book Google has majorly updated their products, with the recent Google Classroom changes being one of them, causing me to have to completely re-write sections and chapters. If you find anything has changed or looks different than I have presented it I would like to apologise in advance but unfortunately that is always the problem with putting anything like this in print! Whilst I am apologising I should mention that writing is not something I am naturally good at and I have tried my best to write this book so that it is easy for you to read. I even created a lot of it using my phone and the voice to text feature of Google Docs to do it so if any of it is written as if someone was speaking it that is why.

I hope that you found reading this book useful and that the new tools you've taken away will help you in your life as a teacher. Please do share your experiences and things you learn from this book with the colleagues in your school and by doing so you all save yourself countless hours of time and improve the learning of your students.

As a final plug please do read through the Acknowledgements and the Links and Resources following this chapter as you will find useful websites that you can go to as well as groups for support and more information. If there is something that you think that this book was desperately missing please do join one of the groups and leave me a comment or send me a message.

Links & Resources

Get more out of G Suite - A Teacher's Guide website https://sites.google.com/view/gsuite-teachers-guide

Not so Magic Apps https://sites.google.com/view/notsomagicapps

Education Scripting https://sites.google.com/view/educationscripting

Tech Problems for Teachers techproblems.co.uk

G Suite Teachers UK https://www.facebook.com/groups/1065687116830636/

Google Educator Group for the UK
https://plus.google.com/communities/103265062805023338577

ICT and Computing Teachers https://www.facebook.com/groups/ict.computing/

Flowchart Maker Software https://www.draw.io/

Gmail Search Operators https://support.google.com/mail/answer/7190?hl=en

Acknowledgements

Google and the Google logo are registered trademarks of Google Inc., used with permission https://www.google.com/permissions/using-product-graphics.html

App Launcher permission granted by Carlos Jeurissen https://apps.jeurissen.co/

Not so Magic Apps permission granted by Hywel Stayte for:
- Digital Badges
- Magic Mail Merge
- Magic Cell Notifications
- Magic Make Copies
- Magic Link

https://sites.google.com/view/notsomagicapps

Flubaroo permission granted by Dave Abouav http://www.edcode.org

Draftback permission granted by James Somers http://jsomers.net/

Pear Deck permission granted by Kate Beihl https://www.peardeck.com/

Unsplash Photos permission granted by Annie https://unsplash.com/

Easy Accents permission granted by Daniel Baker

Screencastify permission granted by James Francis http://screencastify.com

Essay Metrics & Doc to Form permission granted by Oli Trussell http://schoolsmartcloud.com/

Random Student Generator permission granted by Tristan Kirkpatrick

Google Meet Grid View permission granted by Ryan Meyers

Mute Tab permission granted by Thomas McNiven

Mote permission granted by Will Jackson - https://www.justmote.me/

Google Meet Attendance & Google Classroom Grades Filter granted by Allan Caughey

NOD - Reactions for Google Meet

CloudLab (Part of New Vision Public Schools) permission granted by Jefferson Pestronk

- Doctopus
- Goobric
- autoCrat
- formRanger
- docAppender

http://cloudlab.newvisions.org/

I would also like to acknowledge Simon Lemieux who has helped me with advice and guidance during the creation of this book.

Rhys Richardson who runs the Tech Problems for teacher's website that is listed in the resources section has been a great help with checking and offering advice in the creation of this book.

Dan Lee for being an excellent friend and colleague. Many times, you have been there to bounce ideas off as well as listen to me moan and put the world to rights!

Finally, I would also like to thank my family, especially my lovely wife Helen for all her help and support. I think she did laugh when I suggested I wanted to write a book but hopefully she is impressed with what I managed to create!

Updates 2020

- *Google Drive - Update to Shared Drives & Sharing Settings*
- *Google Drive - Hiding Shared Drives*
- *Google Drive - Priority Drive*
- *Google Drive - Right Click Options, Create shortcuts to files*
- *Google Drive - Activity Dashboard*
- *Google Docs - Compare Google Docs against each other*
- *Google Sheets - Remove Duplicates, Trim Whitespace*
- *Google Slides - Audio clips*
- *Google Forms - Import / Reuse Questions*
- *Google Sites - Duplicate Site, Photo Reels, Announcement Banner, Buttons, Version History, Favicon*
- *Google Classroom - Marking Tool and Comment Bank*
- *Google Classroom - Gradebook*
- *Google Classroom - Rubrics*
- *Google Classroom - Originality Reports*
- *Google Meet*
- *Add-ons - Magic Exercise Book (Slides and Docs)*
- *Extensions - Mote*

About the Author

Hywel Stayte lives and works as a secondary school Computer Science teacher in Portsmouth in the United Kingdom. He has been a teacher for over 10 years and has always been a passionate advocate for G Suite for Education. Hywel is married with two young children and enjoys nothing more than taking time out to spend with his family.

He is a Google Certified Trainer who has just started his development of Google add-ons using Google Apps Script with many of his add-ons developed being presented in this book. Many of the elements to this book have come from resources he has developed whilst teaching and training other staff in the uses of G Suite.

The idea for this book has come from a real need for teachers to have a little more guidance on all of the possible advantages that G Suite can offer to an educational organisation with step by step demonstrations and ideas. He initially wanted to purchase an existing book which he could advise his colleagues to buy but found that there was nothing available. His aim is for teachers and staff working in education to be able to use this book to streamline their organisational systems and get the most out of the technology available.

Printed in Great Britain
by Amazon